WHAT READERS ARE SAYING, C'TND

"My husband and I read *The Incredible Importance of Effective Parenting* together and learned a lot about our own individual parenting styles, gaining much insight into our combined parenting role. From the very start I found myself making a list of "what's important" vs. "where I spend my time," which definitely puts things into perspective. What also spoke volumes to us was the reminder to be responders instead of reactors, to meet our children where they are, when they are, and to be present in the moment to play, talk, and learn with them. I'm certain that the wisdom will stick with us on our parenting journey." — Renee Shore, health care wellness specialist, graduate student, and Matthew Shore, computer science business executive, parents of two

OTHER BOOKS BY THE AUTHOR

Starts and Stops Along the Way:
Sharing Some Stuff From The Road Most Travel
(2012)
Prose Press, Pawleys Island, SC

More free verse poetry coming in 2013:

Still More Starts and Stops Along the Way

Parenting: The Beginnings

ACKNOWLEDGMENTS

Special appreciation to the readers
for giving me the green light.

Barbara Blain-Olds, attorney, social worker, University of Michigan School of Law Child Welfare Fellow

Karen DeBord, Ph.D., Professor Emeritus, North Carolina State University; owner, Possibility Parenting

Jenny A. Edwards, early childhood teacher, Horry County SC Teacher of the Year, contributing writer to *Momtastic Magazine*, mother of two

Carolyn Ellis, Foundation Director, early childhood education advocate, former school teacher, mother, and grandmother

Bonita McMenamin, BA in early childhood, certified parenting educator and trainer of early childhood teachers, owner of a child development center, and mother of three

Madeleine Ritchie, education consultant, certified trainer for Enriching a Child's Literacy Environment (ECLE), former teacher and school principal, mother of two, grandmother of five, and great-grandmother of one

Alis Sefick, MHEd, National Parenting Education Network, former council member; director, Central Region Prevention Resource Center New York State; Parenting Education Partnership Steering Committee; parenting educator

Renee and Matthew Shore, health and computer science executives, parents of two

Jennifer Stevens, Specialist in the South Carolina Program for Infant/Toddler Care, early childcare teacher for nine years, associate's degree in early childhood, working toward bachelor's in infant/toddler development, full-time working single mother of two

"Children who go unheeded are children who are going to turn on the world that neglected them."

— *Dr. Robert Coles, Harvard Psychiatrist*

Marian Wright Edelman, a native South Carolinian and founder of Children's Defense Fund tells us that:

"The inattention to children by our society poses a greater threat to our safety, harmony, and productivity than any other external enemy."

THE INCREDIBLE IMPORTANCE OF EFFECTIVE PARENTING

PLAIN TALK ABOUT RAISING CHILDREN
FROM A CONCERNED FIELD WORKER

by

Jim R. Rogers

Pp
PROSEPRESS
www.prosepress.biz

The Incredible Importance of Effective Parenting

Copyright © 2012

Jim R. Rogers

All rights reserved.

This publication may not be reproduced, stored in a retrieval system, or transmitted in any form: recording, mechanical, electronic, or photocopy, without written permission of the publisher. The only exception is brief quotations used in book reviews.

Published by Prose Press
75 Red Maple Drive,
Pawleys Island, South Carolina 29585

proseNcons@live.com
www.prosepress.biz

Comments: Contact Jim Rogers at jim@stilllearning.org

ISBN: 978-0-9851889-7-9

Cover/Interior Design: Jim R. Rogers

THESE ESSAYS ARE
DEDICATED
TO

ALL PARENTS, TEACHERS,
AND CAREGIVERS OF CHILDREN,
AND TO THE MANY CLIENTS, READERS OF
ParentsCare, *PARENT NEWS*, DEDICATED
WORKERS IN THE FIELD, AND THOSE IN THE
SCHOOLS AND ORGANIZATIONS WHO ARE
COMMITTED TO HELPING CHILDREN AND
FAMILIES FIND SUCCESS

TO

FAMILY AND FRIENDS WHO SUPPORTED AND
ENCOURAGED

TO

CAROLINE EVANS, WHO
HELPED ME GET IT TOGETHER

AND TO

MY PARTNER AND WIFE
SALLY Z. HARE FOR
GIVING ME THE PLACE AND SPACE
AND HEART
TO START

TABLE OF CONTENTS

1 PREFACE
  1 THE WAY THINGS ARE IN TOO MANY PLACES

8 INTRODUCTION
  8 ABOUT THE AUTHOR
  9 ABOUT THE BOOK
  14 ABOUT THE GROUPINGS

16 PROLOGUE
  16 EFFECTIVE PARENTING IS THE ANSWER!

19 GROUP ONE
  19 UNDERSTANDING THE ROLE OF PARENT
  24 MAKE YOUR TIME MATTER

29 GROUP TWO
  29 PARENTING: WHAT'S THE BIG DEAL?

43 **GROUP THREE**
  43 THE FOUR KEYS TO EFFECTIVE PARENTING
  43 THE SELF
  47 THE CAREGIVERS
  50 THE HOME
  54 THE KNOWLEDGE

67 **GROUP FOUR**
  67 RESPONSE-ABILITY AND PARENTING STYLES
  69 THE DICTATOR
  70 THE EASY MARK
  73 GOLDILOCKS

77 **GROUP FIVE**
  77 THE TIES THAT BIND
  78 THE MIRACLES OF DEVELOPMENT
  80 HOW DOES YOUR GARDEN GROW?
  88 A LOOK AT LIFE STAGES

96 **GROUP SIX**
  WATERING THE GARDEN, ENCOURAGEMENT, AND MORE

102 **GROUP SEVEN**
  102 TEENAGERS: WHERE DID THEY COME FROM?
  114 TEEN TIPS

116 **GROUP EIGHT**
  116 DISCIPLINE: BUILDING FOUNDATIONS AND CONNECTING RELATIONSHIPS
  116 WHY? WHAT? HOW?

120 BUILDING RELATIONSHIPS
122 DISCIPLINE THE DILEMMA
134 DOES ANYBODY KNOW I'M HERE?
140 DISCIPLINE THE SOLUTION
140 TOUCHING ON SKILLS

157 GROUP NINE
ABOUT CORPORAL PUNISHMENT
157 A REVIEW
160 WHAT OTHERS ARE SAYING
171 NO BLAME
174 I TURNED OUT ALL RIGHT
175 WHAT ABOUT CULTURE
178 IT'S IN THE BIBLE?
182 WE HAVE CHOICES

188 GROUP TEN
MONTHLY SPECIALS

189   JANUARY: THE NEW YEAR
YOU THE FOUNDATION:
YOU THE DIFFERENCE

194   FEBRUARY: VALENTINES DAY
CONNECTIONS OF THE HEART

199   MARCH: SPRING CLEANING–BUT
IT'S THE WAY I'VE ALWAYS DONE IT

204   APRIL: TRAGEDY AT SCHOOL –
TIMES TO FORGET BUT REMEMBER

209   MAY: MAY IS FOR MOTHERS! THEY
DESERVE MORE

214   JUNE: FATHERS ARE PARENTS, TOO

221	JULY: SUMMERTIME AND FREEDOMS
225	AUGUST: SCHOOL IS A FAMILY AFFAIR
231	SEPTEMBER: A LITTLE MORE SCHOOLING NEVER HURTS
241	OCTOBER: HALLOWEEN – THERE IS VIOLENCE IN SOCIETY
246	NOVEMBER: THE BLESSINGS OF THE EARLY YEARS
254	DECEMBER: HOME FOR THE HOLIDAYS
261	ABC'S OF PARENTING

262 EPILOGUE
THE GREATEST GIFT

266 BIOGRAPHY & MORE FROM THE AUTHOR

269 REFERENCES, RESOURCES, AND LINKS

> "If a community values its children, it must cherish their parents."
>
> *Dr. John Bowlby*

PREFACE

THE WAY THINGS ARE IN TOO MANY PLACES

They come to class tired, irritable, disinterested, and hostile. They behave in ways that disrupt, retard, challenge, and conflict. They are treated with neglect, disrespect, indifference, disregard, and punitive actions. They are discouraged and uncared for and they drop out and fight back or disappear into a dark, subculture world of degradation and mayhem. They are the extreme minority who cause or contribute to the majority of the serious societal problems.

Then, there are those who are not so severe.

But, they too are disinterested, unmotivated, undisciplined, unfocused, event or relationship traumatized, neglected, uncared for, and passed over as unchangeable or un-teachable. They exit the learning institutions unprepared for life in a world which will require more than they are trained to give and they become a drain on society, unproductive, and lost somewhere outside the so-called mainstream.

They are our children.

And they come from environments where we, their parents – with no intent to harm – daily fail them in ways that cause and contribute to their being who and where they are. We caretakers, as a rule, don't inflict this damage on our children because we want to. We do it usually because we don't know how not to. This lack of knowledge is centuries old and continues to shackle human beings with feelings of low or non-existent self worth, angered acceptance of our place in life, disconnected from those in better places, and with attitudes that become barriers to making choices for change.

We, the parents of these children, are missing from our children's lives. We are so often so self-absorbed with our own complex plights that we have little time for, interest in, or knowledge of our children's presence. Many of us have jobs, but we do little work, being minimally productive, and creating more problems than we offer solutions. Too many of us are irresponsible, undependable, and are often thought of as troublemakers. The fact is, we are having trouble making it, and making it is a daily chore that is a drain on energy and care and hope for a better tomorrow.

Our children and their parents need attention. They are us, the perfect mirror of a society's priorities and principles, and we have to do something. This book of essays is about doing something. It is one field worker's urgent plea for a country's realization that parenting education is essential for future progress.

Some parents have reached their rope's end and started chaining their children as prisoners because they are too "wild." A young girl left her newborn baby in a hotel room to die seemingly because she was too afraid to tell her parents. Another left her self-delivered baby in a bathroom stall toilet at a sports arena. Some of our states have passed legislation that essentially encourages teachers and principals to beat misbehaving school children with a wooden paddle. More than 5 million grandparents are raising their children's children today.

In my most recent parenting class for our department of social services, a couple delayed taking their infant daughter to the emergency room after an accidental drop because they were afraid of the potential punitive actions of the authorities.

Three months later this child was accidentally dropped again by her father. She died, and even though he was mentally challenged, a fact not allowed to be considered by the courts, he went to prison after waiting in jail for more than two years for trial.

A mother and father brought their four-year-old to a private conference. He had no language. He pointed and grunted.

The father in a custody battle held a gun to the head of his preschooler as a threat to the mother standing by screaming for the father to get out.

In another place, the mother held the gun to her head in front of their preteen daughter while the father mocked her and dared her to do it.

Most recently, a newspaper story related the revocation of a pediatrician's license after he announced on his social media site that he had water boarded his eleven-year-old daughter.

A six-year-old girl, essentially raising herself, was placed with protective services and diagnosed with attachment disorder. Her parents lost their parental rights and she was given to a qualified foster family who wanted to adopt her. Due to her melt downs and school dismissals, the authorities took the child from the only stable home she had ever had and put her in a group home. The authorities, impatient and not fully understanding, offered little and only short-term professional aid to the

parents to help them understand
the child's disorder and work with her.
For her.

And these are from the most recent cases. Only a tear drop in an ocean filled to overflow. And they are typical of thousands of cases all over our country every day, every hour.

We should all be ashamed.

There have been so many stories of heartbreak (theirs and mine) over the years, stories that affirm, confirm, and reveal what most of the research tells us about who children are, what they need to survive and grow and how we, the caregivers, can provide for them in the best possible ways. I have seen with my own eyes, heard with my ears, felt with my heart how our fellow beings find themselves off track and lost in life with no map to get back on the road to a life of a modicum of success and hoped-for happiness.

I have not performed controlled studies. I have not done empirical research. As a practitioner, I bring the information from research studies to practice with the families I serve. The situations and the effects of conditions I present to you in this collection of essays are the results of being there and watching research come to life, and death, and traveling along with people whose lives are difficult, even when it appears to society that things are okay. And in the vast majority of cases, their lives are difficult because of what research has uncovered and confirmed.

So, what I share with you is truth; reality, raw, and real. Terrible things are happening in our country to children and families.

Even though the family courts and the human service organizations perform well for the most part, they are in many ways broken. They are inundated with complex cases, brought to them by overworked, under-appreciated, under-trained, and underpaid workers, tended to legally by attorneys who too often appear to be more interested in their fees which drain the clients of even more of their lives and add more stress. Plus, these clients are sometimes erroneously judged by evidence presented which may not always be the true facts, or the facts where true meaning is found. Due to overloads in courts, mediation is often the recommended process and again sometimes due to money, incompetence, and questionable procedural work there are questionable results; results that are supposed to be the best for the families and the children, especially in custody cases, where human emotions are most often the most raw and damaging. Warring biological parents may end up signing an agreement that is actually a ruse just to settle and get the judge, the attorneys, the service organizations, and the guardians ad litem out of their lives and out of their ravaged pocketbooks. And in most cases, the children continue to suffer damage. While much lip service is given on behalf of children, they often receive the least benefit.

Custody cases and abuse/neglect cases are the norm in social services and family courts. In my opinion (without noting statistical data), the primary reasons for this unhappiness is what this book of essays is about. With effective parenting and family management skills, the bulk of these problems could vanish.

I live and work on a Caribbean island. Not really, but it resembles one in many ways. It is a beach resort area, rich and well-to-do on one side of the intracoastal waterway and on the other side, hidden from the tourists, are many of the workers.

The South Carolina county in which these opposites live is the largest geographical county east of the Mississippi, and much of the county is rural and agricultural but driven by the tourist trade. Low tech, low pay and low quality of life exist in too many places. The "hot spots" of the town resemble any major inner city with inner city problems, homelessness, street missions, prostitution, drug trade, human trafficking, domestic violence, crime, juvenile delinquency, runaway teens walking and cruising the boulevard, illegal workers trying to stay hidden and alive. Migrant workers are isolated in the run-down mobile homes where they dig in the dirt for potatoes or crop tobacco, and have no access to telephones, medical care, and in some cases, education.

Case workers for Social Services, child protection services, the handful of LCSW's, psychologists, mental health counselors and other helping organizations, food banks, meals on wheels, for example, operate beyond the maximum make-sense point and often come up short. Foster parents are overloaded and difficult to recruit and train. The task of hiring trained case workers is daunting and with budgets on the run, almost impossible. Thirty cases for one worker is not unusual. Most of these cases come from the expected populations, but more than you would expect come from the well off, educated, "normal" folks who are also having trouble coping with life.

There are hundreds of clients in the Department of Social services rosters, waiting in line for services related to their treatment plans which could include drug and alcohol, psychological evaluations and counseling, anger management, and yes, court-mandated parenting classes.

It's almost too late to try and convince today's politicians and legislators that policy should change and parenting education should have a place at the top of priority lists. But we can't give up on that pursuit. Parenting education needs to be inculcated into the psyche from early life, just as citizenship has been in the past and service learning is now being required in schools. The young people in our society have been the driving forces behind successful campaigns to recycle, stop smoking, and wear seat belts. They can also make the parenting of themselves and their own future children at least as, if not more important, than their other jobs. I believe departments of education have to start offering classes to value parenting and family life as early as middle school, and a secondary course should be required for a high school diploma. Too many of us have taken the role of parent for granted and used trial and error and parenting on-the-run, often at the expense of the children. The desire on the part of parents to gain knowledge has to come from within us, and the more we believe in the importance of our jobs, the more knowledge we will seek. And knowledge is what we all need. Like...

INTRODUCTION

ABOUT THE AUTHOR

My profession as a parenting and family life educator is not just a job or a career to me: It is a passion that became my life!

I committed to becoming an advocate for the children of today and adults of tomorrow. In addition to the obvious involvements of working with children in direct and indirect ways, I work primarily with the parents of children who will be adults quicker than we think they should. If children are in crisis, it is most likely because their parents are in crisis. I am dedicated to working for parents, caregivers, teachers, and all who impact the lives of children every day. I wanted and still want to be your resource, your ally, and your support as you tirelessly raise our children in the most effective, positive, and caring way so they grow into healthy, productive, and caring adults.

I am a member of the National Council on Family Relations (NCFR), with whom I am a nationally Certified Family Life Educator (CFLE), a member of the relatively new associate organization the Southeastern Council on Family Relations, a member and past council member of the National Parenting Education Network (NPEN), a member of The Center for the Improvement of Child Caring (CICC), and a Parent and Family Life Educator for still learning, inc., which has its own education consulting and workshop development organization. I started graduate work at Antioch University in Marina

Del Rey, CA, in psychology and counseling, completing my master of education in early childhood at Coastal Carolina University in 1994. I also wrote a parenting column for a monthly publication, *Parent News*, for more than 15 years, which is where the material for this collection of essays originated.

Most of us parents are doing a good job, the best that we can do with what we know. I applaud our efforts. I applaud your efforts. I am on your side. I ask you to let me share what I have learned. I am a wait-person in a parenting restaurant, and I offer you a vast menu with an open invitation to access a rich treasury of the work and dedication of others in this field. I trust you will find something that will fit your taste. Throughout our journey together, I will constantly remind you that parenting well, helping to grow children into successful adults, is challenging and takes courage. It takes heart. So as we travel this road together, I will support your every effort to continue your growth with a cheerleader shout out...

Don't lose heart!

ABOUT THE BOOK

This book is not intended to be the end-all for the professionals in this field of child rearing, family studies and parenting education. It is definitely not intended to have the specific answers for the countless problems and challenges all families face. It will not be considered an academic or a literary piece of work. It doesn't even have the accepted standards of book writing in style or form with proper footnoting and referencing, even though it does have extensive references, resources and internet links. And while I am a great believer in and proponent of modern research, and even some policy-driven research, I am also a big believer in the wisdom of Albert Einstein when he said, "Not everything that can be counted counts, and not everything that counts can be counted."

This effort is meant for parents and other caregivers and all people who care about our children and the future of our country. It was not written in the halls of the academy but in the not so pretty trenches of the lives of many who are struggling to find their way.

To fellow professionals I say this is not for you because you know all of this stuff already. Many of you work with it and call it by many other names every day, but there are countless parents and caregivers, even teachers, who do not know all of the information and material offered. Even if they do, since they do not work in it the ways most professionals do, they tend to get caught up in the living of their lives and doing their work and lose awareness and forget to follow their hearts and basic knowledge of the heart that will make lives better.

This book is for them. It's a major overview of the importance of parenting well. It is not a "how to do" book with skills galore for parents to learn. There are thousands of those available in bookstores, libraries and all over the Internet, even though I do offer some highlights that parents can dig into deeper. Rather it is a "how to be" book with observations and insights into the workings of successful families and the children who come from them.

> **It's not a "how to do" book**
>
> **but rather a "how to be" book**

Of course, if parenting and family life professionals choose to read it, that will be quite fine with me. And, if by chance, some legislators, educators, doctors, lawyers, judges, human services workers, and business leaders are led to reading, I would be remarkably surprised and gratefully pleased.

The monthly column I wrote for *Parent News* was launched in 1995 with the title "ParentsCare."

> *We are not born with the ability to parent. It is not a biological given. It's hard to think of many professions that don't require some training.*
>
> *Yet parenting is the most important job we have, and can be the most difficult, and...*
>
> *no training required!*

The column was named for my fledgling company at the time which was all about **putting parents and children first through family enrichment programs**. I called it that because I cared about parents, and I cared about parents who care. It's still my mantra. I want all parents and child caregivers to know that you are valued, supported, and cared for in your search to find effective and loving ways to raise our children. Of course, I care about children, too. In fact, I call myself primarily a children's advocate since they are my major concern, because so many of them are not being nurtured and guided in ways that will lead them into adulthood free from unintentional childhood damage. Almost all parents love their children and want the best for them. But the loving and the wanting are just not enough. We have to know *how* to love them and how to help them find and develop what could lead them to be successful in life.

There is a traditional belief that parenting well is a natural-born gift, that simply because a male and a female become biological mothers and fathers, they automatically become good parents, because they, better than anyone else, know what is best for their child. That belief is not altogether true 100% of the time. Parenting should be thought of as having a career, not a job, nor a duty, nor an expectation, not even an obligation. It's a profession. Good parenting is learned. It doesn't just happen. Parenting is not easy, but it can be rewarding, gratifying, and filled with joy. Yes, it can be filled with frustration, heartache, and disappointment, too, but aren't all careers like that? How one deals with those inevitable scrimmages can make them worse, or the attitude and efforts can raise the positives to even higher levels.

Most of us learn what we know about parenting from our parents, and that can be good or not so good. Do you want your children to be parented as you were? Answering that question might take some deep, honest soul-searching on your part about who you are and who you wish you were and who you might become. In most cases, who we become as adults and who we are on our way to becoming adults is often the result of how we were raised. The values that we acquire, the role models we've had, and the ways we are expected to behave help mold us into the people we become. We can take the parts that work for us from our parents, but what about the parts that don't work? What do we do with them? Too often we try to force our parenting, or we leave it to chance, or we raise our children by the seat of our pants, or from talk show advice, or from observing our friends whose children have different needs, temperaments, and surroundings from ours.

There is no question that our communities, our counties, our states, and our country are in somewhat of a mess. And even though there are a lot of children in crisis, they did not cause the crisis. What we have to do is take the responsibility for past mistakes, learn from them, and grow from here. As parents, teachers and caregivers, we have to take action and take our responsibility seriously. We have to take on the role of professional parent and stop looking for someone else to take care of our children. It's a tough job, but, just as we would look for help in performing our money-paying careers, we have to look for help in being an effective parent. There's no shame in wanting to do a good job, especially when it applies to the most cherished people in our lives.

The Incredible Importance of Effective Parenting is a collection of evidenced-based, research-based, research-influenced and research-informed columns offered monthly in a regional newspaper. The columns were taken from my years of being in the trenches with parents and teachers, conducting workshops and seminars, holding private and small group conferences, traveling with outreach home visitors to hard to reach homes trying to invite the caregivers to the learning table and empower them in seeking more knowledge to bring them more family and child success. The teachings are all professional and educationally based with extensive study and reading. But added generously are observations, lessons learned in hard classes, personal opinions, stories from the struggles of others, and suggestions intended to be heartfelt, experiential, and conversationally written; essays of our most important role in life, parenthood.

The *Parent News* columns were distributed to more than 20,000 locations monthly in coastal South and North Carolina. It is my hope that this book will become a bedside fixture for parents who will read from it regularly as they face the hourly challenges and joys of raising children. These ideas are meant to affirm, encourage, support, and guide, and to share information about the behavior of our children as well as ourselves, and how those behaviors are shaped and by whom. Over the course of the offerings we will explore ways parents can best fulfill their mission to help children and themselves become the "selves" they are meant to be.

There will be many ideas and topics you have heard about before, and even some of the subject matter is obviously redundant and some recycled, but in my opinion subjects so important *should* be repeated over and over again until we get it. As written columns, I attempted to present these concerns in the same way I conducted the workshops, speaking plainly and simply, from the heart and in plain language that even I could understand. It is a sitting room conversation I want to have with you. I want to help you make sure you know that being a parent, a teacher, a caregiver is a part of the team raising a child, a human being; a role that you take seriously and with deep commitment and care. Our future depends on how well the next generations grow our children who will grow to parent more children and better assure that we might stay here for a while.

GROUPINGS

The book is organized in Groups. I wrote more than 150 columns and because there were always new parents and teachers and readers, many of the most important topics, such as discipline, corporal punishment, and education were written in various ways, updated and renewed as new information and research were created and discovered. Therefore, several columns on similar subjects are blended into a single essay and put into Groups for organizational clarity. I hope.

These Groups do not make a linear story. You don't have to read them in order or read one group to understand the others. There is a common theme, but with different plots and approaches.

You might find yourself saying "I've already read this," or "He's already covered that." But, please keep reading because in most cases even when it sounds familiar, I try to say it differently.

Feel free to read this book any way you want – from cover to cover, month to month specials or by subject of interest – but please read it, even if you know everything in it. Read it to affirm, to remind, to encourage, to learn more, to dig deeper, to spread the word, and to support your invaluable efforts to effectively raise new human beings, yourself included.

MONTHLY SPECIALS

During the years I also wrote columns for the many special holidays, seasons and events that are celebrated and recognized annually. I collected those special offerings and include them here in monthly order since most of the specials have to do with an event or happening in a particular month or time of year. The specials are complete essays woven from a variety of columns on the topics over time. I hope you enjoy them.

> **When we have a confident sense of self and that confidence is regularly enriched by additional knowledge, we are likely to be more comfortable with all the decisions that we make regarding our children.**

PROLOGUE

Effective parenting is the answer!! The answer to what? The answer to almost everything that's wrong!

Home is where the START is! If our homes are in trouble due to a multitude of reasons, chances are it's because the leaders in the homes, the parents, are in trouble. The trouble of "not knowing."

Of course there are those conditions that impact families from the outside like economic crises, natural disasters, sickness, and death, and all of us have difficulties dealing with such forces and find a variety of ways to cope and to help those in our charge also get through the tough times. But, those are not the factors of life and living that I'm talking about and have talked about ad nauseam for more than 20 years! However, the choices we make as parents, the depth of knowledge that we have about our role, and the ability to influence others while we love and care for them do have a major bearing on how families survive and thrive in these complex times.

Effectively parenting our young will lead to helping us solve a multitude of problems infecting our society and draining our resources. If we are surrounding our new humans with the nurturing and training they need, they will begin their lives in the world eager to get started and with the skills that might be necessary for a successful life. Early childhood education should partner with parents in exposing the children to new pieces of the puzzle of learning and life. The more solid the foundation of effective parenting and teaching, the more success the children will enjoy and that success will attach itself to all of the other parts of the many elements that make up our communities.

If our homes function well, our schools will function better; we will have better educated adults teaching our children; our neighborhoods will be more harmonious and healthy; our workplaces will be more family friendly and stable; our need for human services activities will decrease appreciably and in so doing will enhance the quality of those very services. Our family and criminal courts will have fewer cases as crime will decrease; divorce will start to decline, practically eliminating the growing need for custody cases. School dropouts will become a rarity, and teenage pregnancies, as well as other adolescent miss-steps will return to those that biology alone dictate, those that are part of the growing up process. The need for drugs and alcohol to numb our senses and give us false courage and what we think is an extroverted personality will not be necessary. Cases of child, elder, adult abuse and neglect will also diminish as parents become educated about how to effectively raise their children and teach them about compassion and loving each other including our neighbors. Even the very damaged foster care system will decrease the overburdened and often ineffective services and maybe even get better at taking care of misplaced and damaged children, those whose parents learned too late or chose not to take the role of parenting another human being seriously.

    I can hear you now, "come on, Jim, you are putting way too much emphasis on this parenting thing. You sound like effective parenting will give us a utopian society. Parenting is just not that difficult." Well, I agree and disagree. **More emphasis does need to be put on effective parenting.** If more of us were educated as to how better to do the job and took it seriously, we could indeed get close to a utopia, whatever that is! Parenting effectively is NOT EASY! It is difficult. Doing it well takes desire, commitment, time, involvement, love, care, and lots of knowledge to get those little ones to a healthy spot in the adult world.

Most of us parents do a pretty good job raising our children. At least the family and relationship problems are tolerable, and do little overall damage if you don't count those arguments and disagreements, and conflicts that often arise at family reunions and holiday gatherings. Most of us don't have drug problems, a juvenile record or need anger management. But look at the bulging mental health load, the people waiting in line for treatment by counselors and therapists. Look at the overwhelming and disturbing success of legal drug companies producing miracle elixirs that will heal whatever ails us from obesity to depression, and look what the young people are being given to help them learn and behave and comply. Even knowledgeable parents make mistakes that can create children who are too dependent, inconsiderate, uninvolved, unreliable, irresponsible, lacking self-confidence and the skills needed to be independent and make their way in life.

We have labored for years in the world of parenting education and family life management to help parenting education become a valued part of preparing for adulthood. For those who want to have children, they should want to be the best parents they can be, and there has to be education available as to how best to do that. Some type of parenting and family life education should be required in high school at the latest, and more should be emphasized about being prepared to parent well, so that it becomes just as important as knowing how to feed a baby and change a diaper. Caregivers, foster parents, adoptive parents, early childhood educators get more training in the care of the young than do the biological parents! That doesn't even make good sense. And what we need to do with the knowledge and education that's available is to understand that it makes good sense.

That's what I'm trying to do here.

GROUP ONE

Understanding the Role of Parent

The dictionary defines a "parent" as "a father or mother." That's it. No details, no embellishments, no explanations. We surely know better, don't we? There are almost as many ways to define "parent" as there are actual parents, since everyone who calls him or herself "parent" is unique in that no one else "parents" exactly the way another does.

We all have our reasons for being parents and we all have our own ideas about what kind of a parent we want to be. We are from the start either ready, willing, and able to handle the job, eagerly looking forward to every frustrating and joyful day in the lives of our children, or we look at the little ones as being necessary only to carry on the lineage. Some parents see their children as more trouble than they are worth and as the ones who keep them from doing the things they had planned to do before the children came. Either we look forward to that day when they say "good-bye" and start building their own futures, or we look forward to that day when they finally get out of the house, give us back some peace of mind, and leave us to our own pursuits.

Here's one possibility I hope for: I hope when parents think of themselves, they do so with pride, knowing that they are engaged in the most important "profession" that they will ever have; that they are doing it to the best of their ability; and their ability is constantly being upgraded with new ideas, new ways to be a parent, and new ways to help their children grow up to be the people we all want them to be. I hope parents remind themselves every day that their roles are vital to the future of their children. I hope daily that they rededicate themselves to their role and giving of the best of themselves to the health and welfare of their children.

I have been told that this expectation on my part is too much pressure. I have read that some people are saying that parent educators, like myself, are being too tough on parents today, what with all the other stuff they have to do, like work, and work, and work, and stuff, and make lists, and stay busy, and do more stuff, and take on more stuff. Parents today are indeed leading hectic lives, and they do need to do a lot of other things that don't concern the children directly. But the children exist and they are in the lives of the parents and these parents have the awesome responsibility of performing the second most important role in life and that is to take good care of their children. (The first most important thing is to take care of one's self, creatively and in a healthy way.) This is not to say that parents should strive to be perfect. Nor should parents make themselves nuts over "what to do" at just the "right time" when working with the children. We are going to make mistakes and we are going to cause some conflict and problems.

I like the physician's oath which, paraphrased, says "do no harm." Most "real" parents have a sense of when they are doing harm. They can feel it deep down inside somewhere. If they feel it there, then they can be pretty sure that the child feels it, too. The way parents are as women and men will teach the children who they should be and how they should behave in the world into which they are moving. Parents can't take that responsibility lightly.

We adults are also responsible for keeping our surroundings in good shape. Those surroundings start with our family unit (traditional or not), then our neighborhoods, our schools, our communities, our counties, our states, and our nation. Our children will take over after us. How they handle it will depend a large degree on what tools we give them to use. It appears that the last generation or two have sort of dropped the ball. Our society is a reflection of who we as individuals and groups of individuals decided to be and what we decided would be our concerns. Many of the problems we have today are the results of us adults letting it happen through abdication of our duty and responsibility.

The future of us all is in the hands of our youth, and to be honest with you, that scares me a little right now because of the lessons the youth are learning from adults who carry the bulk of the responsibility for them. Of course, you know I'm not talking about all adults, but unfortunately there are too many parents and even non-parents who have some responsibility for the guardianship of children, who are side-stepping any responsibility.

I'm not just talking about keeping our children out of jail, off drugs, or out of the poor house. I'm talking about being with our children in nurturing and guiding ways that will help them develop solid, independent decision-making abilities; positive conflict resolving and effective problem-solving skills; and the courage to stand up for what they think is right; and the fortitude to take responsibility for their own actions.

In the many workshops I facilitate, I often ask parents what they want their young children to be like in ten to twenty years. Their answers always include educated, happy, independent, productive, kind, honest, caring, successful, dependable and lots more. The fear is that the children will grow to be too selfish, dependent, unreliable, irresponsible, non-caring, defiant, self-centered, disrespectful, and countless other characteristics that often lead to personality traits that are not conducive to developing and sustaining successful relationships, marriages, or career/life achievements. Behaviors and choices that can lead to addictions and other non-coping "numb-ers" are readily available to all of us anytime, anywhere. Most of us happily choose to say "no." Why do some of us choose one way and others the other way? In most cases, our choices are influenced by the role-modeling adults around us and/or by our feelings about whether or not there is a life for us in the mainstream.

The lives of today's children and those of tomorrow are complex. The lives of the parents are, too. Many skills, techniques, gut-feelings, trial-and-error efforts, and ways of raising our children just don't seem to be working today, if indeed we parents are finding the time, energy, and commitment to even try them with our fragile, confused, often neglected and ignored, maligned, and lost children.

We all want the best for our children, of course. We also want the best for ourselves. We want to be successful; we want to have nice things and drive nice cars and live in nice houses. There is nothing wrong with that, as long as those things don't become our reason for existing. How do we strike a balance that's healthy for everybody? We cannot raise children effectively if we are not aware and mindful of their needs and their natural development. We cannot expect children to raise themselves, and we cannot always rely on those skills that we know only from our parents, even if we did "turn out all right."

Parents serve as a mirror for the child as she is forming her self-concept. If the child sees smiles and positive reflections in "the mirror," she learns to smile at herself and feel good about who she is and who others think she is. By the time a child starts school, her self-image is well established as it relates to learning, success, failure, and other ways of being in the world. Research shows time and again that there is a positive connection between self-concept, learning, and success. Children need to feel able, capable, and lovable. When they do, they are encouraged children and will have much better chances in the world of children and in the adult world, as well.

The most effective parents have a foundation of goodness, good intentions, well meaning, and caring. But even though that's true, staying grounded there takes some work. "Good" takes on all kinds of meanings for all kinds of people. What's good to one parent may not be to another. This is why I like to use the word "effective," since it implies that the parents and children are being somewhat successful in their relationships, and no harm is being done in any major way by any family member.

> **We cannot discipline effectively if we are not present in our children's lives.**

We can guide our children to a life of positive skills that help build self-worth. To become the effective parents we want to be, we have to take the initiative with action, be mindful and caring, and involved in the process of our children's lives, and our response-ability level has to be high. Being involved in a loving way loaded with knowledge and the intent to do what's best for the child, to be "grounded in care" is the key.

The day-to-day boo-boos are not the stuff of which failure is made; rather, it is the attitude, the philosophy, the environment, the role modeling a parent does in relationship with the children that make the difference toward finding the best chance of parental success. Examine how you truly "feel" about your children and about yourself as parent. Wouldn't it be nice if all parents could truly "be in love" with their children and actually cherish every single moment of that journey together called sharing a life?

I think we could do a lot better, don't you?

Don't lose heart!

Make Your Time Matter!

Does this sound familiar? You drop by the grocery store on your way home to pick up some mid-week supplies that you need. Not too many items but enough to fill the bottom of the cart. You get home late, exhausted from a hard day at work where nobody seemed to appreciate how much you were doing, and now you're facing an evening of more work, cooking dinner, helping two children with homework and trying to listen to your husband's woes about his boss and how "he just doesn't understand." You're in a hurry to get in the house and get out of the too-tight work outfit and into your comfy clothes. You have your briefcase, your purse and your stack of reading which you also have to try and tackle overnight, and you make a valiant effort to try to take the groceries in with one trip. You use every God-given digit that you have curling several plastic bags around your arm and hooking them on the elbow, and do an enviable job of balancing it all ... until you get to the door and remember that you have the key in the wrong hand. As you try to retain the balance as you maneuver for the key, two of the bags slip from your fingers ... the bags that contain the breakables and the spillables ... and they do just that on your porch, your new welcome mat and your shoes.

Now you have another job added to your already full list. And this one takes precedence. After you turn red, angry at yourself, let out an exclamation of frustration that you're glad no one heard, you get the door open, put the other stuff in the kitchen and start the clean-up mumbling under your breath "why does this always happen to me?"

Why does it happen to us? Why do we continue to try and do more than we sensibly can do? What could she have done to avoid adding to her extended line up of tasks? She could have made two trips! Think of the time she could have saved as well as not adding frustration and aggravation to her mood as she faced the rest of the family and the other duties on the day.

Here's another scene for you. Did you ever get that nice favorite 14k gold necklace so badly tangled in knots that you felt it would never come undone? You pull it out of the mess in the jewelry box to wear, and you spend the next 10 exasperating minutes trying to get it untangled. You give up, disappointed, but you just don't have the time to bother with it any more. The next morning, you decide to give it another try, even though you're confident it will never be wearable again. You work on it for a few minutes, and then all of a sudden, Shazamm! The knot is gone, and the chain falls out in a straight line the way it should. Persistence, effort, and more effort, patience and focus pay off and result in success.

The same approaches can be applied to a lot of situations in our lives, especially as they relate to our relationships in family-with our children, with our spouse and with all of the members of the care-giving team; relatives, extended family members, friends, coworkers, and school personnel. How could our featured player have avoided the knotted chain that affected her life? She could have applied some prevention measures, and stored the chain in a hanging position to keep it from getting tangled in the first place.

One more. Have you ever tried to get a paper towel out of the dispenser in a rest room or restaurant when there is no edge of the paper to pull on? You end up pushing and pulling and grabbing several in a bunch and yanking out more than you need tearing some into pieces that fall on the floor and create a mess, and you end up drying your hands with scraps of what's left. Why? Because someone didn't load the towels into the machine correctly. There is a way to do it which makes it so easy. The correct way, the way someone should be teaching.

The mess on the floor and the inconvenience for you could have been prevented if the right thing had been done. Prevention of problems is an effort that has to be applied to our lives in order for us to be able to handle the day to day challenges more successfully. Why do you think we don't do more prevention work? What does it take? I have some thoughts for you. I think we try to do too much! We are creating a life that's too busy, too hectic, filled to the brim with things to do, places to go, errands to run, activities and events to attend. We think that all those things are requirements for living the full and rewarding life that we see advertised and modeled in our media. We too often don't give the building and maintaining of our important relationships enough of our unhurried time, either. We don't give the proper, mindful, educated, caring attention to what's important, truly important, in our lives. We don't do much planning or responding. We do too much reacting. We too often wait until there is a problem or a crisis, and then we try to do something about it. Wouldn't it make sense to do something to prevent the problems from happening? Of course we can't head off every inevitable problem in our lives, but with some good attention to planning, we can sure reduce the negative outcomes.

Try this. Write down two columns on a piece of paper. One column is "What's Most Important" and the other is "Where I Spend My Time." Make the list in each column. Somewhere on the Important side, hopefully near the top, will be "my children" and/or "my spouse." That's good. Now in what position are they on the Time Spent side? If you're not spending some great amount of your time with what's most important to you, then maybe you should do some thinking about making some changes. Time goes very quickly. The hours in a day are moving faster and faster due to our busy lives and our many involvements. The excessive time your children spend in front of a screen is possible time that you could be spending with them, sharing, giving, growing. Before you know it, your children will be grown and gone to live their own hectic adult lives, and you and they could miss out on the most important years you have to build solid relationships and to help them develop into the persons you want them to be in order to be happy and successful.

We can't provide the best guidance and role modeling and teaching for our children if we are doing it "on the run," shouting orders and instructions for life as we zip in and out of their lives filled with their own stresses and concerns. We can't give them the responsive caring they need if we do it in pieces seeming not to really care and being too busy to sit down and be 100% present to listen, to acknowledge, and to offer assistance and support.

> **GET IT RIGHT THIS TIME. WE CAN'T GO BACK AND DO IT OVER.**

If we want to eliminate as many future problems for our children as possible, then now is the time to try and prevent those problems from happening. And we have to be engaged with them in their lives in effective and productive ways to do that. We have to prepare them for their future. And we have to have time to do that. If we find that we don't have the time to do what we would like to do, what we know in our hearts is what we should be doing, then think about what needs to happen. Before it's too late. They need you now. They need your time and attention. Now is the time to pay attention to prevention. Right now, you are building their future memories of their time with you. What kind of memories do you want them to have?

Don't lose heart!

> What kind of memories do you want them to have?

GROUP TWO

Parenting: What's The Big Deal?

Parenting? What's the big deal? Anybody can do it, right? Not true. Just look around you. There are as many varieties of parenting styles as there are parents. Some are more "effective" than others.

Effective parenting is the most important job any of us will ever have! Notice I use the word "effective" because there are many parents, often through no fault of their own, who do have some trouble being "effective." How do we define "effective"? Here's my favorite definition:

> **"Effective parenting refers to carrying out the responsibilities of raising and relating to children in such a manner that they are well prepared to realize his or her full potential as human beings. It is a style of raising children that increases the chances of a child becoming the most capable person and adult he or she can be."**
>
> **–Dr. Kirby Alvy, Center for The Improvement of Child Caring and the founder of National Effective Parenting Initiative**

Parenting effectively can be the most difficult job we will ever have, but it can bring great joy as well.

Depending on a variety of factors, some parents find themselves "right at home" having children to raise.

They seem to do it with a calm efficiency while other parents are pulling their hair out, wondering "What were we thinking?"

Most parents take on their vital role of raising another human being with little or no training. Almost all jobs in our society require some type of education or training. But all of the parents I have ever asked always put "mother" or "father" in the top five most important jobs while admitting that they have not had a formal course on how to do it and some don't have a clue. Many do not feel "qualified" to be a parent. How do we know how to parent? Biologically, any of us might have the potential to be a father or a mother, but it takes more than biology to be a "professional parent."

Is effective parenting important? Children will be our next leaders, citizens, and workers. Children will be in charge of our world. Don't we want them to be healthy and ready to take on whatever the world delivers? They have a better chance of being successful (however you define success) if they have strong foundations on which to build. And that's what we parents are doing today with our children: preparing them for the world of tomorrow. Look at this chart provided by the Center for the Improvement of Child Caring in Los Angeles. You can see how what we do as parents can indeed affect almost all of life around us, in the present and in the future.

WAYS OF BEING GROUNDED IN CARE

AS AN EFFECTIVE PARENT

- As soon as the child enters the world, start the welcoming, start giving positive attention, love, approval, smiles, kind words, and hugs for appropriate behaviors. For those behaviors that you like, use praise and encouragement as positive reinforcements.

- You are the role model. Do the things that you expect from others: Be on time, pick up stuff, speak softly, be polite, reveal character, and settle disagreements without conflict.

- Create a routine. Create harmony in the home with clear expectations and promote responsibility. Assign everyday responsibilities, discuss needs, make assignments, and change them from time to time. Set time limits and check up on completion. Praise for efforts and guide and encourage strengths.

- Make rules simple, clear, and age- and developmentally-appropriate. Allow some sharing in decisions. Give and get repetition and reminders until the child can do it in a self-imposed way. Children will test, and forget. Expect it and be prepared.

- Make all expectations and consequences clear, and enforce them firmly, kindly, and fairly.

- Share feelings openly and let children be free to share theirs. Strengthen the basic communications of talking and listening with respect.

- Do not hit, spank, yell, or shame in anger or while you're out of control, preferably not at all. Don't get into power struggles with children. Discipline with love and firmness rather than with anger and force.

- Create a warm, caring, and happy atmosphere and use your loud and attention-getting voice for warnings of danger or taking of action. Avoid statements of threat, blame, shame, and ridicule.

- Have a sense of humor; laugh at your mistakes when you can and don't dwell on theirs. Put emphasis on strengths and encourage efforts and individual responsibility at all times.

- Be fair, understanding, patient, patient, patient, and consistent (but not rigid).

- Listen with undivided attention (what I call giving unhurried time), with interest, respect, and empathy. Avoid communication blocks. Don't pity, lecture, moralize or over-protect.

- Expose your children to a variety of life experiences, in the work places, libraries, museums, shows, and elsewhere. Provide opportunities and encourage your child to be involved in community activities that help others.

- Understand the child's needs and adapt to the changes from toddler to teenager.

SHAPING TOMORROW THROUGH EFFECTIVE PARENTING TODAY

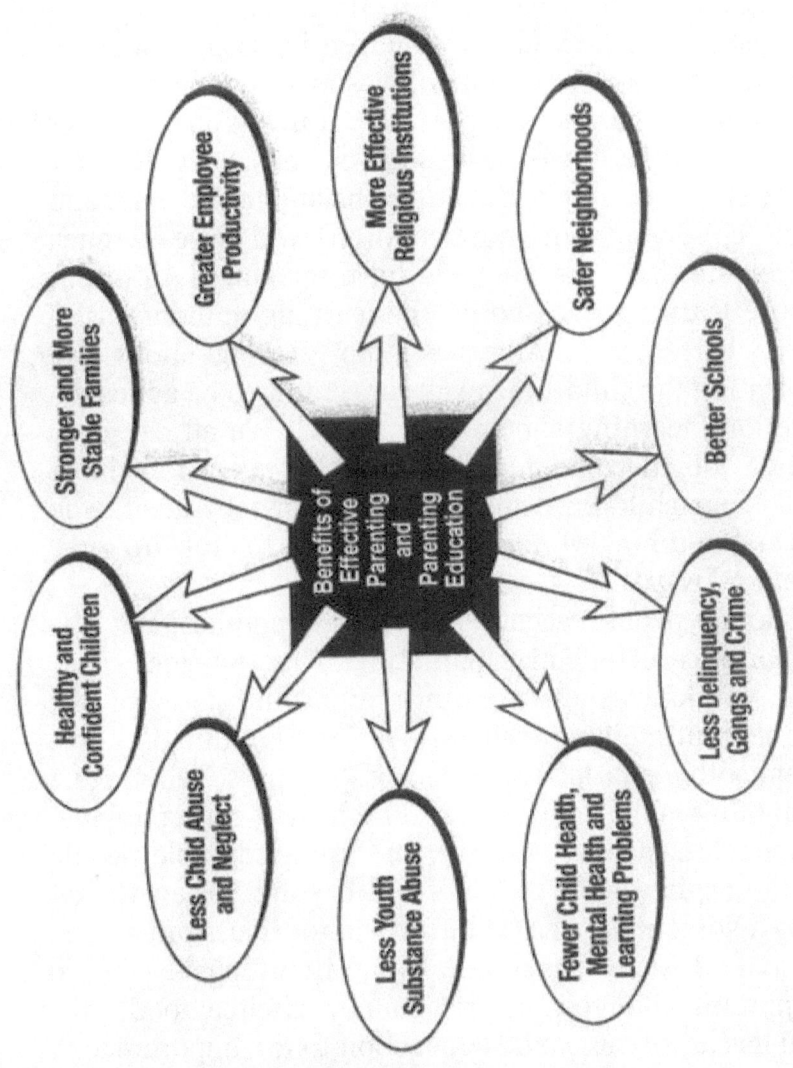

© Center for Effective Parenting (CICC) Los Angeles, CA

Offered by ParentsCare/still learning, inc., SC

Research from more than thirty years continues to point to the importance of parents in the lives of children and the value of the role they play in helping the children find their paths. Caregivers for our children hold the future of us all in their hands and hearts. However, caring for and growing children effectively isn't easy. Our challenge is to be with our children in positive ways so this journey we are all on will result in our homes and our schools being solid places, so our towns and counties will also thrive. If we create solid citizens, we will create a better community with better jobs and better lives, and their children (your grandchildren) will have a much better life than one we could have imagined. All of our future learning is based on the learning foundations of these early years. And we're not talking about just educating the child; we are all continuing to be educated. Life-long learning should be our goal. We all can do a better job, become more effective, if we know more about our children, who they are, what they need, who we are, and how we can best help them to grow up in all the good ways.

Some people accuse me of overemphasizing the importance of effective parenting. They tell me, "Hey, Jim, you know there are other important pieces of life, too. Parenting is not the cure-all for everything!" I give them with a puzzled look and say, "Yes, it is. Tell me one thing that is more important than having caring, loving, responsive, healthy, guiding, and knowledgeable people in the beginning of your life and beyond." Then we get into a sometimes heated but friendly discussion, as one by one, I show them how what they consider more important, like good health, money, shelter, food, etc., still has at its core some connection to the importance of someone in life taking good care of us. It might not be a biological parent but it will be someone or a few folks who are doing the job of effective parenting: Raising children well.

Almost every day, I work with parents who are near "the end of their rope" trying to raise their children. I empathize with them totally. Raising children well can be the most difficult job we have. It is also the most important job we have today and we don't get any training at it; we do not automatically know how to raise children. We get so concerned with and involved in the personal frustrations of our lives that we lose sight of those young ones around us. We forget about their feelings and how our moods and attitudes are affecting their lives now and in the future. With all that's going on, or not going on the way we want it to, it is easy to get so involved that we neglect the children. We don't do it on purpose of course, but we do it. We think they're going to be okay. As long as we feed them, put clothes on their back, give 'em a hug, and tell them we love them every now and then, everything will be all right. Not true. We have to do more than that.

Think about yourself as an adult. What if that was all you got? Would it be enough? We have to be very aware of the fact that we are sometimes leaving our children out of our lives. We have to be aware of them and what's happening to them practically all of the time. We have to give them attention, care, and love all of the time. It's easy for us to feel sorry for ourselves and get self-centered. We shout out in pain, "Hey, what about me?! Does anybody know I'm here?! What about my life?! It's not fair!" Those feelings are also important. You do have to be concerned about yourself, your life, and getting your needs met. But not to the point that you forget about their needs! I know it's tough, but you have to do it. Before you know it, the children will not be children any longer. They will be adults. What kind of adults depends on you. The more you dedicate yourself to your role, whether you want it or not, the fewer problems you will have as the children grow older. The more you give to your children in a sensible and selective way, the less they will need. They will become self-sufficient, able to make the right choices, and able to understand the rules, limits, beauties, and freedoms of life. If you make the commitment and follow through, your life with your children will be much better. You and your home life will be more secure. There will be less stress and that absence will help you be happier in your personal life. If you give, you will get back twice over. You and your children will be blessed for it.

Play with them. Talk with them. Listen to them. Respect what they have to say and feel. Be with them where they are. Let them be with you. Give them the feeling that you think they deserve to be here in your life, that you think they are somebody; that they are special, and you are glad they were born to you.

Compare the job of parent to the job you do for money or to your schoolwork. If you don't attend to the details of your work, you will not do well. You will not get a promotion or a raise or you will make a low grade. If you really foul up, you can get fired or you will fail the course. You can make mistakes in the process, yes, but you will still get paid and you can still stay in school. Making mistakes is a way we learn and get better and better at what we are doing. If you don't pay attention to the details of your work, the work will not get done.

So, when you are working as a parent, you have to pay attention and involve yourself in it. Put down what you are doing. Don't watch the clock. Don't let TV, or the Internet, or a book, or radio, or music, or a phone conversation take your time away from your job, which is being with your child.

In some of the workshops that I facilitate, I talk about the four key elements of effective parenting, which I will touch on briefly here and address in more detail in another group.

In order for families to even have a chance at harmony and happiness, those in charge have to be in charge. I'm not talking about being controllers or wardens or drill sergeants. I'm talking about being good managers of a home, of a schedule, of your life, and of others' lives. The first key is **The Self**. The individual who decides to bring children into this world needs to be a fairly healthy person physically, emotionally, and mentally, and a person who is able to realize the importance of the choice to be a parent. That includes both mothers and fathers to be.

Then the connection between the **Couple, or Caregivers** (the second key), needs to be healthy as well. A parenting style should be discussed and all people engaged in the care of the child should be reading from the same page while supporting and enriching each other. Healthy parents and caregivers will most likely then create a healthy **Home** (the third key), which is a warm and nurturing place with minimum friction, conflict, and combat; where relationships are cooperative, loving, and respectful rather than adversarial, discouraging, and mean-spirited.

The final key to the most effective parenting is **Knowledge**. If we are healthy and our homes are healthy, then most likely we will want to gather knowledge about how best to perform our roles as parents. Which brings us to this point: **Home Is Where The Start Is.** If we do not have the knowledge and health to create environments that allow and encourage our children to grow and find their way to their full potentials, then we are not building the strong foundation of life they need. This failure can lead to future dysfunction and cause unhappy family situations.

I was motivated to write about this subject because of some new research on the importance of the early years of life. The science of early childhood development calls on parents, teachers, family educators, and the nation to thoroughly re-examine policies that affect children and bolster our investment in their well-being. Children undergo tremendous intellectual, emotional, and physical development from birth to age five. Providing safe, loving, and enriching environments for children during this stage in their lives is crucial to development. The first weeks and months of life are crucial in setting the stage for what happens later in life.

It is shocking to me that our nation, state governments, and too many parents and teachers are not taking advantage of nearly fifty years of research on early childhood development to help raise and educate young children. Whenever we talk about our children, much of the focus is on their academic advancement, but their social and emotional development are just as important – maybe even more so. If a child has a solid foundation of self-worth, his ability to become educated increases proportionately. The needs of children in these areas have to have the same emphasis, at least. Scientific evidence shows that even very young children are capable of experiencing deep anguish and grief in response to trauma, loss, and personal rejection. Unfortunately, many early childhood education and child care programs have failed to apply such findings to everyday dealings with children. The severe shortage of professionals with training in children's mental health issues makes the situation even worse.

- Early experiences affect the development of the brain and lay the foundation for intelligence, emotional health, and moral development. Those are the basics that help lead us toward fuller,

healthier lives and relationships that build the healthy families that are the very core of our society.
- Healthy early development depends on nurturing and dependable caregivers who are able to focus on the role and gather the knowledge the role requires.
- How young children *feel* is as important as how they *think*, particularly with regard to school readiness. In most situations where a child is having problems in school, there is nothing biologically wrong with the child; there are no apparent learning problems. Most of the difficulty comes from behavioral problems based on emotional instability, which in more cases than not is born in the environment (the home) and in the fragile and negative relationships modeled in the home.
- Although society is rapidly changing, the needs of young children are not being addressed with the change they need in the process. Too many parents and caregivers are self-centered, immersed in work and schedules and to-do lists, and distracted by anything away from the number one priority: parenting the children.

Effectively-parented children are the most likely to succeed at school; be cooperative and helpful in the community; and become productive and healthy adults and parents. Modern parenting education programs, classes, and seminars are the most direct way of helping more parents to be effective and sensitive in raising children. The Center for the Improvement of Child Caring (CICC), under the direction of Dr. Kirby Alby (along with a gracious handful of more pioneers), has for more than 35 years been trying to convince the country that effective parenting is just as important as I think it is. CICC has been a leader in pointing out to the country that several vital parts of our communities, those that seem to always be on the concerned list, show that effective parenting without a doubt can affect them all in dramatic ways. (See the graphic earlier in this group.)

Providing educational opportunities for parents and others responsible for our children is a solution that speaks to the root causes of some of our societal ills. Lawmakers and business and community leaders often work on the *symptoms* of our ills and not the *causes*. While treatment of existing problems has to take place, we also need to spend more time and money to prevent those same problems from recycling generation after generation. We keep doing the same thing and getting the same frustrating results.

One important aspect of our communities is our schools. If we have better students, we will have better schools. If we have better parents, we will have better students. Effective parents should be partners with the schools as team members in helping achieve the students' success. How effective the parent is at home will better prepare the child to be open and receptive to the wondrous opportunities to learn what the schools and the teachers provide. What a loss in life it is when a child does not receive the educational foundation that is available in many forms in our schools. Many dedicated people work hard to provide the best education they can. Parents and other caregivers have to be equally dedicated and caring about doing their part to prepare the child to be a willing learner. That's why it's important for parents to start the learning process early and continue it through the formal education years for the children.

At the root of a learning attitude is liking to read, and what happens in the home in the early years sets the standard for learning. Reading possibilities are all around us, and the Internet and your child's school's media department are full of ideas and materials. As the parent and role model, your interest in learning is critical for your children. Make sure learning and education are important values in your home. Give support and cooperation to your schools and teachers. Let your children know that education is at the top of your priority list with reading, learning, studying, having a positive attitude, and exhibiting self-motivation receiving your attention before most other things like computers, games, TV, playmates, toys, extracurricular activities, and wasting time. It's all important for well-balanced growing, but too often the lists are reversed and the pieces that are not the most valuable outweigh the pieces that will give the best future.

Parents and caregivers play the most crucial role in the success of our children. Helping them be successful in school is giving them perhaps the best preparation for being successful in life. And success in school does not exclusively mean academically successful. There are many other parts of a successful school life that contribute to our total education. It's important that parents, caregivers, and educators understand that narrow focus on intelligence, top grades, rigid schedules, and unrealistic expectations can be factors that could actually hamper positive and successful growth toward adulthood. There are social, psychological, physical, and emotional growth needs, as well. Proper attention has to be given to all of the parts that make us the human beings that we are and will become. Growing up is hard to do. Helping others grow up well is hard, too. But it's our job. We have to know how to do it effectively. It's a big deal. **Don't lose heart!**

If life is a race, then effective parenting is a sprint, a relay, and a marathon. But it is not about crossing a finish line in record time.
Instead, it's just crossing it - with effort, determination, desire, and the foundation work needed to prepare for the run. The effective parenting race is not something that takes place in milliseconds,
but rather over a lifetime. Effective parenting is lifelong learning and teaching
for the parent **and** the parented.

GROUP THREE

The Four Keys to Effective Parenting

Parenting effectively is arguably the most important endeavor we will undertake in our lifetimes. It can also often be the most difficult one we will undertake and we seldom get any training in it. How, then, do we learn to be parents?

There are all kinds of ways, some of them good and helpful, some not. If what you are doing doesn't seem to decrease your frustration and irritation, or has little or no effect on the disharmony in the home or on unacceptable child behavior, then maybe it's time to try something new. Parents often choose to work together to learn how to bring their child into the world, actually taking lessons in "birthing." Then we think that because we were biologically successful, raising the child will be easy as long as we have love and good intentions. We think that we must have some sort of innate ability that guides us to do the right thing when we need to make decisions. Many new parents are discovering the fallacy in that thinking and are frustrated over what to do.

Key - 1 - The Self

> *Perhaps the biggest barrier to our becoming better parents is our own unhappiness.*

Before seriously approaching child rearing, groundwork has to be laid, like building a foundation to a house. The first and most important item on the groundwork list is your "self." It is most important that your physical and emotional health be in good working condition, and that your attitude about your responsibility be a positive one. If we feel that we are making sacrifices in our personal lives to have children, believe me, the children will feel it in the form of our impatience, irritability, lack of focus, resentment, and possibly misplaced anger. I suggest that we look at having children as a privilege and an honor, having their lives entrusted to us for safe-keeping and guidance. The responsibility is an alternative, a choice – not a sacrifice. The business of raising a child should be a high goal in life unto itself, not a result of sacrificing something else or a replacement for something else which we will get to eventually as soon as we "get this child raised." It is a life-long career and an honorable profession.

In the previous group, I briefly went over the **Four Keys of Effective Parenting: The Self, The Caregivers, The Home, and Knowledge.** I mentioned parents as individuals and how important it is for us to know ourselves well before we can truly be effective parents. Individuals in family management – parents and caregivers – must concentrate on their "selves" since the healthy self is the first key toward effective parenting, raising healthy children, and creating harmonious homes.

When you think about self, you have to ask "who am I" and "what am I here for" and "how do I feel about who I am and what I am here for?" To even begin to arrive at an answer, you have to go way back and find out where you came from. How did you arrive at the present place of self with your values, beliefs, and temperament with positives and negatives? Many things about the self came with you at birth, but so much about you has been developed at the hands and hearts of parents and many others who have influenced your life in countless ways, and led you to who you have become. You may be completely happy with your place and all the excellent work done on you by others. You may be the most well-adjusted person in the world and want for nothing. If you are one of those people, you are truly blessed. Most of us are just waking up to the fact that we didn't get everything we needed in those early years, and we are looking for new and better ways to live our lives. No finger pointing at anyone in the past is necessary. It's just the way it is. We are now just beginning to truly identify what the demands of life really are, what those demands might be on us, and how well equipped we are to handle them.

To be healthy, we need some degree of good health and physical stamina. We need emotional and psychological stability. We need some sort of saleable or useful skill or ability. We must find and hold positions that will pay us for our services. A job means to be productive, to engage in meaningful and fulfilling endeavors with one's energies and talents. Personal happiness and social well-being most often rely on the ability to have friends and actually influence others. There is likely to be an innate need to have and give kindness, consideration, sympathy, tolerance, and generosity.

Then for most of us comes the ability to select, win, and hold a mate through a mutually gratifying bond (hopefully one of love). What usually follows is the establishment of a satisfactory family life, one that produces offspring who are successful in their own lives in much the same ways. How does one confront these demands (or suggested requirements, if you will) of life with confident results?

Through all of my readings and research, my favorite description of our human growth is from *Child Development: Physical and Psychological Growth through Adolescence* (Saunders, Philadelphia, 1965). Even though the book was written a few years ago, I feel that these suggestions from Marian E. Breckenridge and Dr. E. Lee Vincent still ring true:

- As a child grows, she must learn to understand her assets and to use them constructively. She

must discover her liabilities and if possible, correct them or if this is not possible, to accept them and make the best of them. (Helping a child to be secure in his "self" while also being accepting and loving of who the child is, is also a major part of the parental duty.) A sense of one's responsibility to others balanced with a sense of self-protection sufficient to keep one functioning at an efficient level must be developed.
- The ability to accept wise authority, to bend one's will to necessary authority without loss of self-confidence or initiative, requires a well-balanced experience with parental and school authority in early childhood and adolescence, and with civil and ethical authority in later years.
- The ability to live an imaginative and resourceful inner life without withdrawal from the realities of the world must be balanced against the ability to mix happily and successfully with people without continual dependence upon social stimulation.
- The ability to control emotion without stifling and repressing it, to express emotion and to utilize the driving power which it provides without impetuousness or personal disaster is also relevant to the growth.

How in the world do we get to be this mature and healthy in our self-hoods? All these lessons require continual learning. The first learning comes from the parents, the caretakers and caregivers, the teachers, the mentors, the friends, the relatives, and the experiences. The accumulation of all influences together impacts our direction to be who we are. The later, more self-conscious learning comes from ourselves as we determine what part of who we have become is acceptable to us and what part is not. That's when we decide to change and work toward a new goal of "self," or at least we think about some closet cleaning and fine tuning. **The true self becomes the authentic self. The person we see in the mirror each morning is welcomed. The person we see is self-confident, highly regarded and self-competent, ready to take on the challenges of the world in positive, healthy ways.** Included in those challenges are, more often than not, loving a partner and together raising healthy children in a healthy home.

Key -2- The Caregivers

Along with a healthy self, the next important item on the foundation list is **the other parent, or The Caregivers.** If there is a couple involved, then that relationship should be a healthy one, emotionally and physically. If it's a single parent, others in her or his life who are involved with the care-giving need to be supporters in a healthy way. The connecting love should be strong and obvious, with respect for each other, shared lives (fun and work) and with cooperative abilities to solve the many daily problems of life without going berserk. Here is a scenario for you to consider:

Jane came to the relationship with a very conservative history. She was raised in a traditional, intact family setting: father worked and mother stayed home and raised the children, Jane and her two older brothers. The father did the serious disciplining, with mother calling the shots and building the boundaries. The boys were allowed a few more freedoms than the daughter; after all they were boys, and boys will be boys, you know. The children's life schedules were pretty much laid out for them: school, work, church, and some play. As they grew older, the children came to realize that their parents were considered "strict." In fact, they often were so rigid that the boys made choices to rebel in strange and upsetting ways. The girl just held in the pain and shame of not being one of the crowd, maturing naturally and feeling deep inside that she was not only not trusted by her parents, her father especially, but also not liked by her peers. She was a better than average student, making grades to please which were never quite good enough for the parents, and she found a bit of freedom being on the school yearbook staff. Her parents were pretty high on the "demanding-ness" scale. They believed their job to be to direct, teach, and control their children with a lot of limits and very few freedoms. They felt they knew what was best for their children and they would provide for them and tell them how to be in the world. As a result, they were not very responsive to the needs of their sons and daughter. They were more intrusive and demanding with their parental power.

Jane, now an adult, has a steady, respectable job as an office manager and lives a rather structured, no-risk life that borders on boring. She finds change and making decisions difficult, so she pretty much stays in her routine with underdeveloped social skills and bouts of depression.

Jane's new husband, Frank, presented quite a different background. He was an only child of older parents who were quite bright in most everything except raising children. They, too, felt that good parenting was about teaching and influencing and control. However, they felt that the best way to control was to allow Frank lots of freedoms and to offer him very few limits. Limits, they felt, were too rigid and might stifle the child's creativity and natural curiosity. Therefore, Frank's parents were responsive, but they did so in non-traditional and lenient ways. They did not require mature behavior, allowed Frank considerable self-regulation, and avoiding confrontation. As a result of his parents' choices, Frank lacked self-control and discipline. He wasn't used to limits in his life, so he had trouble in school and afterward with authority and structure. His grades and behavior kept him from going to college. However, he was very popular with a good sense of general self-confidence, effective social skills, and seemed to be always positive about life, seeing it as something to challenge and enjoy.

Frank and Jane met when mutual friends invited them to a party and surprised their friends and themselves when they actually "hit it off" and began dating. That often happens when two people are somewhat at odds in basic temperament and personality. There is just enough to attract and fill the needs of each other where there was a lack. Too often, the contrast is too great, and the "opposites attract" myth doesn't last for long. A man and a woman are sometimes too opposite and real incompatibility ensues, often with combative temperaments, eventually causing all kinds of trouble in the relationship. But, every now and then, the opposites do support and encourage and a bond is made. Balance is found.

We have already spent some time talking about the healthy development of the first key to effective parenting: **The Self.** The next key is just how healthy **the relationship of The Caregivers** will be as they prepare for a life of raising children. In the case I'm presenting, Jane and Frank both might be considered quite healthy and normal by most of society's standards, but the fact is they both wrestle with some shortcomings in their daily functioning that could impact their relationships with their future children. As long as they fulfill each other's needs and live their lives with each other in the ways that work for them, fine. But if they don't have serious discussions about a parenting style they both will adopt when they have children, they and the children could be in for a long and bumpy ride.

It's difficult. Each parent comes from a different background with different ideas about how one is expected to behave. Each comes with different parental role models. Whose model will they use? Will they use Frank's in one instance and Jane's in another? Or, will they be so inconsistent that they will present nothing but confusion and chaos to the children when it comes to discipline, expectations, and directions – in other words, will they choose questionable family management. If good decisions are not made beforehand, then what also often results is a deep strain on the couple's relationship. There could be frustration that turns into anger that turns into resentment then into dislike, disrespect, and ultimately dysfunction within the family unit. The home atmosphere could become one of conflict, complaints, selfish actions, and screaming for attention to have one's needs met. In the worst scenario, no family member in such a home will have his or her needs met and the family could be torn apart. The potholes of family court come next.

As far as choosing a parenting style, there are many combinations of the basic styles that result from the mix of parents' temperaments, environments, and who they are as people. Their beliefs and values also play a vital part. Parents need to make the important decision about which parenting style they will attempt to use most often. We all vacillate between some of the characteristics of some of the styles, depending on how we feel on any given day, what kind of mood we and the children are in and what's going on in our lives. But we have to make the conscious effort to use one style most of the time for obvious reasons. (I will go more in depth about the different kinds of parenting styles in the next grouping.) **The effect the caregivers will have on the children will depend in a major way on their being consistent in their relationships with each other and the children.**

Key -3- The Home

Healthy individuals together as a couple create a home environment that is warm, loving, and nurturing for the little ones to enter and grow. Most homes that are not harmonious have a major amount of hectic schedules, a lack of routine, inconsistencies in expectations, and unclear communications. Of course, we cannot create nirvanas or heaven on earth, but we can attempt to be mindful of the need to keep an atmosphere conducive to the continued health of all family members.

You've all heard the saying **"home is where the heart is."** I can't find out who said that the first time, but I believe what it might mean is that home is the place where your heart, in the romantic or poetic sense, feels the best, the safest, and the most alive. That is the place where your heart, or soul, or self can best call home. If that is true, then our home is not a particular structure or a geographical place, but rather the place where we would want most to be. Our home could be in a rolling RV, a sailing ship, a pup tent, or a high-rise penthouse. I like to think of home as the internal human development of a dwelling fostered by a connected and loving family whose aims are for all members to be as healthy as they can possibly be in life.

But there is another saying about home that intrigues me more, especially as we talk about the **third Key to Effective Parenting: The Home**. T.S. Eliot wrote in one of his poems "home is where one starts from." I have modified that and use it quite often when I am discussing this topic in workshops. I like to say: "Home is where the start is." I came across another play on those words recently and like it, too. It's "home is where the heart lives." I modify that to say "home is where the heart lives, or dies." I know that's a little morbid, but I feel a need to be serious about this subject, because too many adults responsible for children don't seem to be taking this subject seriously enough.

The quality of a "home," in this case the place where children live and grow, is an extremely vital component in successfully arriving at and

living in that place called adulthood. From the moment the most dependent creature in the world arrives on the scene with no verbal skills, minimal body strengths, limited cognitive abilities, and hundreds of needs to be attended, the quality of the child's environment plays a critical role. And it continues to be critical until the child moves on to build his/her own idea of what a home should be. Many young adults will base their ideas on the same kind of home in which they grew up. Many others will try to achieve the opposite of from whence they came because it was not the best of worlds. Still others will have no clue about what to do. Many get their ideas from television. Not too many real homes there. Others see beautiful families doing beautiful things in beautiful places in magazines and movies. The reality is questionable there, too.

We may have a dream of an ideal "house": a structure to protect us from the elements and give us pleasure and status. Or we may experience one that gives us anxiety attacks trying to keep it maintained and pay the mortgage. But I think the quality of a real "home" comes from within the people who live and grow there together. This is why it is so important that people who want to be effective parents do some work on the self and the caregiver keys before they decide on what a home is going to be like. If the homemakers bring to the house the proper ingredients, then a successful home will most often result.

Different people, based on temperament, personality, values and beliefs, and wherewithal, will define what makes a good home in many different ways. I don't believe that there is an absolute right or wrong way to define it. If the home is a place where one finds comfort, cooperation, safety, nurturing (for the body, heart, and soul), security, support, warmth, love, care, and connection, then the people there experience the truth of the saying "home is where the heart lives." If, on the other hand, the house environment is one of fear, conflict, arguing, irregularity, unresponsiveness, non-support, minimal love and care, then it hardly qualifies as a home at all and falls into the "home is where the heart dies" category. Of course, those are the two extremes of conditions. In most homes, the reality falls somewhere in the middle. If the majority of the time the environment falls toward the positive pole, then the chance of eventual good adulthood for the children and a successful life for the adults will be better. In either case, the environment plays an enormous part in shaping the behavior of both the children and the adults and pretty much determines just how the home functions. **Home is where the start is**.

Our homes should be havens, respites, retreats in which we find solace from the trials and tribulations of the everyday grind of work and school and stresses. We want to go there for support and encouragement and to heal our wounds that come from competing in the battles of life. In our homes, we should learn about loyalty, compassion, ethics, citizenship, and how to be concerned about our families as well as the larger family of community. **Our homes should be places where we long to be, where we celebrate victories together, and comfort each other in times of disappointment and despair. We find new energy and new hope from the very act of being connected with loving others who care about us and return our love.**

Too often, though, homes are not those wonderful places. Many experts feel this void is at the root of the violence in our schools. I agree wholeheartedly. Adults work more hours than they need to work sometimes, or hang out on bar stools, or get over-involved in extracurricular activities just to stay away from a house that presents them with more problems and demands. Children connive and manipulate and lie to avoid coming home. They would rather be some place, any place, else. If they cannot physically leave or run away, they will often leave emotionally, presenting just a shell of a self with feelings of isolation and worthlessness. Or, just the opposite, radical, rebellious, bizarre behavior might result due to the unhappy surroundings and responses.

Using simple logic, if a human being depends on his/her environment to not only survive but to also thrive, to grow well, to advance in all ways toward a positive and healthy life, then the home in which that human dwells is perhaps the primary factor that determines who that person will become. It will also determine who that person will be in the workplace, in the community, and in the lives of others. It will help determine who that person will seek out; who that person will marry and have children with; what kind of a home those people create for their children ... and on and on the life cycles go. It all begins in the home.

Indeed, home is where the start is. What kind of home are you in? What kind of home are you providing for your children? What childhood memories are you providing now? Is it a place where all family members like to be together, loving each other, caring for each other, wanting the best for each other? Or is it a place filled with battling egos searching for some meaning in desperate ways and so self-centered that nobody's needs get met? Think about your home. Is it all it needs to be? Or does there need to be a revision, a remodeling, or an awakening? To know that requires some good degree of knowledge, which is our fourth effective parenting key.

Key -4- Knowledge

The more we know about our children, how they develop and why, what their needs are, why they behave the way they do, and how we should respond (not react) to their behaviors, the better we will be able to do our job and the higher our

level of response-ability. We will be better informed, more mindful, and more present in the moments when our guiding and teaching are all important.

The knowledge that we already have and can build on will determine just how we put the health of self, caregivers, and home together to surround our children with the care, guidance, and love they need to reach their full potential. It's not simple. There is no quick-fix formula, no magic bullet of parenting. There are many skills that can be developed, and there have to be many since there are so many different kinds of children with all sorts of temperaments in all manner of environmental and physical conditions. What might be a good skill for one parent with a certain temperament and personality might be response-disability for another parent and child combination.

For more than 100 years, many smart people have been studying children through scientific methodology, observation, and applied research. Because of those efforts, which continue even more widely today, we now have a much better understanding of why children do some of the things they do, and we now know better how we in management and guidance roles (parents, teachers, caregivers) need to respond to those behaviors. There are countless behaviors which change and change again; therefore, there have to be countless skills and approaches to those behaviors, a sort of mix-and-match activity to find the best course for helping the children grow into adulthood with the least amount of damage to themselves and to their care-giving adults.

The very foundation of our knowledge has to be our beliefs and attitudes about being responsible for and responsible to another human being. **If we are serious about the job, we will want to learn all that we can in order to be the best at that role. We will want to find out how children tick and how they tock and how we get in sync with them to help their human clock run as smoothly as possible.**

Some parents and caretakers and teachers simply do not care about the children. Oh, they put up with them and do what they can to keep the little "troublemakers" in line and on task, but there is no love for some of these children. Some adults actually think parenting is about making children obedient, compliant, and conformant to adult commands and wishes. They think that it is all children need to grow up. They're going to grow up anyway, whether the parent wants it or not. Just **how** they grow up is the issue.

Let's have a little workshop session.

How do we become who we are? That's a question I ask at many of my ParentsCare workshops and classes. There is always a very interesting list that invariably includes: parents, peers, friends, teachers, schools, music, TV, trial and error, books, geography, churches, relatives, and the like. Other factors that are often mentioned include: our financial situation, our home life, our choices, our spouses, our education, marital status, illness, natural disasters, and so on. Many times, the reason of nature or biology or genetics is left off the list, but who we *are* is very much determined by what we came into the world *with*.

What we have and what we do with what we have are both critical to our development. Since we are mostly talking about children in these writings, perhaps it's more appropriate to say that what *others* do with what we have is critical to our development. We don't have much to say about what others do to us and with us or for us in those early years of life. We are totally at someone else's disposal for them to do with as they please. Many do not do well, often due to a lack of knowledge. They don't know what to do or whom to ask. However, rest assured that our biological makeup has a lot to do with our becoming us. We are short or tall, thin or not, with hair of curls or straight as nails, dark or light skin, strength of muscle, musical inclination, good with numbers, agile, active, calm, curious, persistent, and distractible or focused, and on and on the list goes with physical, mental, emotional, and temperamental differences that move us toward our true selves. How people respond to those unique parts of us impact us in ways that influence our growth and help us to determine our way of living in the world. If the influential ones in our lives respond to our unique selves carelessly or without knowledge as to how they should respond, then their response might become a barrier to our finding our true selves. We may be lost forever, or we may in later adult years discover ourselves for the first time due to a self-help program, a caring loved one, a mentor, or by re-parenting ourselves, trying to give or receive for ourselves that which we never had.

It is from the combination of our biology and our environment that we truly become who we are. Those people in our lives teach us our values and our basic beliefs. They teach us about manners, about consideration, about kindness and citizenship, work ethics, and loyalty. They supply us with role models for honesty, emotional maturity, and caring for others. They fill our needs and guide our steps. From all that we learn, we develop our feelings about all that there is, and from all of those values and beliefs and feelings come our practices and our behaviors.

Now we are getting to the core of knowledge. What we know and how we practice what we know leads us (and those for whom we are responsible) to how we act in the world. How do we solve problems? How do we settle conflicts? How do we get along? Who are we really and how proud of us are we?

If you have children, think ahead to their future when they are young adults. They have been away from home for a while and they are visiting you this Sunday afternoon. What type person do you want to see standing in front of you? Will he hug you, tell you he loves you or will he brush by you with coolness in an effort to get this obligatory visit over with? What kind of character do you want that child to have? What kind of personality? This list often takes half an hour for workshop participants to compile. They want so much for their children. It's not always what the children might want, but the parents love making a wish list of expectations.

The list includes items such as: successful, happy, educated, self-confident, independent, kind, religious, giving, loving, caring, considerate, dependable, trustworthy, helpful, hard worker, respectful, respected, self-starter, family man, good mother, good father, self-fulfilled, and lots more. Add your own. Who would you like for your children to be when they grow up? When do you think they start becoming who you want them to be? The answer is either "as soon as they were born" or "never." If who they want to be (their true selves) and who you want them to be is close to the same, then the answer is "as soon as they were born." If you fight them and turn them from themselves toward some image of what you want them to be, then the answer could be "never."

Children by themselves cannot get to where we want them to be or to a place at which they would like to arrive. They need our help. Their job is to grow up to be independent, productive, contributing members of society; our job is to help them get there. Our roles are hard and challenging, but rewarding and joyful. Now for the news you don't want to hear. Even when all the foundations are laid and the structure is going up, there are still going to be conflicts between parents and children. We know that the goals of children and those of the parents will often not be the same. The needs will be different, and the fulfillment of those needs will often butt heads. Natural disagreements arise because parents and children want different things. The parents' difficult task is to determine the needs of all concerned, and which are most important at that moment, and for future moments, to the well-being of the individual or the relationship or the family unit. Needs, values, and desires are often in opposition, and it is the parents' job to help children understand how to settle differences the most sensible way, or explain, or simply set up a rule with definite and specific consequences that lead to a settlement so that no one feels like a loser and everyone's self-worth remains as intact as possible.

> **Discipline and punishment are NOT the same thing. Punishment is done TO a child; discipline is done FOR a child.**

Most often conflicts arise around behaviors, usually ones that the parents deem inappropriate or unacceptable. Change of the behavior is what the parent wants, but the child behaves a certain way for a reason. In fact, we all behave in certain ways for certain reasons. Our role is to address the behavior, and have the response-ability to change it, modify it, redirect it, or nurture it. Yes, there are behaviors that we like, and it's just as important to reinforce a good behavior in a response-able way.

We want our children to behave in ways that will require little, if any, punishment, because there are very few parents who really like to punish their children.

The answer to finding ways to decrease punishment is to discipline well. *Punishment and discipline are not the same things.* Punishment is usually thought of as coercive action, which means to cause one to undergo pain, fear, suffering, shame, harsh or injurious treatment for a wrongdoing or a "not-doing." It is usually verbal, emotional, and/or physical treatment or retaliation done *to* a child. Discipline means to teach, and is something done *for* or *with* the child. There are many alternatives to coercive punishment, which is usually an action with short range or immediate perceived benefits, an external influence, and most often to satisfy the needs of the parent. Discipline is an action with long-range benefits which are internalized by the child. It is of greater benefit to children if coercive punishment is never used.

There are other kinds of punishments labeled compelling, persuasive, or effective, but most child rearing experts are now putting more emphasis on the use of consequences. There are good and bad consequences that exist or can be created for good and bad behaviors. These are skills and techniques used for long-range good and are for teaching the child how to "be" in the world in the most acceptable and successful way. When we add this kind of knowledge to our foundation and accept that it is real and can be effective, then we are beginning to arm ourselves with what we need to manage our homes and our families in the most effective way.

There are **Affirming Consequences** and **Correcting Consequences**. Affirming Consequences are those that result from acceptable or desirable behaviors that have positive pay-offs or rewards. They include the parental skills of praise (with purpose), encouragement, verbal appreciation, shaping or "show and tell," privileges, unhurried time, approvals, reinforcing, valuing, and listening, to mention some of the more acceptable ones. We will discuss praise, encouragement, punishment and discipline, and listening in some detail in later groupings. Parts of affirming consequences also include other areas like modeling, attending with smiles, and rewards (vs. bribes). We will also dig deeply into the details of correcting consequences.

Until then, please keep working on the foundations of yourself and your "others" and your home. Parenting effectively is a very tough job, but the joys and rewards usually outweigh the bumps in the road.

Don't lose heart!

> The elements of successful child rearing are numerous and complex. Thousands of books have been written on the subject. It's not an innate talent that comes with the biological ability. As a professional parent, you can arm yourself with the information that's available. Knowledge is guaranteed to lessen your frustration and confusion.

Strangers in the House

Many years ago, Thornton Wilder wrote a beautiful, classic play called "Our Town." A scene in the play profoundly spotlights one of the tragedies playing out in homes all over the world. It's the scene where little Emily has died. She goes to the graveyard and is told, "Emily, you can return to earth for one day in your life. Which day would you like?" And she said, "Oh, I remember how happy I was on my twelfth birthday." All the people in the graveyard say, "Emily, don't do it. Don't do it, Emily." But she ignores their warning. She wants to see mama and papa again. So, the scene switches and there she is twelve years old, back in time to that wonderful day she remembers. She comes down the stairs in a pretty dress with her curls bouncing. But her mother is so busy making the cake for her birthday that she cannot stop long enough to look at her. Emily says, "Mama, look at me. I'm the birthday girl." And mama says, "Fine, birthday girl, now sit down and have your breakfast."

Emily just stands there and says again, "Mama, look at me." But mama doesn't. Papa comes in and he's so busy making money for them that he has never looked at her and neither does brother because he's so involved with his interests he can't stop for her, either. The scene ends with Emily standing in the middle of the stage lamenting, "Please somebody just look at me. I don't need the cake or the money. Please just look at me." But nobody does so she turns to her mother once again and says, "Please, mama?" After a long wait, Emily turns and says, "Take me away. I've forgotten what it was like to be human. Nobody looks at anybody. Nobody cares anymore, do they?"

The poignancy in that exchange which took place many years ago still rings too true today. Our homes are filled with family members who are strangers to each other. Strangers because they hardly know each other, barely spend time together, scarcely ever look, really look at each other and often have no clue as to the interests and feelings of the other persons living under the same roof. We sometimes know more about people in the work place than we do about our blood relatives. I think one of the reasons is that we have never learned how to build relationships with our own family. We often take each other for granted, or compete for time, or grow too selfish and too self-centered. We get to the point where we over-expect or under-expect, and we quit trying to truly communicate because it's easier to give short answers and get lost in television or work. We think our loved ones will understand our disconnect because they love us. We can get away with near murder because they are family. And we often do.

Relationship building is hard work, but it is rewarding and fulfilling. How do we build relationships, anyway? If you wanted to build one with a potential new friend, here are some things you consider doing. You might start off by sharing information about each other. You know, birthplace, job, education. As the process develops, you might ask questions, show interest, and be supportive. You would certainly listen and be responsive. You might ask questions like, "My best friend is ... You know why? Who's yours?" Or you could ask about favorite stuff, like TV shows, movies, foods, games, singers, teams, and so on. "Where would you like to visit if you could go anywhere in the world?" How about, "What's your best and worst quality?" Or, "What are (were) your favorite and least favorite subjects in school?" "What books do you like?" "What are you best at? Worst?" "What makes you sad, or happy? When do you feel most alive?" And depending on age, "What would bedtimes and curfews be if you could make them?" Or, a real conversation developer: "If you could change one thing about yourself, what would it be and why?"

Of course, you wouldn't do all these things at once, but they are great ways to show interest and disclose "self" stuff and have it returned to you. This kind of dialoguing is solid "getting-to-know-you" material and can be used in a variety of ways with our mates and our children as we make the effort to eliminate the strangers in the house. There are just too many families whose evening routine finds each member of the family off in his/her nook doing her/his things and finding it irritating if another invades the privacy. I know private space is important at times, but being together in a loving, cooperative, warm, and nurturing way as family is more important. From the solid base of healthy relationships come more effective discipline, cooperation, responsible behaviors, respect, and honoring rules and expectations. There will also be less conflict, less need for punitive actions, and a home life where "other-centeredness" is the order of the day. A healthy family whose members know each other looks something like this:

There will exist a high level of quality **communication skills**.

There will be a **life space** where people feel safe to be open, honest, direct, and disclosing with abilities to listen, to engage, to understand, to critique, and to forgive.

Lives will be **flexible** rather than rigid. The flexibility is found in the roles being played, the rules being followed, the practice of finding balance, the solving of problems with team attitudes and fairness, and the belief that together the family can survive and grow.

Family members will be **bonded.** Each will care about the other. Each will know favorite things of the other, likes and dislikes, strengths and softness. Each will be connected to the other emotionally, respectfully. What makes one happy will make all happy, and what makes one sad will bring support from all the others.

Here is a checklist I put together through the years, ten suggestions for you to think about that can lead to family success. I believe these to be solid goals to strive for as you move with your family through your lives together. Some of the ideas have come from a collection of program information at land grant colleges like Clemson University. These university extension services are some of our strongest proponents of family health in the country. As you read each one, don't hurry. Take the time to ponder the depths of each, what each one could mean to you and how you might put these ideas to use in making sure that you are not living with or contributing to keeping strangers in your house.

ATTITUDE. What's important? Who's important? Gloom or hope?

COMMITMENT. To whom? For what? How deep? For how long?

APPRECIATION. In what ways? How often? How sincere?

COMMUNICATION. How honest? How diplomatic? How caring? How careful?

STRUCTURE/STABILITY. How much? How clear? How flexible? How fair?

COPING ABILITY. How effective? How damaging? How honest? How lasting?

PROBLEM SOLVING/CONFLICT RESOLVING. How difficult? How cooperative?

SPIRITUAL WELLNESS. How valued? How meaningful? How enduring?

RESILIENT. How quickly are come-backs? How truthful? How permanent? How responsive?

UNHURRIED TIME. How much? How often? With whom? What purpose?

Resolve to let the song "Getting to Know You" be your theme song for the years ahead. Continue to seek knowledge that will lead to building better relationships in your family, at your work, in your life. Life is too short to live divided. Get connected and stay connected. Children are as parents do, and children are as parents be. Parents need to BE, to know self, before they can DO. And, as you continue to add to your knowledge collection, **don't lose heart!**

Children <u>are</u> as parents be; children <u>are</u> as parents do!

"Adults need children in their lives to keep their imagination Fresh and their hearts Young and to make the future a reality for which they are willing to work."

– *Margaret Mead*

GROUP FOUR

Response-Ability and Parenting Styles

During the first year of a child's life, most serious, nurturing, and mindful parents respond to the needs of their child in responsible ways. They use what I call a good level of **Response-Ability**. Mother especially gets to know just what the "baby sounds" are about because she tunes in and listens. Does the child need a clean diaper? Does she have an earache? Is he hungry? Does she need to be comforted? Many children get most of what they need that first year, like comfort, care, affirmation, trust, lots of hugs, and love. Thankfully, much more of it is coming from the dads these days, who finally understand the importance of their roles as parents and they are doing it with a sense of pride! They are beginning to know the incredible rewards of an enriching relationship with their children. However, it is a sad commentary on our society that there are also too many children who get little or none of those essential human contacts, and they and the world around them end up paying for those omissions for the rest of that child's life. When that happens, the parents, or caregivers, are in the mode of **response-disability.**

Even well-meaning, well-educated parents can develop response-disability if they are not mindful of the necessity to *respond* to an action or behavior as often as possible rather than to *react*. Responding effectively is not easy. Reacting is easier. First of all, responding takes more care. A parent has to care about the child and want to respond to the child's behavior in the best possible way. Responding takes more awareness that a child (or an adult) is behaving for a certain reason and not just being mean because she/he is monster-possessed or just out to "get you." Responding takes more knowledge as to how one should assess the behavior going on, whether it is a developmental-, environmental-, or temperament-related behavior. Responding takes more patience and takes more time.

Of course, there are instances in emergency or imminent danger situations where one's quick reaction is called for, but those times don't come often. Sometimes we create those emergency situations ourselves, depending on how we feel or how serious the offense is of which we feel the child is guilty. When we find ourselves backed against a wall or at the end of our rope, we too often resort to the "screech and hit" or "knee-jerk" method and accomplish little. We all find ourselves at the end of that rope from time to time, since we are, after all, human, and far from perfect. There is no shame in it. There is shame, however, in sticking to that reactive method and not realizing it. How we respond to a behavior, or a given situation in a given time in a given place, will most often determine what happens next. When someone initiates an action – negative or positive, physically or verbally – how we choose to respond sets the cycle in motion or turns it in another direction.

If, for example, we are criticized and we choose to criticize in defense, then conflict ensues. If we respond in an accepting and inquiring way and don't let another's critique push our buttons as we are operating from a position of internal strength, then we remain in charge of ourselves and act responsibly. That's when our self-esteem is in high gear and our response-ability flourishes. This way of responding to the behaviors of our children throughout their lives is the way of good health, cooperation, responsibility, and independence.

The types of responses you learn to develop are the roots of your parenting style. There are, according to most authorities, three basic styles of parenting, perhaps four. In addition to my own views on these styles, I will use some ideas from Dr. Louise Hart, author of *The Winning Family,* and Mr. Tom Carr's *A Parents Blueprint.* Even though some educators will tell you that these books are outdated, I still highly recommend both of them. Some truths never change.

The Dictator

At one end of the spectrum is what I call The Dictator. Also known as autocratic or authoritarian, this style imposes all limits and allows no freedoms. There is a rigid structure and there is little flexibility. These are the "do as I say do, not what I do" and "children are made to be seen and not heard" parents. This style shows itself in punitive, restrictive, and controlling characteristics. **These parents make all the rules, sometimes changing them on the spot for reasons of their own; offer few, if any, choices to any other family members; and expect children to toe the line, no matter what, no questions asked.** These are parents who have the power and they want to keep the power. Depending on innate temperament and other biological factors, children who are products of this kind of environment can be aggressive and rebellious, and may even lean toward the bizarre, wild and weird, and revengeful. Or they can withdraw deep within themselves, have ineffective social interactions, and live their lives in fear of being wrong, blamed, or criticized for just being themselves.

Some parenting experts define another style as rigid autocratic, which in my opinion is not a style at all, but rather an abdication of the role as parent. The results are doling out physical punishment at the drop of a hat, reinforced with emotional and verbal abuse.

Unfortunately, this "style" is in use much too much by unhealthy parents. Other parents or caregivers go totally in the opposite direction and basically neglect the children to the point of abandonment. Neglect and abuse can take many forms and none of them are worthwhile in any way, so I'm not even going to talk about it here except to say: Don't do it!

The Easy Mark

The parenting style at the other end of the spectrum is what I call The Easy Mark. It is also called laissez-faire, indulgent, and most commonly, permissive. Children from these parents are allowed to believe pretty much whatever they wish and behave according to their own whims. Here there are nothing but freedoms and no limits. Family members aren't interested in each other and there is a lack of involvement among the family unit. There can be professed "love" and it may be shown, but this type of loving is not enough. There are few appropriate rewards, if any, and minimal punishments or discipline which are most often inconsistent and unreasonable. Adolescents emerging from these surroundings can be immature, have poor self-restraint, and have weak, if any, leadership skills, although their manipulative tools may be fine-tuned. Parents who allow children to always have their way have already thrown in the towel and abdicated their role. They have turned all of their power over to the children. They have given it away. The children are in charge and they can become amoral, impulsive, egocentric, and totally ungrounded. This can result in a difficulty cooperating and getting along with others.

Parents who are in the excessive permissive mode are parents who are so self-centered that they have trouble relating to any other people in

a caring or interested way. They are absorbed with their own problems of life to the degree that they seem always frustrated, indecisive, and often hostile about the cards they have been dealt. They are either defensive and always angry, or they retreat within themselves and mope, pout, or just disappear in a black cloud of discouragement and despair.

Of course, I'm painting the extreme picture. There are less severe cases where the parents are just weak-willed, low in confidence and self-esteem, and just don't know what to do with children who naturally need some firm but kind guidance. None of these people have a healthy self (the first key) and as a result they will create an atmosphere in the home (the third key) that is not nurturing or structuring.

Permissive parents who seem to be disinterested in what their children do often defend their position with remarks like "I trust my child. I know she can take care of herself." The truth is that these parents are often physically and emotionally absent from their children and uninvolved to the point of neglect. The parents, overwhelmed with the demanding logistics of life, think they have no control over their lives and consequently think that they have no control over the lives of their children. The children in The Easy Mark family are also confused and discouraged, having learned those behaviors from their parents. They, too, have a lot of anger, have low self-esteem, feel out of control, insecure, unloved, overly dependent, powerless and helpless, and they feel as if no one is taking care of them. They are surrounded by confusion and inconsistency and do not feel that they can trust their parents.

Some characteristics of children from permissive parents are that they have trouble living with limits (although some at the same time crave them); they lack self-discipline and responsibility (or some may have had to assume too much too soon); or they may take on the unhealthy role reversal of taking care of their parents because their parents won't take care of them. These children are often on their own before they are ready because the parents push them to be; they think they have the right to do exactly what they want to do with no regard for others or social responsibility; they may be attracted to cults, or rebellious groups, or to drugs and alcohol; and it is possible that they may become violent toward their parents and others.

The permissive parents who aren't in the extreme mode of virtual neglect but are "trying" to do what they think is right may become a slave to their aggressive or withdrawn child. They try to make the child happy and compliant by giving things to him, like material things or privileges that offer more freedom than a child his age should be allowed to have. Often, these parents are the ones who were not blessed with effective parenting themselves, who were also raised by permissive parents; or whose parents were just the opposite and practiced harsh, dictator methods. In the case of the latter, these parents swore that they would not do to their children what their parents did to them. This is an admirable desire, but they go overboard and their response-ability becomes response-disability. Gaining knowledge (the fourth key) as to what the best responses might be is often "too much trouble" for these parents, or they "just don't have the time." (Remember that having knowledge about parenting is a key to helping achieve harmony in the home and guiding children through the perils of growing into healthy adults.) Some of these parents don't even know, for example, about real consequences and how consequences teach responsibility because they don't want their children to suffer any negatives in life. For example, if Billy forgets his lunch box five days in a row, and Dad brings it to him at school five days in a row, Billy might then believe that he doesn't ever have to take his own lunch box to school because Dad will bring it later. These parents also don't have expectations of their children, like doing chores and taking care of personal areas and belongings. Too often, children from these homes are allowed to regulate their own activities. The parents often don't "know where their kids are." (Just as often, the children have no idea where the parents are!)

Goldilocks

The third and mid-spectrum style is what I call Goldilocks. Yep, "just right." In *Goldilocks and the Three Bears* she kept trying chairs and beds and porridge until it was "just right." I gladly borrow this approach from Goldilocks to finding the best of what's available for parents. This approach is also termed authoritative, and most popularly yet most misunderstood, democratic. I like the term "responsive." Here, growth in independence is encouraged. The atmosphere is warm, responsive, loving, and nurturing. There are freedoms, but there are also limits, and responsibility is taught by showing the children how to predict or anticipate and then deal with the consequences of their actions. There is control – better called management – but it is control with explanation, fairness, and kindness, and the children are allowed to express their views, even though their views are not always accepted. The parents with the power mindfully decide to share it when they can. Social competence, cooperation, and healthy self-esteem are the resulting behaviors. Children raised by parents with this style can be the most well-adjusted adults, able to make decisions, follow rules, and change the rules effectively, if and when it's necessary.

In the authoritative Goldilocks families, everyone's needs are considered important. Parents offer choices and treat children as capable, worthwhile human beings and not as possessions. With encouraged responsibility to make decisions, consequences are established and the child learns from the consequences. Structure is provided that is not rigid, just firm. These parents invite children to participate in planning and rule making but still remain the family team leaders when it comes to enforcing the rules. Children are allowed to have their say, but they are not always allowed to have it the *way* they say.

Democratic parents function as counselors and as coaches. They have the healthy attitude of cooperation with their children. They manage the family as allies to their children and don't use adversarial tactics. They feel respectful and respected. They most often trust themselves, their knowledge, and their motives, and they have high self-esteem and response-ability. The children from the authoritative parents feel capable and able, worthwhile and useful, self-confident, self-respecting, and above all, cared for and loved. They are rich in global self-esteem and most often excel in several specific self-esteem areas. These children are eager to cooperate, they respect rules and authority, they are learning self-discipline, and they are responsible.

These children are in no small part this way because the parents use "two-way" communications and create many opportunities for the family to do learning and fun things together. They are responsive to the needs of the children on every level. These parents respond "just right."

But, of course, they don't do so all of the time. Parents are not perfect, just as children are not perfect. When we are healthy, motivated, and committed to the tasks, we continue to learn how to perform our roles better and better. The parent/child relationship is a journey that goes on for life, not a race, as some people seem to think. But if it were, it would be a sprint on some days, a rely on others, but mostly it would be a marathon. It takes work, preparation, and, of course, it takes time. A life time. And all of this is adding to the storehouse of knowledge.

To complicate the selection of a parenting style even more, as if it needed to be, there are few parents who are able to "practice" the best style all the time. There are days when life has disappointed or stressed us out to the point that our normal responsiveness to our children is colored darkly and we find ourselves being too permissive, with "I don't care what you do…just don't talk to me right now." Or what may be an okay behavior one day will shove us off the cliff the next. We can only hope to stay the positive course as much as possible, and count the days we can't, or won't, as learning and teaching times; the times to reveal the human in us all and how we grow through it and upward.

My explanation of these styles is of course offered in a generalized way. There are many more opinions, labels, spins, and additions about parenting styles and the effects of them all. Today's electronic world offers countless types of just about everything. The secret is to know which ones to accept. There are degrees of each, some parents being more one way than another and others having a combination of the styles. There are always exceptions, modifications, and differences of opinion.

I encourage you to make a concentrated effort to pick and develop The Goldilocks style to use as your primary way of "being" and "doing" with your children. The rewards are great, and the only possible down-side is that it will require you to re-arrange your life and schedule in order to "fit" your children in more and in more effective ways. They're your children. You only have this one crack at it, and it lasts for a very short time.

Don't lose heart!

> # ARE YOU THE PARENT YOU WOULD CHOOSE FOR YOURSELF?

GROUP FIVE

The Miracles of Development

The Ties That Bind

The word "attachment" has several different meanings. To some it means those odd little things that come with your vacuum cleaner, or it could be hook-like thingies that hold your hanging baskets, or to others it could mean a strong liking for another person, a pet, your old letter sweater, a blankie, or a teddy bear. But for all children a solid attachment to a caregiver in the early years can be life-saving.
The attachment that children find and nurture with their adults is in most cases the most important connection that children will ever have. Attachment in the context of care and well-being of our young describes the state and quality of an individual's tie to another person. Some see attachment as being an invisible string, or rope, that ties two people together, and in some cases the attachments can be to several people, if a child indeed finds that kind of good fortune. We are not talking about "bonding," which is what the adult does with the child, but "attachment," what the child does with an adult. Solid, positive attachment offers children a secure life and a safe life. Attachments are made when caregivers attend to the basic emotional needs of children-protection, nurturing, supportive of explorations, encouraging growth, and being watchful and joyful in the unfolding of a child's life. In these days of living life fast as most young parents are doing, it cannot be stressed too much that those young parents must be aware of how vital their being

positively present in their children's lives is to the future well being of the children. And, it's not just about love, it's about survival. When we feel that the our world is constant, consistent, dependable, predictable, possible, then we feel that our needs are being met or are in the process of being met and we learn how to be patient and wait, the core of delayed gratification. We learn that we cannot always have our cake and eat it, too. If ever. Secure attachments are the solid foundations for our intellectual potential, our identity formation, our socialization, and our relationship skills. We internalize our belief system to say, "I am safe, I am secure, I am me, and I am somebody who can do stuff, and I am loved." For a child with strong nurturing attachments, discipline is a relatively easy job for the parents and teachers. Children who are not fortunate enough to find early attachment to caregivers are most often in for some major challenges in life, and are those who become major challenges to those adults who are to care for and teach them.

The Attachment Disorders come in sizes called Ambivalent/Resistant, Avoidant, and Disorganized. I encourage your research on the Web or in the library as to what these types mean. It boils down to the fact that the children with Attachment Disorders will not be leading lives of joy and growth unless there is intervention and help. Children develop in basically four areas: Let's look at those areas as spaces to be filled. There is the space of Physical, one of Cognitive-Creative, one of Social, and a last one of Emotional/Psychological. These spaces need to be filled with enriching and nurturing experiences. When they are, success for children can be expected. When they are empty or near empty, successes for children will be few and far between. They will have trouble focusing; they will constantly scan their environment being super alert to threats and dangers; they will often overreact to any and everything, they will be spontaneous, may strike out for no apparent reason, have higher levels of stress hormones, and will be hyper-vigilant and find it difficult if not impossible to trust anyone.

Why do parents, caregivers, and teachers need to know these things? Children come into this complex world having no idea as to what lies ahead of them, trusting in the adults in their lives to care for them, respond to their needs, keep them safe, encourage their growth and simply love them. The child who enters to find a world that embraces her with an atmosphere of warm affection and loving protection has an advantage from the beginning. If her initial caregivers are knowledgeable parents at that point, a sound foundation will already be in place upon which she can build. Don't you parents and teachers want to be those prepared, knowledgeable adults? **Don't you want to give children the best that you have in order for them to give the best that they have?**

If our children are surrounded by an atmosphere of affectionate care, kept comfortable, and have their basic needs met, they tend to feel satisfied and secure. They develop an attitude of trust because their first contacts with persons in the world give them assurance that their needs will be met. This feeling of security, and trust is probably the most basic requirement for the development of a healthy personality. These human qualities impact all the other human qualities with strengths or weaknesses. Any measure of accomplishment in any of them gives us more of this feeling of security, makes us feel better able to function in a world that holds many kinds of insecurities. All of these attitudes and feelings are characteristics of maturity. They are learned, or not learned, from the experience each of us undergoes from the day of birth. **Our children are here. We are responsible for them! What are we going to do? We can and must make a difference!! As the motto of the Children's Defense Fund states so poignantly, "The Sea Is So Wide, And My Boat Is So Small." Think about our children, help them row, and don't lose heart!**

How Does Your Garden Grow?

So, your "green thumb" is throbbing to be of use and you decide that you want to grow a beautiful flower. You go to the store and buy some seed, go home, dig a hole, throw the seed in the ground, and wait for the unfolding. If you're lucky, it may rain, and your seed will take root and begin its trip to full blossom. Chances are, because it is the nature of plants, the flower will at least survive. But what kind of life will result? The plant may be ravaged by weeds, blocked from the sun, undernourished due to lack of water and fertilizer, and devoid of any tender love and care. The expected beauty could instead be small and frail, without leaves or rich color, and with blossoms that are barely there. In short, the product of your efforts becomes only a hint of what it could have been. And then it dies. Its powerful potential was never reached. And, you wonder, what was wrong with that seed? It just didn't do what it was supposed to do. Perhaps you'll go to the store and demand your money back.

I use this story to begin our next look at **child development.** Just as it is vital to know something about the care of plants if you want them to thrive, it is even more vital that we know something about the care of our children. Not until around the turn of the 20th century did scientists begin in earnest the study of how and why children grow. In the beginning, those researchers were mostly psychologists (who were trying to determine how people tick and what to do when the tick got out of whack), and educators, who were concerned with how best to educate the future workforce. Only three or four decades ago did science start to study how to possibly prevent the problems that keep children from growing to their full adult potential. In addition to the study of biological and physical elements of human development, pioneers began to incorporate observations and explorations of motor, intellectual/academic, emotional, and social categories, as well.

From the work of all of those dedicated visionaries, there have emerged basically four popular theories of child development. Each one has its avid proponents and a supporting body of research, and each one proposes a unique approach to child development and structures information about the world in a particular way, and focuses on somewhat different aspects of development.

First, there is the **Maturational Theory**, which deals mainly with physical and intellectual matters. Two of its leaders were Arnold Gesell and Lewis Terman. Sigmund Freud's work laid the foundations for the **Psychoanalytical Theory**, concerned with the development of the personality, which has been adapted and modified by such notables as Erik Erikson, Alfred Adler, Rudolph Dreikurs, Carl Rogers, and most recently by parenting gurus, Robert Carkhuff and Thomas Gordon.

J.B. Watson was the father of the **Behavioral Theory**, which claims that all behavior is learned and deals with intellect and personality through programs of behavior modification. Albert Bandura took this theory even further to include other processes. In the 1950s, interest in cognition as a factor in determining behavior grew rapidly. Jean Piaget's **Cognitive-Interactionist**

Theory sees knowledge constructed gradually as people interact with their environment. This theory has become very popular in many school classrooms.

Excuse me for drifting perhaps too far into what may seem to be unnecessary territory for everyday parenting, but it's important for you to know that a lot of smart people have been studying the development of children for many years. There are many more today digging even deeper with the motivation to help us be the best we can be. Useful parenting programs have emerged from those efforts and resulting theories, programs that vary in approach, but that use various elements of one or many of the most accepted theories. Which possible solution to apply in any situation depends on one's orientation and the nature of the problem. There is never just one way to "skin a cat": The best solution is the one that works! If something is not working, then either the skill or the application could be wrong, or the uniqueness of the person or the situation requires a different approach. Other sources for the current "truths" of child development have come from homes and classrooms. Decent, thinking, sensitive, caring people have hunches, and through trial and error, have come up with methods "that work," depending, of course, on what is meant by "working." I use the term to mean effective parenting skills. Those skills are also incorporated into most of the parenting programs of today. Much valid research goes into finding out the effectiveness of many programs. And while research and the accepted processes and procedures are necessary, attitude, orientation, and the ability of the teacher to connect with the learner is also crucial.

It is an inevitable fact that children grow. The seed is planted and internal clocks of nature begin ticking. Under what is accepted as "normal" circumstances, children will grow according to the clock. They will go through various "stages" of development pretty much right on schedule, if they are not blocked, discouraged, side-tracked, or derailed by some external force, which can be anything from inadequate care-giving to a natural disaster. The scientific study of children helps us understand our children better, and you know how important understanding is to being able to give and receive love. It will help us know what to expect and when to expect it. Knowing that, we will then know how to respond more effectively.

But, the first and most important questions to existing and future parents are:
- Do you actually want to be a parent?
- Are you prepared to give what it takes to help your children become successful?
- Do you want them to be successful?
- Do you want to know how?

Before we get into the specific skills of parenting, I want to quickly offer you another point of view on some of the ideas I have previously presented, thanks to one of my favorite authors, Jane Brooks, who is quoted here from *Parenting For The Nineties* (Mayfield 1994). She says it so well, I wouldn't even try to paraphrase, but I want you to see her powerful comments. I have read nothing more up to date that is this clear and profound.

> "Development during infancy and early childhood years is more rapid and dramatic than during any other period of the life cycle. Basic patterns of emotional, social and intellectual, and physical development are formed during these years. The child whose earliest environment surrounds her with an atmosphere of affection and tender protection has an advantage from the beginning. If she is guided by wise, understanding parents in these early years, a sound foundation is

laid for later life. If she is surrounded by an atmosphere of affectionate care, kept comfortable and has her basic needs met, she tends to feel satisfied and secure. She develops an attitude of trust, because her first contacts with persons in the world give her assurance that her needs will be met. This feeling of security, this sense of trust is probably the most basic requirement for the development of a healthy personality." (The result is a secure attachment and a solid bonding process.)

"Inner security is more than just desirable, it is necessary for happiness and a healthy personality. When this security is present, the child has more confidence in his belief about the important things in life. He is better able to understand himself and others. His attitude toward life's problems is more realistic. He is more able to face facts. She is better able to learn self-discipline, to assume responsibility. She has fewer fears and anxieties. She is less afraid of change simply because it is change."

These qualities – or the lack of them – can affect others with strengths or weaknesses. Any measure of accomplishment in any of these qualities gives children more of that feeling of security and makes them feel better able to function in a world that holds many kinds of insecurities. All of these attitudes and feelings are characteristics of maturity. They are learned-or not learned- from the experience each of us undergoes from the day of birth. The first experience we have as helpless infants is with security.

Every infant is born into the world with needs which he has no ability to satisfy. The human creature is completely dependent upon others and cannot survive unless his basic requirements are met by adults who accept him as their responsibility and welcome him warmly into this world and assure him that his needs will be met. The infant has no comprehension of the world about him. The parents are his world.

Gradually, during the first year of life (and as he grows older), the baby finds that his own needs and desires sometimes conflict with the world about him, and with the needs and desires of others in his family. As he leaves infancy and begins to take a more active part in the world, he continues to have the need of this feeling of being loved, of belonging. If those needs are neglected or mismanaged, the child's life will be affected in different ways, and he will begin to behave in certain ways and will have no knowledge of why the behavior is emerging.

However, let me make it clear that a single action or a limited series of actions will not necessarily have a long-term effect on who the child becomes. It is more important to know the accumulated social-emotional environment, especially the mother/infant relationship in which the baby begins life. Also, any so-called mistakes are not necessarily final. Even though things cannot be undone, it is possible to do something about them. The past is not entirely unchangeable, because the effects of it often can be changed by what is done in the present and in the future. Children are extremely resilient, but they have to have damages repaired.

Children will grow best if they are assisted in the process by attentive, caring, and knowledgeable caregivers who take the time to know what they need and how to provide in the best possible ways. If they don't get good care, their lives will most assuredly be different. They will be the product of the unique birthright gifts of biology impacted for good or bad by their life experiences. Caregiver homework is necessary in each stage. Each child grows in his/her own unique way.

Human growth is complex and it will help us to know what to expect and when to expect it. If we don't, we may find ourselves expecting too much or not enough.

The job of children is to grow up. They will grow in certain stages and not always on the same time schedule. But they will grow. How they grow is determined by a lot of factors, both internal and external. We know that children develop in these areas: physical, motor, intellectual/academic, emotional, and social. And not a single one of these areas of growth happens in isolation. They are all interconnected and develop in relation to each other. One does not happen without the other. However, there are times when one area is more evident than another. There are general times when certain areas are expected to be "ready" (i.e., developmentally appropriate), but every child is like a unique snowflake moving at his own pace in his own place.

Stages of human development are similar to building a house. You can't build the roof first, or erect the studs. You have to start with a foundation. Most educators agree that there are three major areas that influence parenting:

- the temperament of the child, who she is biologically;
- the environment and the people in the environment, what degree of health and knowledge they bring to the child; and
- the circumstances surrounding the family psychologically, sociologically, economically, and educationally, and what their resources are.

The child comes with his/her own temperament, brain paths, biology, birth order, gender, and physical being. Parents also have their own unique temperaments, and theirs may

present similar to the child, or almost exact, or they may have qualities that could be contrasting, even opposite, plus they would have unique stories of their own and a developed pattern of living their lives. Traditionally, there are a mother and a father. Two people come together with different experiences, and how they merge can affect the home atmosphere. Support for parents can come from each other, the quality of the marriage or partnership, extended family and friends, and the community in which they live. All of the caregivers and potential caregivers can offer great support and positive influence or they might influence in a negative direction. The development of children and the continued development of the adults can be stifled or encouraged depending on the support available. The more informed and caring these influences are, the better the chance of success all around. (See Group 3 for more on the Four Keys of Effective Parenting.)

Most child experts agree that humans do indeed go through certain stages. Perhaps the most widely accepted view of these complete life stages comes from psychoanalyst Erik Erikson (*Childhood and Society,* WW Norton & Company 1963). Jane Brooks, in *The Process of Parenting* (Mayfield 1996), is also helpful in understanding how Erikson identifies each stage as having an unfolding crisis that must be met and resolved. We can have positive and negative experiences in satisfying needs and both kinds are important for the best development. If we have only positive gratification, we may have difficulty learning how to cope with difficulties. If we want to have healthy growth, the balance should be on the positive side. When this occurs, a **strength or virtue** develops.

> **Children will grow best if they are assisted in the process by attentive, caring, and knowledgeable caregivers who take the time to know what the children need and how to provide in the best possible ways.**

Stage One

In the first year or so of life, the child will develop a sense of **trust or mistrust**. If caregivers meet basic needs – like giving love and affection and being responsive – the baby feels she deserves good care and is valuable. The strength or virtue of hope is seeded, and the child develops a feeling that needs can be satisfied, dreams can come true, and wishes and desires can be achieved. In short, what develops is a feeling of belonging – one of the most important basic goals of human beings. Noted theorists Alfred Adler and Rudolph Dreikurs state that the primary human goal is to feel as if he or she belongs, and they have the driving desire to feel significant. In other words, our basic needs as humans are to feel loved, cared for, important to others, knowledge of being able and capable, and developing and maintaining a sense of self-worth. All interactions with primary caregivers provide the actual blueprint for infants' future relationships with others and with the world. Children need answers to the questions "Who am I?"; "How does the world work?", and "What do I need and need to do to survive and grow?"

Those early patterns of attachment create the inner working model of having a sense of self and a sense of the world we live in. We develop our abilities to have relationships and learn how to behave in the expected ways. We learn causal thinking, knowing that one thing leads to another, or causes another thing to happen or not happen. We learn who to trust and how. We learn how to feel, to empathize, to have compassion, and we learn right from wrong. Secure attachments are the solid foundations for our intellectual potential, our identity formation, our socialization, and our relationship skills. We internalize our belief system to say "I am safe, I am secure, I am me, and I am somebody who can do stuff and I am loved."

Children who are not fortunate enough to find early attachment to caregivers are most often in for some major challenges in life, and are those who become major challenges to those adults who are to care for and teach them. Children with attachment disorders will not be leading lives of joy and growth unless there is intervention and help and that's not guaranteed. Their successes will be few and far between and they will have trouble focusing. They will constantly be alert to threats and dangers, will often overreact, they may strike out for no apparent reason, have higher levels of stress hormones, will be overly cautious, and will find it difficult to trust anyone.

However, if our children are surrounded by an atmosphere of affectionate care, kept comfortable, and have their basic needs met, they tend to feel satisfied and secure. They develop an attitude of trust because their first contacts with people in the world give assurance that their needs will be met. This feeling of security and this sense of trust is probably the most basic requirement for the development of a healthy personality.

Stage Two

In the second stage, children are ready to develop a sense of **autonomy** (being able to act independently).

The dark side of this stage is **shame and doubt** about themselves and their abilities. If the positive wins out, a strength of will begins to emerge, meaning the ability to make free choices and to have self-control. This achievement is a result, in part, of having passed through stage one well, trusting that most needs will get met by the caring people who are guiding the new life with a sense of hope. The children feel they are worthy.

Stage Three

The third stage occurs around the fourth and fifth years. Children have gained control of their bodies, have learned language, and can produce self-initiated activity. Language skills and explorations of their world start to bubble. If most experiences are positive, children learn **initiative.** They develop strength of purpose, the ability to set and pursue goals, and they are free of fear, failure, punishment, and criticism. If parents criticize and ridicule their children and their ideas, or are just not responsive to inquiry, children develop guilt and feel that their efforts and thoughts are not good.

The successful completion of this stage leads to a second goal of all humans – a driving purpose to grow in knowledge, to learn about the world around us, and determine our place in it.

> *Growing up is not a piece of cake! Parenting well is a complex task. The more we know about what we are doing, the less complicated and frustrating it will be. And there will be joy!*

Stage Four

In the fourth stage, from the ages of 5 through 12, children's abilities and skills increase. They begin to read and write, develop new activities, and join groups. They become **industrious** and experience pleasure in what they can do and produce. If they don't have a sense of success and accomplishment, they develop a **sense of inferiority**. They feel that they are failures and useless. If the balance is mostly positive, however, children develop a sense of competence – the feeling that one can accomplish goals and not feel inferior. This leads to the third basic goal of life: contributing to the social structure to which we belong, where we are encouraged to continue learning.

    This cycle of three of the most important basic goals of life in my judgment is the simple basis for our self-esteem. When we feel as if we belong, we feel more capable and worthy of the opportunities to learn; as we learn and feel safe and secure in the learning, we want to contribute; as those contributions are made and accepted, we have even deeper feelings that we belong.

    There are four more Erikson stages of a full life span that deal with adolescence and adulthood, and we will talk about those a bit later.

    Knowledge of these early development stages and why they happen and what's expected to happen can be guides for us as we create a home environment that will support and encourage successful learning for our children. If we aren't sensitive to the needs and abilities of our children, we might mistakenly create an environment for them that is not a good mix and will not be the fuel they need to grow and develop on schedule and on their own paths.

    Before we take up the final four stages of Erik Erikson's Stages of Life Development, please remember that the reason we review the developmental how and why of who we are is so we can better understand ourselves and how important our responses are to the well being of our children. I encourage you to peruse other wonderful sources on the development stages that are available at libraries, schools, hospitals, and of course the holder of all information, the Internet.

According to Erikson and other developmental specialists, a healthful and mature outlook is arrived at by the results of our many trips through each stage of development. As you recall, if we pass through a stage with positives outweighing the negatives, a virtue or strength emerges that equips us for handling the good stuff and the not-so-good stuff of life. No one, however, will solve each crisis once and for all. Experiences can change earlier positive resolutions or negative omissions. That's the purpose of learning and growing.

Stage Five

Stage five of development is the **adolescence stage**, and it's one of the toughest and most important. It's almost like a repeat of the pre-school years, the beginning of another **search for self.** The teen's tasks are to incorporate sexuality into that evolving search; to integrate all previous experiences with an emerging sensuality and growing intellectual competence; and to form a psychological and social identity that helps to deal with the potholes of adulthood. This identity refers to the "real inner self" who has the ability to incorporate his new "self" into the world around him and do it with competence and success. Then he starts to feel good about his choices, about who he is and what he wants to do in life. If he hasn't had enough success in previous experiences to merge well with the new sense of self, and if he does not get any affirmations of accomplishment for becoming the new self, **role confusion** will result. He will not be clear about who he really is and where he is going. He suffers from **identity confusion** and the strength or virtue of **fidelity** is weakened or lost. The truth of his self disappears. If a negative identity emerges, what may result is a school dropout, a delinquent, a runaway, and a person who feels unable to do anything positive and wants to hide from the difficult challenges of life.

In these first five stages, children grow from dependence on others into individuals who are able to trust themselves to function independently in the world and are able to initiate and maintain productive activities and to form stable, realistic identities.

Stage Six

The **first stage of adulthood**, the beginning of intimate, personal ties is Stage Six. I include these adult stages here since adding knowledge about one's self can help us as parents when we better understand our own strengths and weaknesses and how they may have become what they are. We may get a good look at who we are, really, and why. Once an individual knows who she is, she can enter into a relationship that she chooses for herself. Intimacy is not only necessary for romance and marriage, but also for relationships with friends, family, and even co-workers. Knowing how to be close to others leads to the **virtue of love and the sharing** of self with others. This sharing of self cannot happen without a strong sense of identity. If the sharing can't happen, the resulting negative is **isolation.**

Because of the poor passage through previous stages, adults can be trapped in isolation, which can present itself in many forms. Other adults might get stuck in Stage Seven.

Stage Seven

The Seventh is the second stage of adulthood. This stage is the beginning of generativity, or creation of new life, to be creative and productive. The virtue that should develop here is one of **care.**

Care is concern about and attention to what has been created and what one must do to take care of the creation. Here, one begins to work outside of oneself and to care for others. If we remain indulged in the self, it can lead to **stagnation,** where there is no true growth. This stage is a most important one for parents and grandparents. It's about establishing and guiding the next generation and keeping society moving in healthy directions.

Both Stages Six and Seven put emphasis on the **integration of self with others**, with intimate peers and children, and with social and economic activities.

Stage Eight

Stage Eight is now noted as the final stage of life, and the focus returns to the individual and the development of a sense of **ego integrity**. We must take inventory of how we have lived and what we have accomplished or not and how we feel about it all. If we have difficulty in accepting how we have lived as valid and worthwhile, we will suffer from **despair.** As much as we may long to do so, we cannot start all over. The virtue or strength that develops when we accept, understand, and are internally at peace is **wisdom,** a deep gratitude for life and the oncoming end which is but just another part of life.

Erikson and many others believe that children are most successful when they are surrounded by experienced, trustworthy, and caring people; have opportunities for helping the self become the self; and when parents and others encourage and affirm who children are and affirm that they are valuable, lovable, and capable.

There are several educators and researchers who are now working on developing the ideas of a ninth stage of life, or maybe even more. Since we are living longer now with the prospect of even greater health care leading to longer years of productivity and improving quality of life, we are now redefining our late years as we continue our development.

There are many aspects of human development and we have just waded in the shallow end of the deep waters of what we need to know. We've glimpsed enough to see some of the important elements as to why children act the ways they do and why we choose to respond in the ways that we do. We are raising adults, you know.

They are children for such a short time, and what we give them or do not give them now will have a major effect on who they become; we have to know what we are doing (at least most of the time)!

There are always reasons we humans behave the way we do, and to know that **most behaviors are learned lets us know that they can also be unlearned and relearned.**

Moving forward in our learning journey together, we will spend a lot of time on the subjects of behaviors and how they are learned and how they might be changed if indeed they do need changing. Until we get there,

Don't lose heart!

GROUP SIX

Watering The Garden With Encouragement

Noted child-parent specialist Dr. Rudolph Dreikurs emphasized:

> "Encouragement is more important than any other aspect of child raising. It is so important that the lack of it can be considered the basic cause of misbehavior. A misbehaving child is a discouraged child. Each child needs continuous encouragement as a plant needs water. He cannot grow and develop and gain a sense of belonging without encouragement." (*Children the Challenge*, Dutton NY, 1987).

Indeed, encouragement and effective praise are among the first and most important strategies that parents can use in developing and guiding their children.

The parent/child relationship is a journey that goes on for life. What changes are the modes of travel.

Encouragement is the process of concentrating on our children's strengths and efforts and not on their mistakes or shortcomings, which usually takes the form of negative criticism and blame discouraging the children and lowering their sense of self. I believe that reinforcement of the behaviors that we like is one of the best ways to teach them, second only to the way we role model. How else will the children know what is the right way to behave? More emphasis should be placed on positive behavior rather than on negative. That way, the negative most often decreases.

Encouragement and "just" praise are NOT the same. We can praise in many ways, but we have to be careful not to overuse it or use it incorrectly. Using it well can do a good job and certainly should be a frequent parent skill, but encouragement – praise with purpose or meaning – is the better choice most of the time. Children can never get too much constructive and honest encouragement, and you can never start encouraging your child to early. (In other words, your child is never too young to hear encouragement!)

With incorrect praise, children may get the impression that their personal worth depends upon how they measure up to what the parent wants or expects (and sometimes our expectations are developmentally unrealistic). It can create anxiety in the child, insecurity, and often misbehavior. The child feels that she is worthwhile only when she behaves or performs in a certain way. It doesn't help to praise children by telling them that they are wonderful because they do something. They could become praise junkies and think they only count in life when they can get approval and attention. This

> **Praise with purpose and meaning, highlighting the behavior.**

can cause a mindset of "what's in it for me?" or a drive to be perfect. They decide that what they do is who they are and they have to do it better and better to be accepted and get the positive strokes. Misdirected praise will say to the child that "you are a fine boy because you did something." In order for praise to be effective, we have to praise the behavior and not the child. Praise with purpose can be as simple as "good job," or a high five, or a thumbs-up, or a hug. Any remark or action that says "I like what you did" provides praise with a purpose. In many cases, a smile that says how you feel is worth its weight in gold.

When we use encouragement or constructive/purposeful praise, we describe and appreciate our children's efforts and achievements without judgment or evaluation. "You're a good boy," "you're the best," "you are just the sweetest angel" statements focus on the character of the child rather than the efforts of the child. It tells them who we think they are because they did such and such a certain way. But then what happens when they don't do it that way? They might wonder if they are still a "good boy." Will they still be loved? A certain behavior does not make a child good or bad. The behavior itself is what is acceptable or unacceptable.

Effective encouragement describes in specific ways what we see and how we feel. Instead of saying "you're a good boy" to a child who has picked up his toys try "I thank you very much for putting your toys away. It looks so neat in here!" This says to the child that he is responsible and can take care of his things. This approach is a reinforcement of a behavior and action that we liked, and when we tell people that we like something they did, even in the adult workplace, their desire to repeat the behavior that was appreciated and acknowledged increases. Encouragement does not focus on the child and simply (and perhaps insincerely) tell her how great she is. Instead, it focuses on what the child needs to do and the internal satisfaction she feels when she gets the job done. An encouraged child will internalize for himself that "mom and dad value what I do, they have confidence in me, they appreciate my work, I am a capable person, I can make good contributions to my family, I can figure things out on my own, I can do it!"

Incorrect praise recognizes the "doer" and is presented as a "you" message: You are good, you are nice, you are able ... as long as I say you are. This is an external approval and is only effective when it is given for things done a certain way. Effective encouragement and purposeful praise are "I" messages that let the child know that the actual action is what's good; there is no direct judgment put on the value, quality, or worth of the person. It says, "I am pleased with this nice work; I appreciate your thoughtfulness and efforts." Children are then left feeling that whether they succeed or fail, they can always try without fear of being criticized, scolded, or demeaned. "I feel as if you are not giving it your best effort" is a lot better than "you are so lazy and you never will get this job finished."

Our children need to know what's expected of them in order to feel capable of being successful. When we appreciate their efforts, we encourage a repeat performance, or we motivate them to keep on trying. Children will then develop the ability to recognize and appreciate their own strengths and abilities and work to improve in areas where needed. Encouragement fosters independence, self-esteem, a willingness to explore and experiment, and an acceptance of self and others. Effective praise needs to be a way of celebrating our children rather than evaluating them.

Our words and actions let our children know that we are pleased that they are who they are. We may not always like the way they behave, but we always love and respect them.

Dr. Stephanie Marston offers these five keys to using encouragement from *The Magic of Encouragement* (Pocket Books 1990):

- Build on your children's strengths by "catching" them doing something you like.
- Express appreciation when your children are cooperative and helpful.
- Give positive support for each step along the way to achieving a goal or new behavior.
- Show confidence.
- Nurture successes.

Try it for awhile. Start with one act of purposeful praise or encouragement each day. Selectively add attention to an accomplishment, an effort, or a desired behavior over time. Change will not happen overnight, but eventually, many undesired behaviors will begin to decrease. Try this for the school-aged children: write them a note. Send them a text message. It works really well with most teenagers, even though they might not admit it. When one of your children does something you are especially pleased with, write down your feelings and mail it to him, or slip it under his pillow or in his back pack. Even when you just want to remind them of how much they are loved and how proud you are to be their parent, the effect is rewarding. How many of us as adults would like to have a note of encouragement from one of our parents tucked away in our special papers box? That's where a lot of them end up because they can become treasures to our children. As Dr. Marston says, "Our beliefs about our children have an enormous impact on their self-concept and behavior. Believe in your kids. Expect them to cooperate and to excel, and they will fulfill your expectations." And as you challenge yourself to be consistent and aware of how and when you encourage and praise,

Don't lose heart!

**Children are
as parents be and do.
How we believe in them
can lift them up or
tear them down.**

GROUP SEVEN ❦ ❦ ❦ ❦ ❦

Teenagers! Where Did They Come From?

Who am I? Where am I going? Adolescents spend a lot of their time wrestling with these and similar questions as they look for their identity. Psychologist Erik Erikson tells us that establishing a sense of self is the major job of adolescence. (See Group 5 for more on the stages of development.) To do that in today's rapidly changing world is more difficult than ever before. There are many more choices from lifestyles to occupations to role models, to technology and how and when to use it. And when there are more choices, there is more confusion. A teen's identity is developed through lots of experimentation. S/he will audition new personalities, hoping to find one that fits; one size will not fit all. This is normal and necessary in the process of self-development, but the process can be most trying for parents at times. Teens can be quite moody and rebellious in their search. They may be friendly one moment and argumentative the next. Personalities, clothing, hair styles, and friendships can change frequently. The periods of search time are often called "phases" that can last for a few days or much longer. Chances are some of the phases will be undesirable ones from the parent's point of view. Some experienced parents advise that you just stay calm and wait for the phase to pass: The more you fight it, the deeper footholds become. Good advice. But while you are waiting, you still have to be present in supportive and caring ways.

Parents can offer support for their teen's frustration and confusion by giving him the time and the space to explore his options, roles, and personalities. That, of course, doesn't mean that you should allow your teen to get involved with individuals, groups, or activities that you believe might be dangerous, illegal, or unhealthy. Many psychologists believe that parents should promote their child's sense of individuality while at the same time maintaining connection to the family, which will provide the teen a secure base from which to explore. One minute they want to run away from you, and the next they want to sit in your lap. The Authoritative or Democratic (or what I call the Goldilocks) parenting style best fosters the identity development (see Group 4 for more on parenting styles). The Goldilocks style actually allows and encourages teens to be involved in family decisions.

Identity development is a long process and is revised many times through the years, but its most turbulent time is usually during adolescence. So parents need to watch in wonder with lots of patience and understanding as the child's teen sense of self emerges. As a parent you may feel that your child doesn't need you as much as when she entered elementary or middle school. The fact is she needs you just as much, if not more, but in a different way.

There will be conflicts and disagreements as your relationship evolves, but chances are, if you were good together during earlier times, you will still be able to have positive and warm connections. That's why it's so important to build solid relationships and keep them nurtured. Believe it or not, the vast majority of teens and parents do get along. Many surveys have shown that the majority of teens consider their moms or dads, or both, to be their best friends. They remain connected for life.

Adolescence is that time to move forward, to try on new parenting approaches, and to get to know and understand that new creature emerging from childhood.

Parents need to keep in mind always that a new relationship is forming, because slowly but surely, your "old" style of parenting will not work any more. You, hopefully, will still be using the "Goldilocks" style, but even it has to be modified for the new age. Instead of keeping the child dependent on the parents, you have to promote and encourage that growing need for independence, and you have to do it in a caring, thoughtful, and knowledgeable way.

For example, some parents feel threatened by their teen's normal and necessary quest for independence and react (not respond) by pulling in the reins even tighter. They might even fight to hold on to that "child" they nurtured so well when they felt comfortable in their role as parent. They may even say "Where is that nice young boy (or girl) we used to know so well? Where did we go wrong?" The problem does not rest with the changes the teen has made (it's his job to change), that's who he is now. Rather, many of the problems come from the lack of changes the parents make to adjust to this new person in the family. The sooner parents establish changes in their own behavior that are more appropriate for responding to adolescents, the less conflict they will have during this transition. When they refocus attention from the child's behavior to their own behavior, the relationship will usually turn the corner for the positive. Saying good-bye to the childhood years is difficult for all parents. But the job of the child is to move ahead. With every ending there is a new beginning. Remember, it is how the parents *respond* to behaviors that often determines what happens next. If they have that high level of response-ability, they can actually impact the behavior of others in the most positive ways.

When children are infants, caring parents are attentive to the child's needs. In very short order effective parents learn to identify what the infant is trying to communicate to them. They know when she is hungry, when he needs to be changed, when she is tired, when he is in pain or discomfort, and a variety of other signals. In short, they learn how to *listen*. They pay close attention, and through mindfulness and knowledge, they respond to the needs in satisfying ways. Then, as the child grows older and begins to talk, they, too often, stop listening and instead become talkers, fixers, ignorers, preachers, lecturers, moralizers, and psychologists in roles that tend to block communication with the child.

How many times have you heard someone comment that such and such a person is a very good conversationalist? Think about the qualities that you like in other people, your mate, your best friend, your boss, your employees, your children. Somewhere on that list of qualities, and one of the top reasons someone is thought to be a good conversationalist, is the ability that all those people have. The ability to listen. They not only let you talk, but they also appear to be interested, even encourage you, and they don't judge you or tell you how to fix things. They just listen. When someone listens to you, that tells you that they care about you, that they value your opinions, that they respect your feelings, and that you have the right to express yourself in healthy and constructive ways.

The first duty of love is to listen.

– Theologian Paul Tillich

There are many "healthy" people in this world who pay their hard-earned money to counselors, therapists, and other healthcare workers to listen to them. If we can't afford that or if we don't feel we need that type of listening, we often settle for the ear of a good friend, or, if we're lucky, a significant other. Often, whenever we are troubled or in need of counsel, we turn to those who will listen, sincerely, with quiet interest and let us just "air it out"; often we find that is sufficient. We are lucky indeed if we have someone who will just listen, and not judge, fix, advise, or moralize.

Everyone wants to be listened to! We love the attention, the feeling of being valued, and the feeling of importance when someone actually gives us the time to listen to what we have to say. To give someone your undivided attention, your time, your genuine presence at that moment is a gift to both the speaker and listener.

Those moments are few and far between in the hectic schedules of today's families. Too often in this 24/7/365 society we are distracted and pulled in a hundred different ways that do not allow us to take that so-important time to just "be" with our children when they need to talk with us. Teenagers especially yearn for this kind of attention from their parents, although, admittedly, they most often need it on their own schedule. We can't force them into talking with us just because it's what we want. This simple act of listening can actually transform the parent/child relationship from one of combat to one of peace and cooperation. Also, the tip most often given parents by parents is "listen to your teenager." One mother commented, "When I take the time to concentrate on what my daughter is saying, I understand her world better." Parents who try and understand their child's world, his thoughts, her feelings, dreams, and fears are very high on the wish list for most teenagers, although, according to teens themselves, it doesn't happen very often. They say, "Our parents should at least listen to what we have to say about things, and respect our right to have an opinion, even if they don't agree with us."

The art of listening is perhaps the single most important skill of parenting. Good, open, honest communication is the foundation of healthy relationships, even in adults. Listening honors and respects the other person and is a great tool for helping children, young and old, to make their own decisions and build their self-worth. To do it effectively takes commitment and lots of practice. There are two types of listening at the basic level of communication tools:

<u>Basic or Attentive and Care or Empathetic</u>

Basic Listening

Sometimes, all we need to do is just give our time and attention. Children will come home with an angry or hurtful story to tell, and all they want to do is to air out their feelings and have them affirmed by the most important persons in their lives, the parents. In this case, try to get physically close to your child and be "with" him. Teenagers need a little more space and sometimes no eye contact, but the younger child needs you to be close and feel involved. Try to be on their level, not looking down at them. Try to give them your undivided attention without distractions. Be in the present moment with the child and actually feel her emotions. Be really "tuned in." Keep your mind and heart open and put your personal opinions on hold. Seriously consider the child's point of view. In fact, encourage her own opinions and beliefs rather than making her feel that her thoughts and ideas are simple and meaningless. You can offer a word or two from time to time, like an "oh," "wow," "really," or

"I'm sorry" just to let them know you hear them. Quite often, after they let it out, they will feel better about the situation; you will have helped them feel better about themselves because you allowed and listened to their reality.

Basic listening, being attentive, is not a time for fixing and solving things, but you can make an effort to "hear" what your child is saying, connecting the feelings to an event and being mindful of what might really be going on with your child, which s/he may not even really know. An argument with a playmate or a teacher may result from feelings of jealousy or inadequacies. If you determine that it is, you might begin to pay more attention to the causes and not only the results. If what you hear is way off track in terms of what you are trying to teach your children, then, at a later time, when the child is calmer, you might want to discuss what was going on and give your input.

Care Listening

Care or empathetic listening requires more from you. All of the elements of basic listening come into play, but you can also give small, unforced invitations for your child to share more. You can begin to ask questions that don't place blame. You can start to feed back your interpretations of what you think you are hearing to determine whether you understand. For example, "Tell me more about..." She may not be able to express exactly what she is feeling, and you can help her get to her real area of concern and frustration. **Don't start giving her advice unless she asks for your help; and even then, turn it back to her, asking what she might do or how she might solve a particular problem.** Eventually, you could offer some alternatives from which she might choose a possible solution. If you and the child reach a possible solution that the child wants to try, encourage him in his efforts and then, after a time, check back with him to see how things are going. You can review with him, praise him for his efforts and solutions, or modify for another try.

Listening is not only important when the child approaches you. The parents should regularly take advantage of opportunities for discussions that involve listening to the child and for the child to listen to the parent. It's a great role-modeling skill for the children. Try and let the times for discussion happen naturally, like when riding in the car, taking a walk, doing chores or playing together, at bedtime, at mealtimes, or just hanging out. We parents should be brief with our own stories and input. We should be aware of our tone and body language, be specific about our points without dragging up past grievances, and as we are able and it is relevant, disclose our own "stuff" and admit mistakes and changes.

We can't listen well if we are:

- Too tired
- Too involved in the problem
- Having a problem of our own
- Late for work, or an appointment, or hectically getting dinner ready
- Not feeling accepting of the other at that moment

If any of these exist, we don't just blow the child off; instead, we might say things like "I'm sorry, I'm so tired that I'm having trouble listening. I can't concentrate, and I know this is important to you." Or, "I'm too angry (worried, upset, scared) myself to listen. Give me some time to chill out, and I will try to understand." Or, "I have to leave for work, but I want to talk with you about this. Can we talk about it right after dinner tonight?" If you have to postpone the conversation, make sure you set aside time to resume the talk with your child, and re-initiate the talk on your own without waiting for the child to remind you.

Try not to throw up barriers to communication, like:

- too much advice
- blame
- threats
- lectures

Avoid phrases such as:

- "You're always complaining"
- "Shape up, or you'll really be upset"
- "Just forget about it, you cry baby"
- "Don't let it bother you"
- "Oh, why don't you grow up!"
- "You never take responsibility for anything, do you?"
- "Why, when I was your age..."

For some unknown reason, many parents think having a conversation with a child is supposed to include nagging, lecturing, moralizing, advising, and criticizing, all amounting to "always telling me what to do." One-way conversations are not conversations, and they are certainly not listening; rather, they are downright disrespectful. Some teenagers I see are totally estranged from their parents, many not being able to remember the last time they had a good talk with their mom or dad. "They're too busy with all the stuff in their lives" is the usual explanation.

The truth is that we have to listen to our children. It's the only way we really get to know them, what they think, and how they feel. The better we know them, the better we can respond to them in helpful ways. Building relationships anywhere requires some people skills, and one of the most important people skills is learning how to listen. We sign up for this kind of training at our work all the time to help us be better at what we do. Doesn't it make perfect sense to train ourselves at building relationships in the most important of places – home – with the most important of people – our children? If you agree, then maybe some of the following ideas will appeal.

At least once a day, at dinnertime, bedtime, or some other special time, use some listening skills with your teen, even if only for a few minutes. At least once a week, have an extended listening time (thirty minutes or an hour) with him or her.

Although it sounds a bit repetitious, I'd like to offer you the ideas of two other parenting teens educators who might evoke or affirm even more good ideas for you. Some folks might think that *Teen Tips* by Tom McMahon (Pocket Books, 1996, www.kidtips.com) is a little dated, but from what I've seen and experienced, Mr. McMahon's listening tips are still very current and can be very effective. I share them here. You will recognize how similar these skills are to the styles we have already covered above when discussing basic and care listening, and I have updated them a bit, but these tips are somewhat more specific to dealing with teenagers.

Parent Skill Builder 1: Attentive Listening

The purpose here is to practice listening with undivided attention. It's not easy. It takes energy, concentration, and commitment. A good time to start this practice is when your teenager seems to be interested in talking, or whenever you are alone together. Turn off the TV, ask for the computer, the phone, the iPad, or the e-reader to take a back seat for a while, shut down the Internet or shut the door for privacy if necessary.

- Give your full attention.
- Maintain eye contact if it's not uncomfortable for the child, and get close if it feels right.
- Concentrate on what your child is saying.
- Don't change the subject. Let the child lead the conversation. Don't force it.

Notice how your child responds to your listening. Did she seem more talkative than usual? Did he seem pleased with your attention? Did you find him more pleasant afterward? What other observations did you make? When this skill starts to feel good to you and you get in the groove with it, move on to:

Parent Skill Builder 2: Listening with the Heart

This listening skill goes deeper and involves understanding and looking for the feelings and what's behind the feelings. It's listening with your heart.

- Use the simple listening skills to begin.
- Try to put yourself in your child's shoes. If you were your child talking, how would you be feeling? As the child talks, what are her words and body language telling you about her feelings?
- Instead of telling her "I know how you feel," let her know that you are really hearing her by saying something like, "you must feel so confused, or angry, or upset" about whatever. Responses to

positive feelings work the same way: "you must be very excited"; "I can see you are very happy about that."
- If and when she asks for your input, give it carefully, ending up with something like, "that's one way to look at it ... and might be a solution ... what other ways do you think might work?" Express your reasons for your position and move on. The children most likely hear you. Don't cram it down their throats or spoon-feed them.

In other words, have a conversation with careful, mindful responses on your part. Don't block his efforts to talk with you by doing all those typical parent things, because if you do too often, the chances of your child's ever talking with you and confiding in you and asking you for guidance during these turbulent times will be few and far between. You listen to your friends and co-workers, don't you? Your spouse? Why not respect your children the same way? Keep 'em talking by "hearing them into speech." That's one of my all-time favorite quotes about honoring others by listening to them. It comes from theologian Nelle Morton quoted in the writings of Parker Palmer.

Parenting teens is, indeed, a tough assignment. But how parents take on that assignment is critical to the teen's getting through what is probably the hardest part of the journey to adulthood.

Here are some more valuable tips for parenting teenagers from adolescent specialist Sue Blaney (www.parentingteensinfo.com) with a few of my own added.

Tips for Parenting Teenagers

- Be a good example of what you want your teenager to learn. Your behavior is your single most powerful tool, and they are noticing everything you do and say (and how you say it). They will learn values and beliefs from you, as well as how to deal with conflict, success, and how to behave in relationships.
- Strive for connection even more than communication. When you connect, you share experiences, and it provides the conditions under which communication can occur. **You can't have good communication without being connected. Make sure your child knows you are listening, want to listen, and that you are there to support.**
- Heighton your listening skills, because their communication skills will change as they grow. Your teens may begin to withhold information and not share the way they once did. Don't take it personally or be hurt by this because it truly doesn't reflect on you. You will still need to have a good idea as to what is happening in their lives, so begin to focus on non-verbal cues and other ways to gain information (honestly and carefully).
- Expect indirect communication. Don't be too disappointed if the close talks you hoped for don't last long or go very deep right now. You are not the person you used to be to them, but you will be again some day, so don't worry. Stop, look, listen, understand, and above all, be patient.
- Encourage your teens' connections to the school; make this a priority. School performance is the single most important determinant as to whether a teenager will engage in destructive behaviors.

Connections to the school can come in many areas, not all of which have to be academic. Clubs, sports, and music programs are some examples.

- Do not lessen adult influence in your teens' lives; rather, gradually adjust your parenting style from being a manager to being a mentor and consultant. A mentor rarely has real control, but is able to influence, educate, and facilitate development. This shift is important to help your teens develop responsibility and autonomy. Make this a gradual change that spreads over several years.

I also highly recommend what I think is the ultimate work regarding raising adolescents offered by Dr. A. Rae Simpson of The MIT Work-Life Center, Massachusetts Institute of Technology. Her excellent Raising Teens report can be found at http://hrweb.mit.edu/worklife/raising-teens/?q=worklife/teens-young-adults/raising-teens.

Don't lose heart!

> "What people really need is a good listening to."
>
> – *Mary Lou Casey*

GROUP EIGHT

Discipline: Building the Foundations for the Connections to Solid Relationships

Why? What? How?

Sometimes I shift into my short-of-patience mode. I am digging deep into my logic and good sense of how important it is to try to understand and accept how others choose to live their lives, but I must confess to you that my rope gets a little short with parents who put almost everything in their lives ahead of their children. As a children's advocate I choose to work with the parents of children, knowing that parents and homes are the very foundations, the roots for the character, and success of children. So, I want to start this offering with some questions.

WHY? Be honest with yourself now and think about just why you had your children in the first place. Who are they to you? How do you value them? Are they a daily joy to you, or do you look at them as some sort of burden or barrier to your getting all of your needs met? Of course there are going to be conflicts and disagreements, and on some days you will wonder what in the world they are doing to you. But, that's natural. That's the way we truly get to know each other, children and adults, by loving and honoring even in the growing pains of life. Some people had children because it was the thing to do; others because the clock was running out; some to carry on the lineage; still others to have someone to love and to love them; and some others even had them by accident. Even in the latter category the parents usually look at the child and say, "she's no accident, she's a miracle and a joy." At least that is the case most of the time, but often it is not. There are some parents today who really would rather not have children in their lives at all. You are a parent, for whatever reason, and you have one heck of a responsibility raising another human being into becoming an adult. So, get over being upset that they take up too much of your time, they are too demanding, they are stifling your life and career goals, or whatever self-centered notion you might have. These children need you and they need you in many ways. The younger they are when you begin being effective in their lives, the better and the longer you stay with them in the growing years. Then, you can be selfish.

I'm not suggesting that you ignore your needs. You have to take care of yourself, of course, and stay healthy; but part of being healthy is putting the welfare, well being, education, and love of your child high on your priority list. That leads to the second question.

WHAT? Now that you have these little ones or one in your life, what do you plan to do with them/him/her? Just what is the job of a parent? What do you do with these complicated beings who never seem to do the same thing the same way two days in a row? We do not know how to be effective parents naturally. We think we do, because we were raised well and we'll just do what our parents did. Are you trying that? Is it working? I have parents tell me all the time that they would never talk back to their parents the way their children do to them, or that they would never disobey an order from their parents and their children don't (or won't) even listen to them, much less obey.

These parents also say they are parenting the way they were parented, and they are frustrated that it doesn't seem to accomplish what they had hoped. There are reasons for all that and even more of the discoveries of modern parenting that frustrate and irritate parents today and ultimately drive wedges between them and their children.

The world is not the same as it was even twenty years ago. We have to parent children in smarter ways today because of all the environmental pushes and pulls on all the lives involved in family living. We all need new tools and skills and new ways of "being" if we are to successfully maneuver through all the pitfalls and barriers. If we adults are not very good at it, then how can we expect our children to be? So, what do we plan to do about it? Keep doing the same old thing we have been doing whether it works or not, whether the children or the family are in turmoil or not, whether we are at our last straw of acceptance, love, and understanding or not? I hope that is not the case, for that would mean that you have given up, given into the pressures, and have decided to just coast and let the chips fall where they may. That's fine, if you want your children to grow up with all kinds of troubles and problems trying to make it in a world that we adults created for them. But, if you want to give yourself and your children the best shot at a good life, then parents have to take action, make decisions about family health and the proper development of their children's lives. And that takes hard work, which is why a lot of parents can't bring themselves to do it. You have to. You have to.

HOW? How are you going to do what you know you want to do? We have to stop fitting our children into our lives when it's convenient for us, with little regard for the life that's developing in them and their need for our guidance. Children do not raise themselves, at least not very well. Unfortunately, too many of them do have that chore, since those who are often unsupervised, shown little interest, or not given care, develop their own ways of behaving and most often the behavior is not acceptable to anyone. It happens too often and often too late. We don't do anything about it until the schools or the police, or we parents are just sick and tired or afraid of the behaviors that the children have designed for themselves simply because it got them what they wanted. Not what they needed. What they **wanted.** They need what we adults can give them. Children need to feel that they are loved. They need to feel safe and cared for with daily talks and hugs and "I love you's." They need to feel capable, like they can do for themselves and get praised for it or certainly for their efforts. They need to be encouraged in their pursuits and interests and trials and mistakes and successes.

Little successes can mount up to

GREAT ONES!

When children feel capable, that feeling grows; their self-worth can blossom and endure for life. That leads to a solid feeling of being able to make decisions, become independent, follow and develop values and beliefs from the role models around them, and function in life in a happy and productive way.

All of this can come from committed efforts on the part of parents who sincerely care about doing their jobs well. We have to actually build relationships with our children. And, we do that by being with them more, cutting down on the talking and nagging and pointing out mistakes and shortcomings. Instead, we listen more, are truly interested in what's going on in their lives, give them our **unhurried time** and attention; we concentrate on the good stuff they do, the good qualities they have and the joy they bring to our lives.

Vital keys to building relationships

1. Work to calm down the home and life. Cut out some of the activities; simplify schedules and to-do lists.

2. Bring order to the family, with structure (not rigid), routine, and rules (clear, and specific).

3. Install a system of consequences, nice ones for good behaviors, and not so nice ones for not so good behaviors.

4. Create and clearly communicate expectations of behaviors and performance (within reason).

5. Follow through with what you say you're going to do. And make that clear. Say what you're going to do or not do, not what you're going to make someone else do. For example, "I am not going to pick up your dirty clothes and put them in the hamper again. If you want them washed, you know what you have to do."

6. Practice consistency. Don't be wishy-washy. If you don't mean what you say, don't say it. Learn to say it once, then act. Act more, talk less.

7. Try not to yell much. Or give orders, or commands. We all do sometimes. Try to keep it to a minimum. Instead, ask, correct, guide, show the way you want it to be or ask them how they think it should be and involve them in finding the acceptable way.

When we yell and punish, children most often will hear only what we don't want them to do rather than what we do want them to do or what we expect. Be sure to reinforce with positives any good behavior that you like. And do it as soon as possible and be consistent. Ask questions rather than fussing all the time. Like, "hey, what's going on here? Something I should know about?" "What's the rule about throwing things in the house?" Don't send mixed or nixed messages or "take-back compliments" like "the bed looks really good, now why haven't you been doing that all along?" The praise is offset completely by the criticism. Too much criticism will stifle the desire to try. Or use an approach like, "are you frustrated? Mad? Would you like to be less mad? What can we do? Tell me how it could be better." Always try to be kind and respectful. Certainly, we can't always be, but the more we are, the better relationship we will have, and parenting results will be better. Not necessarily easier, but better.

Finally, we parents have to do our work. For whatever reasons, we have children. We have a job to do. It is not easy. It will drive us nuts at times. But, if we commit to it, learn about it, want to dedicate our selves to it (while not sacrificing our selves), be responsible, then our life will be enhanced and rewarded, not to mention the lives of the children involved. If you don't like children, don't have any. If you're not taking good care of the one you have, don't have any more. Commit. Learn. Grow. Raise your level of **response-ability.** To those of you who are working hard at it...keep it up and

Don't lose heart!

EFFECTIVE PARENTING:

HELPING OUR CHILDREN

FIND THEIR WAY.

Discipline: The Dilemma

Picture yourself as one of five employees sitting around the conference table at your company's weekly staff meeting. Your boss is holding court and opens with an edict: "Sales are off, and what I need here is a little more discipline!" He moves to Employee 1 and in a loud, commanding voice states, "I don't like the way you behave with your clients. I want you to change it, now." With that, he directs the employee to bend over a chair, and he proceeds to beat the backside of the worker with a wooden paddle.

Employee 2 gets, "Your opinions stink! Your ideas are dumb. You are to be seen and not heard. DO YOU UNDERSTAND, YOUNG MAN?"

The boss gets skin-to-skin close to Employee 3 and almost whispers, "If you don't get with the program posthaste, your butt is out of here. Make no mistake about it, you can be replaced."

Shy and withdrawn Employee 4 hears almost in passing, "You're not worth even talking to, or giving you my time. You can do anything you want to with your joke-of-a-job...just don't ever bother me with the details. You're only here because you're blood kin, anyway."

And, finally, an anxious Employee 5 relaxes cautiously as the boss pulls up a chair close to her and calmly confides, "What do you think we ought to do about our sales slump? I know I can always count on you to come through for us. Let me hear some of your good ideas so I can make a better decision for us all."

Which employee would you rather be? How your boss treats you pretty much determines how you feel about him or her and how you perform your job. If your boss creates a company atmosphere where you do not feel battered, shamed, threatened, or ignored, but rather one in which you feel safe, respected, appreciated, encouraged, and recognized, chances are you will respond to your boss' requests in an entirely different way.

I make this comparison for you to keep in mind as we think about one of the major concerns and frustrations and controversies of parents, educators, and the general society today:

What are we going to do about discipline?

If you ask 100 people how to discipline, you're likely to get 100 answers. Most people usually talk about control and often equate discipline with punishment. Discipline and punishment are not the same! As you probably know, "discipline" comes from a lot of different roots, almost all of them meaning to instruct, educate, teach; the word "disciple" means "follower, a learner," and comes from a similar root.

> *Punishment is done TO a child.*
>
> *Discipline is done FOR a child.*

So, discipline then should be about learning, teaching, instructing, and training. One of the main duties of a parent is to do all of those things, thereby creating some followers; as in, "these are the house rules, the ways we behave here." The children that we see today – misbehaving and acting out in all sorts of undesirable ways – are a reflection of society. They are doing what they are doing because we, as parents, teachers, educators, ministers, businesspeople, politicians, media giants, and legislators, have allowed them to act that way.

Each one, of course, has to take ultimate responsibility for his/her self and for any actions, but the adults have actively or passively created this mess in which we all find ourselves: frustrated, enraged, and pointing fingers toward somebody else, anybody else.

We adults too often sidestep our responsibility. If we are looking for someone to blame, we have to assume a big share of it ourselves. It is true that today's children do need more discipline. But, we adults, who perhaps didn't get any from our parents, or perhaps got the wrong kind, just might need it, too. In order to hand it out, we have to have it ourselves and know what it is. And it's *not* punishment.

Discipline is the teaching, training, and guiding that parents must do **for** their children. It is to help their children feel capable; to respect the rights of others; to learn acceptable rules of behaviors and coping skills to use throughout life; to accept responsibility for their own behaviors; and to develop self-discipline, the ultimate goal.

Punishment is most often verbal abuse and physical retaliation done **to** the child, usually resulting in feelings of fear, anxiety, resentment, rejection, and shame. When a child is punished often and severely, the child can become devious, aggressive, hostile, or extremely shy and withdrawn.

When we get discipline and punishment mixed up and punish when we should discipline, we can cause more harm than good. We get so frustrated with our children's behavior when they are young that instead of **responding** in a knowing, caring way, we **react** emotionally and proceed by the seat of our pants and resort to punishment. We do that usually because it's the only thing we know.

Why is discipline so important? Because it is one of the main keys to the way your child will behave today. Appropriate and consistent discipline can make life smoother and more pleasant for you, your child, and everyone in the family, the school, and the community at large. The way discipline is handled in your family today will help shape the kind of adult your child will become tomorrow, and how he/she will survive and thrive in the world.

When something we do doesn't work, why do we keep doing it? Although most child behavior experts differ on details of discipline strategies, they do agree that children respond best when the parents are comfortable with their own methods and use them calmly and consistently, rather than angrily and inconsistently or rigidly. Children also fare better when they understand the consequences of breaking rules, when parents are firm and fair, and their follow-through can be pretty much predictable.

Surprisingly, corporal punishment is still being used by a lot of parents today because – I believe – that they see it as a quick, band-aid solution in their hurried, hectic lives and because, to them, it does appear to "work" for the moment. But parenting is not just about the moment. We have to consider what long-range effects our actions are going to have on the child, too. We are building relationships. We are raising adults! What kind of life-skills are we passing along? The experts are pretty much split on using corporal punishment, but the split is based on degree. Almost all agree that when corporal punishment (usually meaning physical punishment) is the only means of punishment, and it becomes a way of life for the child and if it is used to the extreme, it is never good. Some say that a slap or two on the hand or the buttocks on occasion is acceptable. But I believe that there are just too many good alternatives, even to slapping. However, the alternatives take patience, thought, planning, and time – something parents often choose not to work into their busy schedules. The more I have learned and the older I've gotten, I am now at the point where I can think of no rational reason for one human being to bring physical pain or emotional shame to another human being, especially one for whom love and care are professed. Exceptions could be in the matter of self-defense or dealing with life-threatening conditions that usually don't involve one's children or other loved ones. (Read more about corporal punishment and specifically spanking in the next Group.)

OK, so just what are some alternatives to physical punishment when seeking discipline?

> **Discipline is not just keeping your child from doing something you don't want him/her to do. It's about teaching your child how to behave in certain ways and to internalize that knowledge so the child will grow in self-discipline.**

You won't always be around to direct, coerce, punish, or pick up the pieces. The best way to develop a good plan of discipline in the home is to first try to prevent situations of conflict from getting out of hand. Some degree of conflict or disagreement is natural and desirable; it's *how* those situations are resolved and guided that are critical. This takes awareness, mindfulness, planning, and sensitivity on the part of the parents. What you decide to do and what parenting style you use when your children are small will in a strong way determine what kind of relationship you will have with your child when she/he is a teenager and later, an adult. The atmosphere in the home is critical. Is it a place you would choose to live if you had the choice? If not, then change it!

Be cautious, though. Don't expect change overnight, especially if children have been used to other methods or parenting styles for years. Also, don't be doom and gloom. Lighten up and cultivate your sense of humor.

Sure, raising children is serious and extremely important, but you're supposed to enjoy your children, not dread them.

Effective discipline is a positive process. Parents who are serious about being the best that they can be know that they need to take action, and be mindful, caring, and involved in the process. It's very difficult to be an effective parent with an absentee vote. You have to be present, and I'm not talking about just being physically present; you have to be emotionally present, as well. That may be even more important.

George Scarlett of the Eliot-Pearson Department of Child Study at Tufts University sums up effective parenting nicely: "Try to implement the least possible amount of force and work on supporting those things in the child that will make him or her know how to, and want to, behave."

Parents need to try and maintain loving familial relationships, create orderly routines to minimize conflicts (especially at times of transition and stress, like morning and bedtime) and help children learn how to take responsibility for their own lives. We must try to look at how we can help organize a life for the children that minimizes the need for parental control tactics and gradually help the children understand that they are partners in a small community, within which there are duties, responsibilities, and rewards.

We all want answers. We all want to fix whatever it is that seems to be broken. I'm sorry, but effective parenting just doesn't work that way. If indeed something is broken, or more likely just in need of an adjustment, then it cannot be repaired overnight. It probably took awhile and major effort (or lack of it) to get that way; therefore, it will take some time and effort to make any kind of effective change. Part of this change process might include going to local workshops, writing for advice, or developing your own self-help program.

Today's electronic vastland offers endless opportunities for learning and finding those specific skills that can be applied to specific situations. There are countless "experts" online who can be helpful, if you are careful in selecting the right ones.

In the meantime, I will offer you some "general specifics" to supply you with some more details about effective parenting skills.

- Establish a home atmosphere that is as harmonious as it can be with a team of caregivers together giving time and attention to the most important roles they will ever have.
    - Establish regular and familiar routines, yet allow freedoms for choice.
    - Define expectations of family members and create secure, safe, and loving foundations.
    - Promote responsibility by giving chores and duties. Explain the jobs of all family members. Discuss the needs, make assignments, and make changes if necessary. Set time limits for jobs. Follow up on completion.
    - Praise for efforts and guide and encourage strengths.
    - Have at least one meal together during the week. Talk the good talk.

- Be a good role model. The best way for you to get your child to do something is to model what it is you want. Children are natural copycats. If you want to raise an honest, truthful child, it will be wise to let them see you return money when the store clerk gives you too much change. Or let them see you following rules in preparing your tax returns.

    - If you want promises kept, keep them.

- o If you want good manners, use them.
- o If you don't like yelling, don't.

- Be ready to give immediate approval and encouragement for behavior that you like. Thumbs up will do. Love, kisses, hugs, notes through the mail work wonders; smiles and thank you's go a long way. Use positive reinforcements to increase desired actions: social and other rewards and enticements!

- Concentrate on your child's strengths, not the weaknesses. Make sure your expectations are realistic and age appropriate. Remember that there is no such thing as perfection. There is only great effort and a process of learning. To immediately point out a report card "C" when there are all A's and B's elsewhere to admire is not pushing your child to do better; it's most likely sending a message that no matter what he/she does, it's not good enough. Know what happens then? The child can quit trying for one thing. The child can put entirely too much importance on external approval for another. Encouragement is key to development. Discouragement will cause stagnation.

- Share your feelings openly, with and within reason, and create a space where the children will feel free to express their own feelings as you teach them how to do so creatively and in a healthy way.

- Do not threaten, shame, name-call, or abuse any living creature. These are all dangerous negatives and will cause harm.

- Make rules. Set limits. Create structure and order. Make it all clear and simple and appropriate for the age and developmental stage. Make boundaries realistic. Explain that they are for safety and harmony. Define all consequences of behavior, both good and bad. Enforce them firmly, consistently, and fairly. Also, offer freedoms that foster trust and independence.

- Of the top three "ways of being" for effective parenting, none is more important than listening. Listen, listen, listen. (See Group 7 for more on listening.)

If you incorporate any of these skills into the life you have with your children as often as you can, stick with it, giving good effort, you will be amazed at how the discipline in your home improves. At the same time, the need for punishment will decrease. The positive results at home will carry over into the schools and in the community. When children feel loved, safe, valued, respected, and cherished, they will knock themselves out to respond to you in the way you'd like. They love you, you know. Or, at least they want to love you. Let them.

The following four basic skills are at the core of effective discipline and they can be best applied by a parent being authentically present in the life of the child. Your children will be out of the home and on their own before you know it!

**Don't waste a single minute that you're with them.
They'll love you even more for it.**

Highlights of Disciplining Effectively

1: Effective consequences are one of the best skills in the parent skills-box. Our lives as adults and children are shaped by consequences. Most behavior is learned, therefore it can be unlearned and re-learned. Consequences help us learn how to behave.

They can be natural or logical.

Natural consequences teach children a lesson when they rush without caution into the ocean's surf for the first time only to be knocked down, tossed around, and filled with salt water. Caution or pure avoidance results next time. <u>Logical Consequences</u> are those that are planned with a result in mind. If you leave a bike out in the rain, it will rust, and it will not be replaced. Or, to prevent rusting a bike away, the consequence could be no rides for a while because the bike is not cared for. These are examples of what I call correcting consequences. They are the most difficult to develop and to carry out and to have understood, but they work, as do positive or <u>Affirming Consequences</u>, which should be happening all the time as a way of decreasing conflicts. When we see or hear behavior that we like, we want to reinforce that behavior with an affirming consequence. After a while, children learn that good behaviors result in better stuff than not-so-good behavior. That's the process of internalizing how one is going to behave, and it becomes a natural part of our lives.

2: <u>Role-modeling</u>. Children actually learn more about how to behave by watching adults than in any other way. They learn how to talk in respectful, polite ways or they yell their communications and demand responses. They learn how men treat women and how women treat men. They hear dad tell them about honesty and then listen to dad tell mom to tell the man on the telephone that he's not at home. They see mom live in clutter as she makes them clean their rooms. Parents punish their children to give them respect when the parents offer none to the child. The old saying "do as I say do, not as I do" doesn't work today (if it ever has).

3: <u>Encouragement</u>. Parenting pioneer Dr. Rudolf Dreikurs said that encouragement to a child is like water to a plant. If you really want a child to grow and grow well, offer bundles of sincere encouragement for efforts and accomplishments. A misbehaving child is a discouraged child; one who is discouraged about his self-worth, his abilities, and his lack of acknowledgement from others. Encouragement is a means to promote positive behavior, and some argue that it is more effective than praise (compliments and affirmations for accomplishments) or reward. It implies reasonable expectations (one step at a time). It conveys that you will accept the child's mistakes, as well as her/his successes.

4: <u>Rules and structure</u>. We all need order in our lives. We need routine and structure and the knowledge that some things will always be the same, expected, counted upon, to help us feel secure and safe. Rules provide predictability, consistency, and stability. Rules need to be very clear, clearly understood, simply stated. Too many may be overwhelming. There needs to be an understanding about the consequences of breaking the rules for everybody.

Does Anybody Know I'm Here?

Can you relate to any of this? **"I'm always rushing. It seems I'm always late. I miss deadlines, and forget things. I wait until the very last minute to make decisions and do chores. Sometimes I don't ever make the decisions *or* do the chores. I muddle through daily activities rather than follow set routines, and I often just don't get around to doing stuff. My house is generally disorganized and disorderly...and don't ask me how many times I lost my car keys last week. And my children! Let's don't even go there. It seems that I am constantly explaining, pleading, arguing, threatening, bribing, yelling, punishing, losing my temper, and more often than not, I usually wind up backing down, giving in and feeling guilty."**

Have any of you ever felt like you were in charge? Of anything? Can you remember the last time? Or, do you feel like you are just one step ahead of a train, like you just can't get your arms around all that's required of you? Do you feel like you simply do not have any "say so" about anything? Not at work, not at home, not with the children, not with the spouse, not with your parents? Well, get in line.

There are lots and lots of moms and dads who express these feelings every day and all too often during the day. When they do, then imagine what must be going on in the lives of their children. I see the results of how hectic, disorganized, and stressful homes contribute to problems between all of the people involved. Stressful lives diminish the quality of those relationships. Stressful relationships can be found in the workplaces, between employees and the bosses, between the workers themselves, and between the workers and customers.

At home, stresses deteriorate marital harmony, and of course are a major factor in how parents and children live their lives together and how the children live out in the world. One key ingredient in reducing those stresses is that **somebody has to be in charge**! Somebody has to drive or the vehicle called family will run off the road, land in a ditch, crash with another family in similar circumstances, or will simply wander aimlessly in its small, confused world until a crisis or a tragedy occurs, and the family unit is destroyed, perhaps along with individual members of the family. There has to be a plan in place, a plan that helps the family live more in harmony, helps decrease the hectic pace, organizes time, activities and responsibilities. In order for there to be a plan, someone, or several someones, has to be in charge. I'm not talking about a bunch of bosses, or dictators, or controllers. I'm talking managers. A management team designs a plan for a better family life that will result in all members being happier and more in tune with each other and with life's meanings. Everybody needs organization. For the children, it is critical.

The first step to being in charge is to restore or to create a **sense of order**. This has to begin with the adults who are supposedly the responsible ones in the group. So, putting order in one's life has to begin with the parent. To be in charge as a parent requires being effective with discipline and problem-solving. That applies to the self as much as it does to the children.

Claim or reclaim parental authority. The parent is supposed to be in charge. I hear parents say that their children run the house, that everything is about them and for them. If you feel that way, then change it. Be in charge. But do it in smart ways. Yelling and barking orders for everybody to follow is not good management. Your associates will abandon you, either physically, emotionally, or both, if you choose that style.

Develop and maintain a living structure that mostly works for everybody. We often find ourselves stuck in the goo of **response-disability**. We have to change that. We have to stop what we are doing. Calm down. Breathe. Think. Observe. Listen. Then take action. Create a strong level of **response-ability**, not only about behaviors and feelings that present themselves, but have a pre-behavior **response-ability** plan, too. Another word for that might be proactive, or preventive. If we slow down and become present in the places we find ourselves, we can do better.

Good discipline is always a blend of kindness and firmness. As those in charge, we can be kind and firm to ourselves and to our children. Being in charge is leadership that involves all those affected by change and participation. It requires structure that has flexibility. Children need parents to be in charge. They won't admit it, but they want it even if there are arguments and disagreements. Young children become fearful when they have very few limits and expectations for behaviors. They need some thoughtful, caring, guiding hand to lead them along the paths to adulthood. If they are left to their own devices, they will create their own paths and behaviors that may not be acceptable and may impact parents, teachers, and society in negative and harmful ways. Children do not know how to behave when they join us in this life. Who told them? Many children feel very much out of control and lost because they don't have enough caring structure to maintain their behavior and keep them on track. In good homes with effective parenting, most children internalize parental structure and expectations for proper behavior as safety and security.

> **They often cannot express themselves, but they do accept reasonable limit setting as a message of love and caring.**

The roles for parents get set: the parent is the dictator; the parent is a peer; the parent is a doormat; or better, the parent is a guide, a teacher, a caring, responsible adult. The parents need to become allies with their child, which has to be done in some form of relational structure. A lack of order in life creates an adversarial relationship which can become a pattern, a way of life.

"I've told him a hundred times"; "she can see how angry I get"; "he's always being punished for that"; "I've explained it over and over again"; "he just never listens!" Do any of those statements sound familiar? If you find yourself often making them or something similar, then your child doesn't think you're serious. If your discipline in a relationship is not working, then it's not effective and should be changed. For example, if your child is too demanding, he can be told simply that he will never get what he's asking for if he is rude. If polite, he might have a chance. Mean it. Stick to it. Don't give in. Hold your ground. Be firm. But, be kind and cool.

Here are some things you might choose to do:

1. Create a home where everybody feels safe, secure, comfortable, loved, respected. Role model how these feel and look. Talk about them and how the family working together can make it happen for everybody. Point it out when you see others-neighbors, TV shows, movies – doing what is important to you.

2. As the leader, the parent, take charge of yourself. Get healthy; get cleaned up, in every way-hygiene, medically, physically, emotionally, spiritually.
Be confident. Get organized. Reallocate your time priorities and put your children and your time with them in the right place. Seek to balance your family life and your other life (whatever that may be) so your family life does not take a back seat.

3. Create a structure in the form of routines, clear rules and expectations, organized time structures with predictable things to do, and consistencies with flexibility.

4. Have family meetings. Plan and prepare them. These are places for group focus and discussion. Structure and routine can be designed and implemented with input from all. Allow and encourage impromptu meetings when appropriate.

5. Plan **response-ability** to misbehaviors using early interventions (but not too early), watching out for warning signs and triggers.

6. Say "yes" more often than "no," but when you say "no," do it with conviction.

7. Respond quickly and clearly. Take a stand right away to stop behaviors.

8. Learn to say: "I love you very much ... and the answer is no." Along with that can be, "I know you are angry at me. I'm sorry. Maybe tomorrow you will like me again." "I know you are disappointed that you can't go. If I were you, I'd feel the same way, but the answer is no."

Affirm the child's feelings (also works wonders with your spouse) and affirm how you feel and stand your ground. You're in charge. Somebody knows you're there and are doing the job. And, above all,

Don't lose heart!

THERE WILL BE MANY DAYS WHEN YOU THINK:

I'M DOING THIS ALL WRONG. I MUST BE THE WORST PARENT IN THE WORLD. MY CHILDREN WILL SUFFER ALL OF THEIR LIVES AND WILL HATE ME.

BUT REMEMBER, NONE OF US IS PERFECT AND WE JUST KEEP TRYING AND LEARNING AND GROWING!

Good Morning!

I love the way a new day feels.

Those few moments when

Yesterday's memories

Are slept into a docile file for later.

When rest gives birth to new eyes

That see a life

With energy and hope

And a chance to try again.

Discipline: The Solution (Touching on some skills)

We have talked about getting to the point in parent/child relationships when the wants and needs of the parties cross into conflict. That's the time when a parent's level of response-ability comes into play. That's when the degree of a parent's knowledge about his/her children's development and behaviors becomes most vital. How do we as parents help our children grow well, physically and emotionally, and at the same time teach them appropriate and acceptable behaviors?

Effective management of a family unit is the key. What best leads to that, beyond the good health of the caregivers and the environment, is **effective discipline**. When we discipline effectively, positively, then negativity in our lives and homes decreases.

Positive reinforcement

The best and most effective way to decrease inappropriate behavior is to positively reinforce the behaviors you do like. We seldom point out to children how pleased we are about the really good stuff they do. But we jump in a split second when we see something we don't like. So, I say "surprise" the child doing something you are pleased about and in some enthusiastic way let him/her know it by encouraging that specific behavior. There is effective encouragement and there is proper praise. Remember to praise the behavior, not who the child is or isn't, and be creative with statements and questions that briefly dig deeper into the child's efforts and understanding of what he did. Proper praise and encouragement (words, hugs, smiles, time with, special treats, privileges, or approvals) most often will lead to positive reinforcement of desired behaviors.

Add to those skills the art of listening. Sincere and dedicated listening and being present with someone are most respectful, honoring, valuing, and are true gifts that we can give. Empathetic listening is hearing what the other person says and hearing what is meant. We don't interrupt, put down, belittle, criticize, demean, or discount another person when he/she is trying to talk to us, if we truly want to communicate with him/her. We don't have to agree, we don't have to allow inappropriate words or behaviors but it helps if we do let them express opinions and listen authentically.

Affirming Consequences

Affirming consequences are incorporated with the positives and desirable behaviors. They affirm the behavior in children that we like with such approaches as effective praise and encouragement, basic and care listening, valuing, concentrating on strengths, proper rewards, and attending with smiles.

Attending is one of my favorite words. "AT" means to "go to," "be there," "be present," "to show up." "TEND" means "to care for, take care of." **Attending with smiles**, therefore, is what I call a "first level" practice of **approving consequences and positive reinforcement.**

Attending involves moving to your child, in his space, up close and personal, down on his level, eye to eye. Touch him in a warm and gentle way and with a smile tell him with an "I" message how you feel about his good action or behavior. "I want you to know that I am very happy about the way you picked up your toys. Don't you think the room looks nice now?" He will get the message clearly that you are pleased with his behavior and that this is something that you like. Children do want to please the people they love the most (if the relationship is a good one).

- "I feel so good when you and your sister play so well together. It looks like you are having a lot of fun."

- "I think your drawing is interesting. Why did you decide to use that color? It is really a good choice."

A formula you can consider in developing a new way to respond might be: "I feel ... when you ... because ... and I would like ..." For example: "I feel so happy when you come in on time because I don't worry that you might be hurt and I would like to give you a hug." Be creative and do what feels right for you and your child. The point is to reinforce with appreciation and approval, value the behavior, and respect the effort. Usually the opposite of this approach is yelling something across the room, telling the child long after the event, or not doing anything to reinforce the positives.

When attending, do it during or immediately after the behavior occurs; be brief, clear, focused, and to the point; and be aware of the body language and expressions. A parent once told a child, "I love you." The dubious child then replied, "Then why don't your face show it?"

Rewards

What about rewards? Some people think they are bribes or threats. To clarify, a bribe is an offer of something to stop a behavior you don't like or to do something you want done. A threat is a promise of something unpleasant if something is not done or is done. A reward is giving something for deeds well done. Of these three, only a reward should be used and only after the fact. Usually, a reward should not be promised; it should be given because of some effort or accomplishment after the fact when not expected. It becomes reinforcement for desired behavior, a consequence for good stuff, and it should be given soon after the action and needs to be meaningful to the child. It should rarely be a material thing; rather, something more intrinsic, like a handshake, a thumbs up, a hug, a huge smile, words, special time together, a trip to the park, staying up later, a video, or a dinner which the child chooses and at which he is the honored guest. These are called social rewards and are often more effective, longer lasting, and are great for building positive relationships.

Most parents don't like to punish, whether it's coercive punishment, or the more thoughtful and more difficult compelling, persuasive, or effective punishments, which from now on I will call consequences of action or behavior. However, the consequence approach to discipline is the most effective practice for "management" of the relationship. Consequences are a natural part of life. When we behave in certain ways, good things befall us; when we behave in other ways, things not-so-good crop up. It makes sense that the earlier we start this learning, the more socialized we will become. It makes for good management. Lots of experts tell us that when we humans feel valued, we are more cooperative. Children are more likely to obey rules if they have a clear understanding of what the rules are, what is expected of them, why the rules are necessary, and what the consequences are for breaking the rules. It also helps if the child is allowed to give input into making the rules. Age should not be a barrier against input. Figure out a way for even three-year-olds to contribute. They will be quite happy. You don't always have to let them have their way, but they can certainly have some "say-so."

Correcting Consequences

Most often, corrective consequences are used when we are trying to change behaviors that are negative or undesirable. No matter how well we parent or how well our children are developing, there will still be some negative or unacceptable behaviors to which we will have to respond. There will be some child mistakes and misdirected actions. That's one way children learn and a way parents can teach. Whenever consequences are used to correct behavior, they should be used immediately if possible. Ideally, consequences for certain behaviors should be predetermined from earlier discussions so there is no doubt in the child's mind. There is a recipe of ingredients to follow in order for the process to be most effective:

- Control your emotions.
- State the reason for the consequence.
- Ask for child input. ("What do you think we should do about this? Is that what you want to happen? What do you want to happen and what needs to be done to make that happen?")
- Set limits on the consequences.
- Communicate love, not fear. Talk about the behavior, not the person, and no name calling.
- Avoid empty threats. Don't say you're going to do something you can't do.
- Show respect.
- Make corrections in private, even at home.
- Think before you act. Stay focused in the moment, not the past.
- Try to make your tone of voice light and kind but firm.
- Give one statement at a time and then act.
- Expect testing. Hold firm.

Make the consequences real, natural, and attached to the misbehavior. If a curfew is missed, a consequence could be making the curfew earlier or not going out at all for a few days, not two months or not going on a camping weekend with friends.

Consequences are also about choices. There is a formula for giving them, too: "this/that" or "before/must" and "after/then." For example, "either this happens...or that happens." "Either you finish your term paper or you (natural consequence) will get an 'F' or (logical consequence) you don't go out tonight. It's your choice." "Before you go to the pool, you must finish your homework. No homework, no pool. You have a choice." "After you take out the trash, then you can go to the mall. Not before. No trash, no mall. You can decide for yourself." Always offer a choice. It develops responsibility for one's actions, plus it helps children learn how to make decisions. It honors them rather than demeans them. Make sure, however, that you stick by your directions. If you're wishy-washy, you might drown.

Natural consequences are those that naturally result from a particular action or behavior. If he doesn't keep up with his cell phone, it might get lost or stolen. If she doesn't keep up with her things, she won't know where they are when she wants them. If too many potato chips are gobbled down while no one is looking, chances are an upset tummy will tell the tale. That's what consequences are – the results of some action taken or not taken. Our behaviors are shaped by consequences. They are great tools for all of us learning how to take responsibility for our actions. We parents have to allow the child to experience the results of his/her behavior. If behavior is positive, there will be pleasant or good consequences which will be a positive reinforcement of positive behavior. If behavior is not positive, there will be undesired consequences that will not reinforce the behavior.

Logical consequences are those that can be created and predetermined. When rules or expectations are set up for the home, they need to be simple and very clear. There should be no question about certain expectations. Some may be negotiable while others are firmly non-negotiable, like bedtime or curfew hours, or homework, or chores. Positive reinforcement of negative behavior (like too much attention, overreaction, being unreasonable) will result in a "pay off" for the child, but not for the parent. We can actually give negative behavior more "life" and the child could respond with even more and more drastic behavior to "get even." Negative behaviors need to result in undesired consequences, where there is no "pay off" for the child. **She won't do what doesn't work for her.**

There are several skills and techniques that can be used when **practicing correcting consequences,** the first being the simplest and the most effective, especially when your children are young.

Attending with frowns. When your child is misbehaving (like banging a metal toy on the good table), try not to yell at him across the room. It's a disconnected communication and after a while goes in one ear and out the other. It has very little effect. Instead, use attending, but this time with frowns. Go to your child, get on his level, make eye contact when possible, put your hand or hands on him with firm but not hurtful pressure, and deliver an "I" message. The message should be a calm, firm, very clear and positive direction. "I want you to stop hitting the table with the toy right now. Toys are for playing with, not hitting things. I don't like it when you do this." Remember, the longer you are with the child, the more time and undivided attention he has gotten from you, which may positively reinforce his undesired behavior. So, just let him know that what he is doing is unacceptable. If the behavior is repeated, go to him again, and say, "I said I want you to stop hitting the table. If you do it again, I will take your toy away and you can't play with it any more today. So, you decide: you stop or you lose your toy." If it still continues, take action and remove the toy. Be prepared for the fuss, and big, teary, contrite eyes, but be firm and consistent. That's the way they learn what you do and don't want from them and whether or not you were serious when you said you would take action.

Some more examples are: "I can't stand all of this bickering. My head is beginning to hurt and I want you to stop right now, please." "It hurts your little brother when you pinch him like that. I don't like to see him hurt. Please stop." "I am really bothered by all these cookie crumbs on the floor. I want them picked up and put in the trash right now." Each of the misbehaviors can have consequences if they continue. Some can be predetermined and explained to the children, like if the child hits a sibling or parent, you explain that an unpleasant consequence will happen, like losing a privilege or going to time out (a popular but mostly misused skill which we will discuss in the future).

Planned Ignoring

This sounds pretty awful, but it's really not. This is not neglect. It means to decide beforehand not to look at, talk to, or touch the child when he/she misbehaves. This is best used when a behavior or act is just beginning. It can be used on such behaviors as whining, pouting, certain types of tantrums, or crying to get one's way. As you ignore, the behavior will most likely get worse before it gets better, but the ignoring must be strong and consistent. We cannot give up or give in because if we do, the behavior will have "worked" for the child, and she will use it again and again. Children often need an audience for their behaviors. If no one is paying attention, if his efforts are not getting a rise out of the parent, then there is no benefit. Eventually, he will stop and try something else.

Part of planned ignoring can be to isolate the child simply by leaving the room where he is and taking his audience away. He may follow you with the behavior intensified, but you can still (with determination) impose the ignoring approach. This practice is also effective when new words are being tried out for effect. If a new "bad" word is suddenly introduced to us, we must try to ignore it and not let our reaction fuel the child's desire to attract focused attention and to manipulate the parents' reactions. If the child's use of the bad word has been reinforced in some way and he continues to use the word, then a direct disapproval and statement that your family doesn't talk that way and you expect it to stop is the right direction to go, but it will take consistency and firmness.

Show and Tell or Shaping

This is just a form of teaching a child how and why to do what it is we want. It is most effective for the preschool and early school years especially, but the same method can be applied for older children with modified approaches. Using "I" statements, we tell the child how we feel about a particular behavior. For example, we have just put the grocery bags down on the table, and your child immediately goes for the cookies on top. We tell her/him calmly, "No, I get upset when you snatch the cookies that way. You might knock all of the groceries to the floor and it is not polite. You may not have a cookie if you try to get them that way. I like it when you ask me, 'Mom, may I have a cookie when you empty the bag, or may I take the cookies out for you?'" Then, you ask them to repeat what you said, and when they do, say, "Now, that's the way to do it. Thank you, and yes, you may take them out and you may have one." Of course, you don't have to use my words, which may seem silly in your home, so pick your own.

Here's another example. The child wants something from the refrigerator and is whining. Say, "I really am bothered when you whine like that. It's not the way for you to ask for anything. Also, it's too close to dinner for you to have a snack. If you ask without whining, like, 'Mom, may I please have a snack,' then I would let you have one. Or, I may let you have some extra treat after dinner. Now, let's practice. Let me hear how you will ask so I can understand and not be bothered by your whining." When he has done so, tell him how much better it sounds and when he asks that way, he will definitely be allowed a snack. You might even say, depending on the situation, "I'll tell you what, since you asked in such a clear and nice way, I'm going to change my mind and let you have one small snack right now, anyway." Surprise rewards for good behavior go a long way to reinforce the behavior that you like.

I have previously suggested a possible formula using the "I" message, and I suspect you have already heard a lot about this approach if you have been looking for effective parenting input. "I feel ... when you ... because ... and I would like..." We can make this formula fit many situations. The more we practice, the easier it will become until it is a respectful, normal way for us to use correcting consequences.

Before we move on to our final two specific approaches, here is a word or two about consequences inspired by parenting authority Jane Nelsen. One of the mistakes we parents make when applying consequences is that we too often think of them only in terms of some form of "punishment" for a behavior or for not doing something expected. It would be helpful if we could modify that thinking and **think of consequences also as a way of finding solutions to the problems which we confront.** For example, when a child fails to pick up toys, a logical consequence might be to not let him play with the toys for a day or two, followed by working with the child to help find a solution as to why he is not picking them up: "Do you need more time?"; "Do you need more warning as to when I expect them to be picked up?"; "Would it help if I let you play with only a few toys at a time?"; or "How about if you put away the things as you finish playing with them and that way there wouldn't be so much to pick up at one time?" In other words, with some thought and effort, we could turn a correcting consequence into a problem-solving situation that encourages the child to find his own solutions and take responsibility. A combination of logical consequences and child-involved solutions might just lessen the need for further application of consequences. Also, a reminder that when you do choose or together with the child decide on a certain consequence, make sure it fits "the crime." Keep the consequence reasonable, age-and developmentally-appropriate, and above all make sure it is connected to the misbehavior.

Time Out

The use of time out is an example of a popular method of behavior management that is often misused and overused. Time out can be an effective approach with some children from about 2 ½ years old to 6 or 7, but it is not effective when it is used as punishment. When used as a teaching and child-empowering action, it can achieve results. A positive approach is that time out is for "cooling off" so we can all feel better. This is important because when we feel better, we do better. Misbehaving children are often discouraged children, so our job as parents is to encourage them to behave in more acceptable ways.

Time out is best when used to help the child calm down and think about other acceptable ways he should behave. It is a "social isolation" move, taking the child out of an attention-getting or attention-causing situation and putting him into a calming and thinking place. Time out should be used for major infractions of rules or for major misbehaviors, and the child should know in advance, if possible, that certain behaviors or misbehaviors will result in going to the time out place for a period of time. The place can be a corner, a hall, a chair facing a wall, any place where there is nothing to do or see or play with; in short, a place where the child would rather not be, as long as it is not dangerous, scary, dark, abusive, or feels like punishment. You could even designate a time out place for the whole family because even adults need to take a time out periodically and it could be the same place for all members. When children are older, or when the misbehavior is less major, like just being angry about something, you might consider letting the child go to her room where she can quiet herself and get it together. The child's room is not, however, the place for a regular time out.

If a child is directed to or put into time out and she complains and cries loudly, plan to ignore her, if possible, while she is there. Some parents use a timer to signal the end of the time out period, setting one minute for each year of age. Some let the child set it for herself for however long she feels she should be there. The child should know that the "time" doesn't start until she is quiet. Others let the child decide when she is ready to come out and behave in the expected way. If the child were removed from a situation where she was misbehaving, return her to it after the time out, and tell her you expect her to behave in an acceptable way now; when she does, reinforce with praise or use affirming consequences of appreciation verbally or physically, as in hugs.

After the time out period, find an opportunity to talk calmly with the child about the infraction or behavior and the purpose of the time out. Ask her some questions, rather than lecture, and try to get her to tell you why she thinks she had to go to time out and what you can do together to correct the situation and solve the problem for the future. It then becomes a learning experience. We are most effective as parents when we help children learn from their mistakes rather than making them "pay" for them.

To recap:
- Explain what time out is for.
- Make a list of why and when time out will be used.
- Pick a place for it. (Let others give input.)
- When behavior is heading toward a time out, issue a warning and offer a choice: "Either change

the behavior or get ready for time out." If the behavior continues, the child has made a choice and you might say, "I see you have decided that you need a time out." Take the child by the hand and calmly, quietly, without yelling or scolding or lecturing, lead him to the place.
- Set the time or allow the child to set it.
- Ignore all efforts to get you to change your mind. Remind the child that the time doesn't start until the child is quiet.
- Be consistent and stick by your decision.
- When the child comes out, return to normal, affirm appropriate behavior, and at an opportune calm time, go over the time out reasons and work on decreasing the need for time out. Keep these teaching sessions short and don't make them lectures or scolding. Spending too much time with the child actually reinforces misbehavior if his purpose was to get your attention.

Time out is for calming down and thinking about misbehavior. It is not for punishment. Try to remain calm through the process. If you can't, give yourself a time out, saying that you are too upset to talk right now and you're going to take a time out. This type of honesty and role modeling might even encourage the child to start taking time out on his own when he feels he needs it. It's a way of helping us feel better, and remember that when we feel better, we are better. Remember, too, that time out is just another approach to child management and shouldn't be the only one used. There are other corrective consequences to use before you get to time out, which we have already noted.

Remember especially to use a lot of affirming consequences, that is, praise and encouragement for the behaviors that you do like, which can decrease misbehaviors. Also, time out may not work for all children, but used properly, it can for many. For very young children, time out is too complicated and it feels too "mean" to isolate them. As Jane Nelsen says, "When children have not reached the age of reason, distraction is the most effective parenting tool. This means simply removing children, kindly and firmly, from what they can't do. A short, direct and clear direction of 'I don't want you to hit people' would be in order. If they can't understand reasoning, why try to reason? They can't understand the reasoning behind punishment, either. **Where did we ever get the idea that in order to help children do better, first we have to make them feel worse?"** Often for very young children, a warm and nurturing holding will provide the calming influence and help restore order.

A misbehaving child is misbehaving for a reason. Before you react, think about the "why" and make sure you respond in ways that will help the child learn as well as change the behavior. This is accessing your level of response-ability and avoiding response-disability.

For more information, I recommend "Without Spanking or Spoiling" by Elizabeth Crary or Jane Nelsen's "Time Out: A Guide For Parents and Teachers" to find out more about specifics and procedures. Jean Illsley Clark's unique book, "Time In," is also helpful. Using time out properly is like following a recipe ... if you leave out a step, the effectiveness is weakened and it might not "work."

Family Get-Togethers

The last Correcting Consequence (can also be an Affirming Consequence) we'll cover is family get-togethers, or family meetings. I prefer to call them get-togethers, since the word "meeting" has negative connotations for adults and for children. A lot of parents don't like this approach because they don't think it does any good, and it's just a lot of trouble and takes too much time. It does take time, thought, and preparation, but if done correctly and consistently, these get-togethers do wonders in establishing house rules, expectations, and consequences, creating a space for respectful disagreement, problem solving, and review and modification of situations that tend to cause disharmony in the home. Many children misbehave because they are discouraged, and often they are discouraged because no one ever listens to them. They don't have any "say-so" about anything, and somebody else is always telling them what to do. Get-togethers speak to this situation.

These get-togethers (you can call them anything you want), can be relaxed, semi-formal gatherings held on certain days at certain times. Each member of the family has a turn at conducting the group. Even small children can lead with some help and guidance. It should start off with everyone passing out a compliment or encouragement to one or more of the others, a thank-you, or an affirmation of someone's behavior. There then can be an agenda, like finances; old problems and solutions reviewed and modified; new problems and brainstorming for solutions; family topics; or individual topics of concern and interest. The financial agenda could be a sharing by the parents of budget concerns (as much or as little as they want to share) with the topic of allowances and extra chores. When there is a problem, it is a problem for the whole family to discuss, because it most likely affects the whole family. We can borrow techniques from conflict resolution mediation to help find solutions.

Here is a guide for family get-togethers:

- Agree that there is a problem. Someone is being impacted by someone else or something.
- Agree to solve the problem.

- Everybody gets to talk, with respect. No name calling.
- Everybody listens, with respect.
- Everybody tells the truth.
- Possible solutions are discussed.
- A solution will be chosen that everybody can at least "live" with.
- The suggested solutions will be reviewed at the next meeting and accepted or modified.

This gathering is the family unit working at its best. The system, which is what a family is, is running smoothly with preventive actions warding off potential larger problems. These team get-togethers are for talking, lots of listening, allowing input, involvement, and some winning for everybody, with no one totally losing. This is also an excellent tool in which to review the environment. How are schedules and duties running? It's a time where you can change the things that are causing problems.

Each family and each home is uniquely different, so the type of get-together should be tailored to the needs and schedule of your unique family. There could be called meetings. Impromptu discussions could be held, even one-on-one, with suggestions that the problem or question be brought up at the next gathering of the clan. Time limits can be set. It can be made clear that some items are not negotiable, especially for the young children, and certain rules for children and adults are cast in concrete, like curfews, homework, boundaries, etc. As the age and responsibility level of the children grow, flexibility comes into play. The key words to remember for these gatherings to be successful are: desire, patience, respect, patience, valuing, patience, honoring, patience, and fun.

Parents who are on hectic schedules, who are controlling people, who want to get things done, and who are inflexible will find this approach difficult. It will be a challenge, but if they can commit to wanting change and giving it a good, long, and dedicated try, they will be amazed at how well conflicts are reduced, misunderstandings are cleared up, and how much time will be saved in the long run. Not all of the children will be happy with all of the problem solutions. There will be times when the parents still have to hold fast and be the leaders, but if these times are kept to a minimum with children having a right to their say, even if they don't get their way, children usually become more compliant, more cooperative, and more pleasant.

Speaking of pleasant, it is important that the parents role model attitude about the get-togethers. The discussions should be calm, rational, and non-critical, and there should be an atmosphere of fun and enthusiasm. End each gathering with some type of treat, like pizza or a special dessert someone made, playing a board game, or a night out at the movies. When the team is working together to make things better for all members, a family bond will get stronger and stronger and many lessons of how to get along will be learned.

Remind yourself often that we are talking about raising adults, parents-to-be, creating harmony in the home, and providing guidance and direction for our children's welfare. I hope you will consider it well worth the time and effort that all of these thoughtful and response-ability approaches to home management take. It is not easy but the pay-offs are great! So, get to work and **don't lose heart!**

LOVE

is when the happiness of another person is essential to your own.

GROUP NINE

Corporal Punishment - A Review

First and foremost: I am not going to tell you how to raise your children, and I am not going to tell you not to spank. That is your decision.

However, I do want to present some ideas on spanking and then, perhaps, you can look at your practices with new eyes, with new information about the pros and cons, and see if you feel any differently. (See more on discipline in the previous Group.)

Spanking is such a sensitive and controversial matter that it might be best left to personal discussions in classroom or workshop settings in order for all viewpoints to be heard and explored. We talk about it a lot in the parenting workshops I conduct, but only when we have become friendly and can discuss such a heated issue in a safe space with respect and consideration for other points of view. It is not as simple as deciding whether or not to spank your child. There are many aspects to consider: the specific definition of the action; background knowledge to acquire; religious and psychological factors to explore; and most importantly, the style of parenting involved and the dynamics of the home environment. I believe it to be one of the most important issues of parenting today.

While we are going to concentrate specifically on spanking for this Group, it is important to point out that spanking is only one part of corporal and physical punishment of children. Both refer to a wide range of practices intended to cause physical pain, discomfort, tension, anxiety, shame, and feelings of worthlessness. These tactics are used to change behavior, make someone follow orders, stop doing/saying something, obey, submit to control, or stay in step with the cadence set by the guides, no matter what the cadence might be. Weapons of corporal and/or physical punishment include pinching; shaking; slapping; punching; kicking; pulling ears and hair; switching or caning; burning with cigarettes or matches; or injurious treatment such as making a child stay in a hot car, a dark closet, or in a cage. All these behaviors can be done with or without the use of objects like belts, cords, brushes, sticks, coat hangers, and wooden paddles. Corporal and physical punishment can be mild or severe, depending upon the force, severity, frequency, and duration. Their use can be seen as abuse, neglect, or in some people's eyes, discipline, or "a good spanking."

The debate on this subject seems to come from the need to justify using or not using corporal punishment. It's a debate that has already been resolved in our country when talking about adults in prisons, jails, domestic courts, and institutions. With older human beings, regardless of what they have done, people are not allowed to hit them. It's against the law. Yet with little human beings, the most vulnerable and defenseless of our population, we are still debating whether or not they are here for the hitting!

Dr. Murray Straus makes it clear in his 1994 book, *Beating the Devil Out of Them: Corporal Punishment in American Families and Its Effects on Children,* that violence is defined as an act carried out with the intention or perceived intention of causing physical pain or injury or discomfort or shame to another person. Such acts constitute violence directed toward children.

Here is a research article on spanking and corporal punishment for you to consider:

> "There has been a trend away from spanking or corporal punishment over three decades which is almost certainly the result, to some degree, of

increased national awareness of child abuse. When states enacted child abuse legislation in the 1960s, special provisions were made to allow parents to use physical punishment to correct or control children, so long as it is limited to "reasonable force" (my quotes).

In practice, that includes the right to hit with belts and paddles, provided the child is not injured. (There are no distinctions between physical injury and emotional injury, and my impression is that a "whippin'" hurts like heck.) While most parents understand the difference, some may need a clearer definition of where the lines between disciplinary spanking and child abuse are drawn. That's one of the problems.

Polls and surveys on spanking and discipline conducted over the past 30 years support the conclusions of the decrease. Researchers in 1968 found that 94 percent of the population approved of spanking a child who misbehaves – a belief so universally held that racial, regional, gender, income, and educational differences had little bearing on the outcome. But society's ideas on spanking continue to change. Early in 1997, in a Gallup Poll of 1,036 parents conducted for Parents magazine, 65 percent of the parents polled said they approve of spanking children. A survey done in 1994 by the National Committee to Prevent Child Abuse concluded that nationally, 49 percent of parents use physical punishment. It was the first time in a many-year study that the percentage of those who don't spank was higher than those who do. In 1988, it was 64 percent. In the 1950s, according to the University of New Hampshire study in the article, the percentage

was 99 percent for toddler spanking as compared to 90 percent today (1998). The number of parents who say that sometimes a kid needs a hard spanking has fallen from about 94 percent in 1968 to 65 percent today (1998). The percentage of those who do spank is decreasing overall, but it is still quite high."
Wichita Eagle, Wichita, KA, Roy, Nov. 1997

The research for the article by Dr. Murray A. Straus at The University of New Hampshire, published by the American Medical Association, found that the more a parent spanks (6-to-9 year-olds) for misbehaving, the worse over time that child behaves. To quote the researcher, "We are now able to show that when parents attempt to correct their child's behavior by spanking, it backfires. The more they spanked, the worse a child behaved two years and four years later. It also showed that the more frequently a child is spanked, the worse the behavior."

In the many discussions I have had with lots of people on this subject, someone invariably comes up with this statement in defense of physical punishment: "Well, it's in the Bible, where it says 'spare the rod and spoil the child.'" Then I have the dubious duty of informing them that that quote is not from the Bible! It is from the English poet Samuel Butler. You will find references to "the rod" in Proverbs, but not that specific quote. The book *Spare the Child* by Philip Greven (Vintage) is in my opinion, the definitive work on this subject.

What Some Others Are Saying

There are probably no real parenting "experts," since this field is constantly changing as we learn more about who we are and how our

children grow. There are, however, leading authorities who spend a lot of time thinking about, researching, developing programs, and teaching how to be effective parents.

The aforementioned research was published in 1998 by the American Medical Association Archives of Pediatrics and Adolescent Medicine. It was the first study to point out the correlation between spanking and behavior. Dr. Straus concluded that undesirable child behavior gets worse with more spankings, regardless of how much love, affection, and attention the parents showed the child. He is talking about not only spanking as brutal beatings with belts, switches, iron cords, coat hangers, hairbrushes, buckles, but also even a swat or smack to the rear or on the hand. The data was collected from 1986 to 1990 from interviews with the mothers of 900 children ages 6 to 9 years old. He measured the level of a child's antisocial behavior in 1986 along with the number of times the child was spanked each week. He then tracked behavior and the frequency of spanking over the next four years. Of the children whose mothers didn't spank, two years later, the misbehavior score was better. They had less misbehavior. For those whose mothers spanked once or twice a week, two years later, the misbehavior score was higher. And, highest of them all were the kids whose mothers spanked them three or more times during the week. Antisocial behavior for kids who were spanked three times a week or more increased 14 percent from 1986 to 1988. Antisocial behavior was defined as lying, cheating, bullying, being cruel to others, not feeling sorry after misbehaving, breaking things deliberately, being disobedient at school, and having trouble getting along with teachers.

Dr. Straus pointed out that he is well aware that these research results will continue to fuel the fire about the controversy of corporal punishment. On one side are anti-spank people, child advocates, parent educators, psychologists, and sociologists concerned about child abuse and future violent behavior. On the other side are pro-spank people, among them conservative Christians like Focus on the Family's Dr. James Dobson and psychologist John Rosemond, who fear undisciplined children will run wild. I know the work of both these men and it seems from their writings and publicity that both have softened in recent years and now make sure they qualify and clearly define what kind of spanking they mean.

Fairly, the article in the Wichita Eagle pointed to the fact that the new research report has some perceived limitations. First, it examined the disciplining of children ages 6 to 9 but not younger children, which still leaves unanswered what to do with toddlers who are naturally exploring their world, those tantrums during the terrific twos, and preschoolers who are testing their limits. (There are answers to this, but they don't include spanking.)

Robert Larzelere, PhD, director of residential research at Father Flanagan's Boys' Home, who takes a middle ground approach to spanking, says this study is the strongest to date that linked spanking with bad behavior. He agrees that if parents are still routinely spanking their 6- to 9-year-olds, clearly something has gone wrong with the way parents are dealing with the child. But, he said Straus overlooked at least eight other studies that show some spanking of children ages 2 to 6 has improved behavior. His research, along with that of Dr. Diana Baumrind of the University of California at Berkley, indicates that "authoritative (also known as democratic) parents ... as opposed to permissive (or indulgent) or authoritarian (or autocratic) ones ... who set clear limits, reason with toddlers and use a swat to the rear as a last resort discipline their children best."

Dr. Larzelere also states "if parents only talk and never back up their reasoning with negative consequences with 2- and 3-year-olds, my data shows that those kids are still acting out as much at 4 as they did in the terrible twos." I agree with him. There do indeed have to be corrective consequences to misbehavior, but there are many alternative consequences other than physical ones. He goes on, "parents should not be jumping to use punishment. If a child misbehaves after time-outs and a withdrawal of privileges, backing it up with an open-handed swat to the buttocks is appropriate. The idea is over time, you'll get the child to comply more with time-out, so you don't have to resort to spanking as often."

The University of California at Berkley Campus News media release in February 2007 cited an August 24, 2001, Baumrind study (which included 12 years of long-term consequences in the lives of more than 100 families) that reported occasional spanking does not damage a child's social or emotional development. Dr. Diana Baumrind said, "I am not an advocate of spanking but a blanket injunction against its use is not warranted by the evidence. It is reliance on physical punishment, not whether or not it is used at all, that is associated with harm to the child. What really matters is the child-rearing context. When parents are loving and firm and communicate with the children, the children are exceptionally competent and well-adjusted, whether or not their parents spanked them as preschoolers."

She emphasized that her study does not address at all the damaging effects of abusive and physical punishment, of which she and other researchers have found there to be ample harmful evidence.

In an article featured on MSNBC, "Discipline Debate," by Victoria Clayton in February 2007, Baumrind was again quoted: "Spanking in my view is not more or less harmful than a mild scolding, timeout, or other developmentally appropriate level and kind of punishment. But also, any form of punishment by definition is aversive and so whether physical or non-physical, punishment should be reserved for times when milder methods such as persuasion or distraction have failed."

The article went on to say that the majority of psychologists move to the anti-spanking side. The American Academy of Pediatrics is firmly against spanking and hitting, saying in a policy statement that corporal punishment is of limited effectiveness and has potentially deleterious side effects.

The New York Times article *Findings Give Some Support to Advocates of Spanking* by Erica Goode in August 25, 2001, also noted comments from Dr. Baumrind as she presented to the annual meeting of the American Psychological Association in San Francisco. She asserted that social scientists had overstepped the evidence in claiming that spanking caused lasting harm to the child. She said, "The scientific case against the use of normative physical punishment is a leaky dike, not a solid edifice." Dr. Baumrind said she did not advocate spanking, but she argued that an occasional swat, when delivered in the context of good child-rearing, had not been shown to do any harm.

Dr. Murray Straus was actually present and heard Dr. Baumrind present her study and said that it may be the best single study available in terms of methodology, but he said the findings did not change his view that spanking is harmful. There is not absolutely conclusive evidence but there is strong evidence. And there is strong evidence that other methods work just as well.

Dr. George Holden at the University of Texas agreed with some critics that many spanking studies were flawed. But he said enough studies had found harmful outcomes to suggest that spanking was "a damaging practice in certain cases under certain conditions." The Times article concluded with Holden's observations that some parents spank emotionally while others have the firm belief that it is necessary to socialize their children. It is important to remember that different children react differently to being spanked.

Researcher Dr. Paul Frick at the University of New Orleans in Louisiana warns that "spanking and hitting can lead to later emotional and behavioral problems. Even children who are only smacked occasionally are more likely to show signs of depression or lower self-esteem." Frick and his team who studied the impact of corporal punishment on 98 children and published results in the January 2007 Journal of Applied Developmental Psychology said they couldn't find any positive effects for spanking.

> "Children on the receiving end of a slap can learn that when they are upset and angry they hit rather than understanding their behavior was wrong and that they need to do better. This is a small but significant sample. We don't want to overstate the implications. The vast majority of kids who are subject to mild corporal punishment will not suffer severe negative effects. Our point, though, is that spanking and hitting are not effective and may be dangerous."

The Washington Post, in a June 26, 2002, report "Harm Outweighs Benefits Of Spanking: Information On The Effects Of Corporal Punishment On Children" found evidence of many of the negative interpersonal relationships with parents, family members, and others with whom the children were associated.

What has been called a study of studies was presented by Dr. Elizabeth Thompson Gershoff of Columbia University. It encompassed 88 studies more than 62 years of research. Entitled "Corporal Punishment by Parents and Associated Child Behaviors and Experiences: A Meta-Analytic and Theoretical

Review," it was first published in a journal by the American Psychological Association, (Psychological Bulletin, Vol. 28, No. 4, pages 539-579, 2002). The study found that parental use of corporal punishment was related to such child behaviors and experiences as:

- greater aggression
- poorer internalization of moral values
- higher rates of delinquency and antisocial behavior
- poorer quality of parent-child relationships
- poorer child mental health
- being a victim of child abuse and
- abusing own child and spouse

It also found that corporal punishment was associated with the short-term effort of a child's more quickly complying with parental directions. But it is temporarily more compliant and can cause more problems than it cures by raising the risk that children will become aggressive, antisocial, and chronically defiant. "I would argue parents should, to the best of their ability, avoid using corporal punishment and instead use nonphysical and more positive types of discipline that we know are effective," Dr. Gershoff said.

Dr. Robert Larzelere, from Boys Town and the University of Nebraska at the Medical Center in Omaha, responding to Gershoff's research, states that "severity and context are much more important than whether parents spank. Parents should never resort to spanking as their initial techniques in disciplining their children. But if reasoning does not work and neither do nonphysical punishments like timeout or taking away, a spanking could be beneficial. Children in black families tended to see spanking as motivated by their parents' concern while white children tended to see it as a sign of rejection by parents."

Dr. Gershoff found that spanking was not associated with increased aggression among black children, but it was associated with that risk among white children. Larzelere says aggression in older children tends to rise with spanking. Both agreed that a spank delivered in the heat of anger as a visceral reaction by a parent was less effective and much more likely to slip into abuse than a spanking that was carefully calibrated and used as a technique of last resort.

When responding to the popular defense used by some adults, "I was spanked and I turned out all right," Dr. Gershoff said, "There are no situations where a child should be spanked. Children turn out okay in spite of spanking, not because of spanking." Think about the millions of healthy and productive adults in our world who were not spanked. They turned out all right, too.

Dr. Michael H. Popkin, founder and CEO of Active Parenting Publishers in Kennesaw, Georgia, in the Spring 2008 newsletter of "The National Effective Parenting Initiative" presented "8 Good Reasons Not To Spank." Dr. Popkin tells about a family trip to the San Diego Zoo where he watched a papa gorilla back-hand a bothersome offspring, knocking the hairy child across the large cage. In his seventh good reason, he states, "It doesn't take a high level of intelligence to hit a child, even to spank a child. If it worked, then parenting would not be difficult, because we could all do it. There must be more to effective discipline in our complex society than there is in the primitive society of apes."

Dr. Straus continues to work tirelessly to make his views known. The CICC newsletter in 2008 featured a chapter from the 2007 book *Current Controversies on Family Violence,* edited by Drs. Donileen R. Loseke of the University of San Francisco, Richard J. Gelles and Mary M. Cavanaugh of The University of Pennsylvania which makes a powerful case for everyone making a commitment to stop spanking children:

- Spanking has serious harmful side effects that parents have no way of seeing, because such effects do not show up until later.
- Spanking is no more effective than other methods of correction and control and it is therefore unnecessary to subject children to the risk of the harmful side effects.
- Spanking contradicts the ideal of nonviolence in the family and society.

Noted child-raising authority, the late Dr. Haim Ginott, in his book *Between Parent and Child*, (1969) New York University, Avon, says,

> "...when we punish a child, we divert her from facing herself. There are people who say,
> 'but if you don't punish her, you're letting her get away with murder.' Just the opposite is true. When we punish a child, we make it too easy for her. She feels she's paid for the crime and served her sentence. Now, she is free to repeat her misbehavior. Actually, what do we want from a child who has transgressed? We want her to look into herself, experience some discomfort, do her emotional homework, and begin to assume some responsibility for her own life."

That result is best accomplished with the use of consequences for behavior.

Here are some thoughts from Dr. John Gottman, a professor of psychology at the University of Washington and the author of an exciting book, *The Heart of Parenting: Raising an Emotionally Intelligent Child* (Gottman, DeClaire, Fireside, NY, 1997 Page 103).

> "Another commonly used consequence of misbehavior among American parents is spanking. A 1990 survey of college students revealed that 93 percent were spanked as children, with 10.6 percent reporting physical punishment severe enough to cause welts and bruises. While spanking may be popular in the United States, it is not standard among parents worldwide. Only 11 percent of parents in Sweden, for example, report spanking their kids, a statistic many believe may be connected to the lower incidence of violence in general in that country."

Dr. Gottman also says that many parents who spank say they do so because it makes their children obey.

> "Indeed, many kids will do what they are told to avoid physical pain. The problem is, a threat of spanking works too well in the short term: It stops misbehavior immediately (sometimes), often without discussion, cutting off chances to teach the child self-control and problem solving. And, in the long term, spanking may not work at all. In fact, spanking often backfires because it makes kids feel powerless, unfairly treated and angry with their parents. After a spanking, children are more likely to think about revenge than self-improvement. A sense of humiliation may cause them to deny wrongdoing, or they may plot ways to keep from getting caught the next time they misbehave."

The anti-spank people know that even as well-intentioned human beings we might from time to time "lose it" and apply a physical punishment. Generally, an isolated, mild, and non-wounding spanking most likely will not harm a child for life. On the other hand, one terrible physical punishment in a rage or out of frustration may indeed mark the child and damage the relationship forever. It depends on so much. That's why this is so complicated. Here's more from Dr. Gottman:

> "Spanking teaches, by example, that aggression is an appropriate way to get what you want. Studies show that children who are hit are more likely to hit their playmates, especially those playmates who are smaller and weaker (a factor in bullying). The effects of spanking may have a long-term impact as well. Research indicates that, in relation to the severity of physical punishment received, spanked children become more aggressive. As teenagers, they are more likely to hit their parents (and to be more defiantly disobedient). As adults, they are more likely to be violent and tolerate violence in their relationships. And, finally, people who were physically punished as children are less likely to care for their aging parents. Although a majority of American parents use spanking, I believe most want a better way to respond to their children's misbehavior. Interestingly, studies of parents who have trained in other methods of child discipline show that once they find effective alternatives, they drop the spanking. Families do better with methods of limit setting that allow children to keep their sense of dignity, self-esteem and power. When children are given rules they understand, and a sense of control over their own lives, they are less likely to misbehave in the first place. When they learn to regulate their own negative emotions, parental limit setting and discipline are less frequently needed. And, with fair reliable allies in Mom and Dad, children are more open to mutual problem solving."

I agree with a great deal of what Dr. Gottman is saying. I want to delve into another area that concerns me and share some thoughts about why this issue is so heated and why some parents respond to it the way they do.

No Blame

Talking about spanking is a very sensitive thing. Some parents are very uncomfortable, hostile, defensive, downright rude, and aggressive about their views. I believe that the reason for some of this is that they don't like anyone bashing a long-held tradition, "the American way," "the Christian way," but I think it goes even deeper. To admit that spanking might not be good for children makes parents feel guilty about what they have done maybe even to children who are now grown, or about what they still might be doing. Some teen or adult children may indeed be acting out in ways some authorities predicted they might when raised with corporal punishment, and the parents don't want to own any responsibility in the children's being who they are. It might make them defensive because they don't want to be dubbed less-than-effective parents and don't want anyone to blame them and say that they have failed or are failing their children. They don't want anyone messing with their family and their way of doing things (even at the expense of the children.) Touching on ego matters, they may even think they are being attacked because they are the product of physical punishment, and they don't want to think that they may be lacking in any way.

I work with parents, on the other hand, who readily admit that they know that they are "messed up," because their father used them as a punching bag, and/or their mother, too; and yet they are working to take responsibility, not just

pointing a finger and blaming. Defensive parents may respond heatedly because they feel their parents are being blamed, and they don't want anyone talking badly about their parents. I for one don't blame them. In fact, none of this is about blame. Certainly, it is not in any way a suggestion that a parent should blame him or herself for anything. Rather, it's about learning, growth, and change – if one feels that a change is in order. Blaming just keeps the wounds open; forgiveness and moving on with one's life helps the healing. Changing the way we do something in our lives is very hard to do at times, but there are few of us who would hesitate to change if we felt harm were being done to ourselves, our families, our jobs, or our children. In the workplace, we change procedure mid-stream if it will make things better. We don't dwell on the old way of doing things as a mistake; rather, learning new things is seen as growth and we learn from the past to better our futures.

To my knowledge, there have been no studies on the subject of why caregivers are defensive and reluctant to change. I wish I could cite some research here. I bring my opinions to you, however, based on more than 20 years of working in the field with a cross-section of parents and grandparents, close to a thousand of them, and I share with you my findings and my concerns because of the realities that exist.

There is a lot of talk about the state of today's teenagers, let's say from ages 13 to 17. The undesirable behaviors they exhibit, or are blamed for, are caused by a complex variety of factors, among which may be too much bad TV, bad music, bad role models in the media, bad magazines, access to more bad stuff, and just plain old bad teaching from parents and schools (or no teaching at all.) Note I use the adjective "bad" in all the examples, because there are good elements in some or all of them. One of the indisputable factors in causing some of the problems is home life, how the child is raised and in what kind of environment. Many parents are in ill health, physically and emotionally; society's requirements are stressful and time-consuming; and many still live in a cycle of dependency and dysfunction that carries on to the next generation.

There's another factor within the family environment that may also have had some influence. The teenagers were not raised with any discipline or taught self-control when they were developmentally ready. They have no values or morals. These teens are actually a mirror of society. We adults have created this society in which these kids are trying to grow up, so we have to be careful where we lay blame. It just may not be the kids' fault, although they are responsible for what they do about it.

Consider this. A teen in 2008 was 13 to 19 years old. That means the birth day was between 1989 and 1995, and were toddlers between 1993 and 1999. Let's say at their birth, their parents were approximately 30, which would have made their birth dates in the late 50's to mid 60's. That would make them somewhere between 43 to 49 years old in 2008. During the years from 1959 to 1965 when these parents were growing up, there was a 94 percent approval of the use of corporal punishment. That means that most likely those parents were spanked, and they most likely spanked their children, who might be some of today's teens. There are those who say that today's teen problems were caused by parents being too permissive with their children and following the advice of "liberal" parenting authorities. If we are to believe the numbers I used above, the parents of today's teens were more into autocratic than into democratic or authoritative parenting styles. Permissive parenting can be just as bad as rigid autocratic, and permissive is not what the democratic or authoritative (Goldilocks) parenting style teachers. It's very misunderstood. There is a section in this book on choosing a parenting style. I encourage you to visit. (Group four).

To my knowledge, there is certainly no scientific correlation in what I've just pointed out, but it surely seems to me that there might be a connection. Since the use of corporal punishment has declined in the last few years, for the upcoming teen generation, it will be interesting to see if there indeed might be fewer problems connected with teens.

Unfortunately, it's not that simple. There are too many other factors in the home. The children may not be getting as much spanking, but they may also not be getting any discipline due to several factors: both parents working and not having the time it takes to discipline effectively; being too indulgent with the children because of fatigue; guilt about not being able to spend the time they would like with them; or the lack of knowledge about discipline skills that will work other than spanking. Spanking is a punishment, not a discipline, and it is used for immediate results – to get a child to stop or start doing something right away. It might even work for that moment, but it might not work over the long haul. Parenting is not about the moment only, but also about the future of the child and who the child is going to be.

I Turned Out All Right

"I was spanked, and I turned out all right." This statement is offered to me a lot as justification for spanking children. On the surface, it might seem to make some sense, but if we examine the statement at a deeper level, we might discover that the person doing the claiming wasn't really spanked that often, or was "spanked" in the least severe way. They may be wonderful people whose parents spanked them on certain occasions for certain reasons, but at other times gave the child good nurturing, love, kindness, and skills that developed and maintained a good child/parent relationship where there was respect. Often, a child who is spanked only a few times never has to have another spanking simply because s/he respects and loves the parents; they have a good relationship, and she doesn't want to do things that upset them and anger them. Not wanting to be in conflict may be a part of that child's temperament. There are other children with different temperaments who don't have that kind of good relationship; rather, they have one that is disrespectful, and they don't care whether they please the parents or not. In fact, they will find ways to hurt them back, lie to them, manipulate them, and rebel against them. So, if you were spanked and you turned out okay, then maybe it is because there was a foundation of a good relationship and you knew you were loved and cared for and you had the temperament that didn't require Gestapo tactics.

On the other side, spanking can do great damage if it is used too often, too severely, for every little misbehavior, and out of anger, accompanied often with harsh and hurtful words. In this case, any meaningful relationship between the parents and the child can be seriously jeopardized.

On a lighter side about that "I turned out okay" statement: The person saying it might think it's true because he functions in the world, has a job, isn't in jail, is responsible, makes the house and car payments, and keeps a roof over the family. We often ask the person boasting that he turned out all right what answer would we get if we asked others in his life if they thought the statement was true.

What about Cultures?

Of course, there are cultural differences that have to be considered. Some sectors of our population differ on their approaches based on "that's how we do it in my culture." In my opinion, a person's culture shouldn't even enter the picture until the children are old enough to understand and be influenced by it directly. In the very early years, all (healthy and normal) human children are pretty much the same biologically and all need to have their needs met in similar ways. Children also need all of the other necessities of physical and emotional development. Cultures enter the picture when they start having "minds of their own" and begin to be a major fact in the child's life.

We noted in an earlier research section a comment from Dr. Robert Larzelere that the "children in black families tended to see spanking as motivated by their parents' concern while white children tended to see it as a sign of rejection by parents." In the same section, we also used a comment from Dr. Gershoff who found that spanking was not associated with increased aggression among black children, but it was associated with that risk among white children.

In a recent study from "Teachers College Record" on August 30, 2008, by Jelani Mandara, " The Impact of Family Functioning on African American Males' Academic Achievement: A Review and Clarification of the Empirical Literature," there are some other interesting points made about what we popularly – and in my opinion incorrectly – call "cultural" differences in building and maintaining relationships. The paper reviews and clarifies many of the inconsistencies and misconceptions in the literature regarding the effects of family functioning on an African-American male's academic achievement, concluding that an African-American version of authoritative parenting, which is qualitatively different than European-American authoritativeness, is the optimal parenting style for African-American male academic achievement.

The findings that "authoritative" parenting for African-American parents would be like "autocratic" for the European-Americans are most revealing to me. It makes sense. None of us is doing it right most of the time; in fact, European-American authoritative approaches are way too permissive, but when African-Americans are serious about "keeping you out of trouble and showing you the right way," they mean it and will be tougher on their children. In my opinion, the reason it works is that in the other part of the relationships, there is love, warmth, and good role modeling that goes along with being "strict." And the message is "this is good for you" rather than "I am the boss and you will do what I say." Of course, there could also be the "fear" factor; when behavior is better in school, it could be because of what the child is afraid will happen at home. Then there is always "temperament"; some children will naturally be more inclined to respond one way and others another way.

The best and most effective way to help guide your child toward self-discipline is to reinforce the good stuff. "Find" the good things children do and let them know how you feel, encouraging the behavior that you like. Research studies show us that when humans feel valued we are more cooperative. We all want to "matter" and when we feel that we do matter, we have the basis of a sound foundation with those who help us feel that way. Children are more likely to obey rules if they have a clear understanding of what the rules are, why they are necessary, and what the consequences are for breaking them. It also helps when the child is allowed to give input into making the rules. Children may not always have their way, but they can certainly have their own say-so. So, listen! You don't need to be the one talking all the time. Nagging, sermonizing, moralizing, and psychologizing often fall on deaf ears. You don't need to fix everything. Sometimes children just want to be heard. Don't you? Don't you want to just "matter"?

It's In The Bible?

I have debated as to whether or not I should write about the "Biblical" aspects of spanking mentioned earlier ("spare the rod, spoil the child"). I have decided to do so because I feel it's important for those of you who do base your practice of physical punishment on the Bible, or "Christian teachings," to at least hear another point of view. I am certainly not attacking anyone's religious beliefs, nor am I suggesting what you should believe, nor do I present myself as a theological authority. But I do want to share with you some of the discoveries I made after much research on the issue. The research came about as a result of a newspaper editorial debate I had with the late Mr. Horace Carter, founder and publisher of the Tabor/Loris Tribune, a weekly newspaper based in Tabor City, N.C. He took a pro-spanking position and I took the position that ideally there should be no corporal punishment of children, but if there is, it should be done with knowledge and responsibility. That includes spanking, of course.

Earlier in this group, I wrote that the oft-used rationale for spanking, "spare the rod and spoil the child," is not in the Bible, as an astounding majority of people believe it to be. It is actually a quote attributed to English poet Samuel Butler. I made this point in the second letter to the editor as Mr. Carter and I debated. His final entry in the friendly discussion was his editorial that again affirmed his belief that "whipping is a good means of disciplining your child," and it was based on a letter he received from a Baptist minister in Florida that offered several quotes from the book of Proverbs in the Bible. The verses he listed are as follows:

- Proverbs 10:13 – "In the lips of him that hath understanding wisdom is found: but a rod (is) for the back of him that is void of understanding."

- Proverbs 13:24 – "He that spareth his rod hateth his son: but he that loveth him chasteneth him early."
- Proverbs 14:3 – "In the mouth of the foolish (is) a rod of pride: but the lips of the wise shall preserve them."
- Proverbs 22:8 – "He that soweth iniquity shall reap vanity: and the rod of his anger shall fail."
- Proverbs 22:15 – "Foolishness (is) bound in the heart of the child: (but) the rod of correction shall drive it far from him."
- Proverbs 23:13-14 – "Withhold not correction from the child: for (if) thou beatest him with the rod, he shall not die. Thou shalt beat him with the rod and deliver his soul from hell."
- Proverbs 26:3 – "A whip for the horse, a bridle for the donkey, and a rod for the fool's back."
- Proverbs 29:15 – "The rod and reproof give wisdom: but a child left to himself bringeth his mother to shame."
- Proverbs 19:18 – "Chasten thy son while there is hope, and let not thy soul spare for his crying."

There they are: the verses in the Bible that refer to "rod" as submitted by a minister. One cannot deny that they exist. However, one can take exception to the way the verses are interpreted. I would question the difference in meaning and purpose from the times more than 2,000 years ago and today. I would also point out that literally only one of the verses actually says to beat the son with a rod, Proverbs 23:13-14. Also, what definition of rod is meant in "rod of pride" and "the rod of his anger"?

For example, the "big fat" Webster's Dictionary offers the "Biblical" definition of "rod" as an "offshoot or branch of a family, tribe, stock or race, as in the rod of Isaiah." Another definition: "a kind of scepter or badge, as in the usher's rod, hence power and authority, a symbol of office (to escort or conduct others)." Webster gives eleven definitions of the word "rod" and only one of them defines it as a tool for punishment. From the list of the Proverbs verses, only two of them could be seemingly interpreted as a direction to actually use a rod to beat, and only two of those specifically mention a child. If we used the definition of "power and authority" for the word rod, it would change its meaning in the other verses from beating with a rod to using one's rod of authority when raising a child. (Consider also what might be the meaning of "Thy rod and Thy staff, they comfort me" in the 23rd Psalm.)

The Old Testament has also been a source for those who oppose equal rights for women and minorities and by some groups as a base of belief in white supremacy, slavery, homophobia, and a variety of other ideas and opinions that are now in many cases against the law of the land. There are not too many people I know who want women to return to the submissive roles they lived in for a very long time, which up until only a short while ago included silently suffering spousal abuse. I also don't know many people, even staunch Christians, who would stab to death their only son on a sacrificial altar or literally use a "rod" to punish their cherished children, although a tobacco stick does come close.

And, speaking of Christians (and I try to be one), that same dictionary defines a Christian as "a person professing belief in Jesus as the Christ or in the religion based on the teachings of Jesus, and as one having the qualities demonstrated by Jesus ... love and kindness and understanding and compassion." Why then do so many Christians base the raising of children more on the Old Testament (and only a few verses at that), rather than on the New Testament in which are found many verses about Jesus' feelings for children, love, fear, and punishment? One of them is from 1 John 4:16-19, about God the Father: "God is love and he who abides in love abides in God and God abides in him. In this is love perfected in us, that we may have confidence for the day of judgment because as He is so are we in this world. There is no fear in love, but love casts out fear. For fear has to do with punishment and he who fears is not perfected in love. We love because He first loved us..." Jesus Christ never once spoke a word recorded in any gospel that can be interpreted as advocating physical assaults of children or urging the infliction of painful punishments on any child.

Wise King Solomon, the author of Proverbs, in all his wisdom knew nothing of physical, emotional, and psychological child development and what effect parents or caretakers might have on the child's future. He probably didn't even care. Children were to be blindly obedient to the king, as were the adults. In order to achieve that, the child's will and spirit had to be broken. The children were not encouraged to be free thinkers, independent, or to work for a successful and happy place in life. They were subservient and were programmed to stay that way. The people of those times knew nothing about the ills that could befall the minds and hearts of human beings. They knew nothing about the root causes of anxiety, fear, anger, hate, depression, paranoia, delinquency, sadomasochism, domestic violence, and mental disorders like obsessive-compulsive. People were just called "crazy" or "bad" and put away in places we have long since determined were inhumane and inconceivably cruel. All those ills, and many more, have been scientifically traced to most likely having as one of their root causes early years of harsh and frequent physical and/or emotional punishment.

So, many Christians of today rationalize their use of spanking and other types of corporal punishment from a few verses written by an ancient patriarchal king, with little consideration for the teachings of Jesus Christ who looked at children in loving, nurturing, and protecting ways. Even less attention is paid to the proven facts that children can indeed suffer much pain and anguish in life from physical and emotional traumas at the hands of caretakers who profess their love. We humans listen to and respond positively much better to those we love and respect than to those whom we fear and despise and against whom we may seek revenge. That is a truth.

I am hoping that I will not be misunderstood. I'm not at all talking about "blaming" anyone, you or our mothers and fathers. As I have said before, blame only keeps wounds open. Understanding and forgiveness can heal them. What I am talking about is "growth" in the way that we grow from knowledge and understanding about many things in life that were once another way. Growth is about going on from here with a new awareness in hand, with even more hope for a better life for the adults of the future. We all love our children and want the best for them. We all do the best that we can do with the knowledge that we have at the time. Certainly, we need to truly "raise" our children responsibly, lovingly, and with care. We do that most effectively when we do it with kindness while at the same time setting limits, designing structure, having rules and expectations, living with the consequences of actions, and truly building healthy relationships with our children by treating them with respect and dignity and learning how to increase our "response-ability" to behavior. Discipline is a must and the better and more consistently we discipline, the less any kind of punishment will be needed, especially anything physical.

We Have Choices

The great thing about living in a free democracy is that adults can make their own choices about the way they live and the beliefs they practice. Children don't have those choices. We adults make the choices for them. We just need to make sure that our choices are based on knowledge that we can truly live with in our hearts and souls, and, where the children are concerned, that we do no harm.

Most parents understand and agree that beating a child with fists, belts, sticks, coat hangers, extension cords, or other material objects can be identified as child abuse and that it is the wrong thing to do. Disagreements begin to arise, however, when we replace the word "beating" with "spanking" or "whipping." Then a lot of modern parents today believe it is okay to spank a child. Further controversy starts when discussion begins to define spanking. Some questions need to be asked and answered, like:

- "What is the spanking for?"
- "Who is the spanking for?"
- "How many whacks do you give?"
- "Do you just use your open hand?"
- "Do you just hit on the fat part of the behind?"
- "Do you do it when you're angry?"
- "Do you save it for those really bad things that children do, like disobey or run into the street?"
- "Do you use it for every little misbehavior?"
- "Do you give them hugs and kisses just after you do the deed?"

A lot of parents believe that spanking or the threat of it is the most effective way of getting the child to behave the way the parents want the child to behave. No doubt about it, spanking or whipping can get results. But what results? It might make the child stop or start doing whatever it is the parent wants for that moment. It might get immediate results. It is a short-range tactic that could cause long-range harm.

There are experts who say that it's okay to spank a child and some who say it is not okay, but the split is based on degree. Almost all agree that under no circumstance should physical punishment be the only means of discipline; it should never be used often until it becomes a way of life and it should never be used to extreme. You should not spank when you are angry and out of control, and your target should be nothing but the fat part of the behind, or on the wrist or hand with a light tap that really only hurts the child's feelings rather than causing pain.

Spanking can fill a child with negative feelings about himself. It can teach the child fear, deviousness, deception, lying, and aggression. The act is a physical assault of a bigger person upon a smaller one, yet we adults tell children that they shouldn't hit someone smaller or weaker, and most often teach that the child shouldn't hit at all. A parent has been known to repeatedly slap a child while scolding, "I'll teach you not to hit your little brother." Above all, physical punishment sends a message to a child of total disrespect.

Spanking can be a real hassle for everybody. Tempers flare. There is a struggle for power and control. Words are said that hurt to the core. Bad feelings can be generated and they can last for a long time. A "good spanking" is a contradiction in terms: A spanking is hardly ever good for anyone. It may make the parent feel better, at least for the moment, because it vents frustrations, lets off steam, and lets the parent think that he/she is actually doing something constructive. Destructive is more often the case, especially when done too often and too harshly.

Spanking teaches the child the wrong thing. It teaches that aggressive behavior is a preferred solution to the solving of problems. It tends to make the child aggressive with others, when the child does not get his way, when he desires change or when he wants something. It also teaches intolerance and an unhealthy way of dealing with it at the same time. When physical punishment does appear to work, it's usually only when the parent or the punisher is present or nearby. When the threat is real there is conformity. When there is no one to control or threaten, the child may run wild.

There are times when a spanking is actually a positive re-enforcer of a negative action. The child engages the parent in a power struggle and the child wins when the parent "loses it." Or the child gives in and the parent wins and the child gets the message, if you want to win, hurt others. A message the child receives from a spanking can also be, "If you have a right to hurt me, then I have a right to hurt you." It also sends the signal to "Obey me, or else." Physical punishment humiliates and creates anger and resentment in the child. It erodes his self-esteem and the relationship with the parent. The child obeys out of fear and not out of respect. Spanking teaches that the use of force and strength overcome all. The child learns to avoid the consequence, sometimes at all costs. Physical punishment doesn't change someone's mind. It may change behavior for awhile, but it doesn't change their opinion or motivate their thinking about what they have done. They are too busy being mad at the punisher and thinking of a way to get revenge. Fear is a poor motivator. When the child is blamed and punished, he feels as if he has been attacked and/or violated. The child may react by being defensive, making excuses, trying to protect himself, wanting to withdraw, or run away either physically or emotionally, being afraid, giving in and repressing feelings, becoming defiant, seeking perfection, lying, and cheating.

Parents will usually spank when they are angry and pushed to the limits. They usually regret their actions later, feeling guilty and sad about what they "had to do to their child" or because they felt that they had no other choice. Parents have often been heard to say to the just-punished child, "Look what you made me do!" Every parent feels that frustrated from time to time. The key is to give yourself a timeout and cool down so you can tap into your level of response-ability, and not retreat into the negative reactionary mode of response-disability. Try to find an alternative to using physical punishment. There are a lot of them. Remember, many adults today were not spanked as children, and, "they turned out all right."

As you know from the beginning of this group, the use of spanking is decreasing. Some of the reasons are:

- Social awareness or stigma
- Awareness that it doesn't work
- Learned from education, reading, or personal experience
- Media information
- Parents who don't want to hurt the child's feelings because they never get to spend much time together so they want what time there is to be peaceful so, they let them have their way
- There is also the fear of the abuse issue, from a moral as well as a legal standpoint

Although the decrease is desired, this does not mean that there should be a decrease in discipline. Discipline for a child is absolutely necessary, but spanking is a punishment, not a discipline. If you are a spanker, please do it responsibly and follow these guidelines:

- Not when I am angry and out of control
- Not often and not severely

- Not with anything but my open hand and on the behind
- Not for every misbehavior
- Not when I have reached the end of my rope
- Don't get to the end of that rope

And, above all, **don't lose heart!**

> "In times of change learners inherit the earth while the learned find themselves beautifully equipped
> to deal with a world that no longer exists."
>
> *– Eric Hoffer*

GROUP TEN

MONTHLY SPECIALS 🎀 🎀 🎀 🎀

As I noted in the beginning of this book, I wrote a lot of offerings for special events, most of them in specific months. I invite you to read these special thoughts about certain celebrations and events as it is convenient for you, but I suggest that you not read them all at once, rather at some time in their designated month, since there are topics and subject matter that will seem repetitious, even though that's not a bad thing. Is it? Like this...

Children ARE

as parents

BE and DO.

JANUARY

YOU as the Foundation: YOU Make the Difference

Happy New Year! I hope your holidays were great and you are ready to jump-start your life anew. There may be no other time in recent history when being connected to family in good ways is more important. I don't like to start the New Year off talking about some of the sad parts, but the fact is there are way too many of them all around our lives to just ignore them. Hoping they will go away will not make it so, nor will we be able to turn everything into sunshine and roses, so we have to be able to accept some inevitable troubles and learn how best to cope and adjust. Responsible adults are obligated to make sure that their children don't end up being victims of bad behaviors because of bad times.

During this coming year, my hope is that when sadness attacks your life without warning, those attacks bring your family closer together. Many families count this time as one of reflection and re-evaluation, arriving at the firm belief that what counts most is family, and that whatever comes, the family will get through it together. That takes courage, strength, and knowledge.

Without realizing it, many adults are suffering from the stresses of the unknown: What will happen next? Will more angry and sick people bring death to our country and its people? Will I have a job next month? Will I be able to pay the rent? Will Internet hackers become more of a factor to deal with? Will somebody steal my identity? The new car may have to wait, and the college account may have to serve the whole family.

People walk around every day with those and hundreds more thoughts hidden away from their conscious activity, trying to do routine jobs and pretend that they aren't worried. Emotions run the gamut from denying fears and anxieties to overreacting, supporting violence, and judging and criticizing others. Most people just try to get through each day, and when they are lying in bed at night trying to go to sleep, they are wearily grateful that they have made it through another day.

Through all of this, stresses mount and new emotions begin to present themselves. Tempers run even shorter. Irritability shouts out-of-place words of hurt to those we love the most. Patience is lost and depression sneaks into our senses. We may not want to get up in the morning. We may want to watch TV until the sun rises. We may even begin to behave in ways that say to others in our life, "I don't care, I'm too tired, what difference does it make, what's the use anyway?" If we let ourselves sink to this depth, we will become different people. We will become different parents than we were. Our children will wonder "what the heck is going on here, anyway?" If we allow this "new" self to interact with our children and other family members without being aware of the change, some unexpected damage in our relationships might occur. We have to be open to the fact that we might indeed be stressed, depressed, and different. It is crucial to family health everywhere that adults remain as healthy as possible by recognizing problems, airing concerns, finding solutions, and staying in charge. We can.

Here are some ideas as to what it takes. It is important for us as parents to role model for our children. While it is correct that parents should be real, honest, and open with their children, they should also pull every ounce of strength, courage, love, and maturity together during hard and difficult times. It is vital to the health and continued good growth of the children that parents do so. The first key to effective parenting is a healthy self.

Health is one of those complicated issues which, like love, can mean so many different things to many people. The list includes physical health, medical health, emotional health, mental health, educational health, cognitive health, spiritual health, moral health, and I'm sure you could name even more. All of these areas of health are involved in becoming a healthy individual who becomes a healthy parent and creates a healthy family. The healthier we are in all of these areas, the better our lives will be. Without a doubt, when we feel better, we act better and behave better. When our lives are going well and our environment is not toxic, we are better people, better employees, better children, better citizens, and certainly we are better parents.

The first aspect of a healthy self to consider is self-awareness. Ask yourself: "Who am I really? Am I pretty effective as an adult, a child, a spouse, a worker, a parent? Am I still holding on to stuff from my childhood, still not loving my siblings like I would like to, or still not being as honest in my relationship with my parents? Am I still jumping through hoops to please them? Do my own actions help make my life miserable, denying me the inner strength and courage it takes to get me where I need to be as an individual? Do I respond to others' ways of being with disability or with ability? Do I overreact, jump to conclusions, seek to blame, and find fault to protect myself against my own shortcomings? What is my attitude about myself and my relationships with others? Do I think I am better, and if I do, do I throw it in their faces? Do I judge and measure success by what I have and not who I am? Do I seek to understand others and their ideas, their tastes, their cultures, and their sense of humor, or do I immediately turn away with obvious disdain? The honest answers to these questions will determine your next step. Here are some examples of steps that you may follow in your self-exploring:

- I need to look in the mirror of self and see just who I am and who I am not, and who I want and need to be. I need to eat better, exercise regularly, and look at my "to do" list so I can start to reduce my stress level by knowing just what those stresses are. I want to reduce my schedule so I can have 'unhurried time' with my spouse, my children, my neighbors, and my family.

- I want to be the person I want others to be. I won't expect more from others than I expect from myself and I will not express disappointment if they don't live up to those expectations. I will be supportive and encouraging for the efforts they make to achieve or to improve their lot or make situations better. I need to forgive myself and take on a more positive attitude about myself and others, cooperate, reduce conflict, and truly try to get along.

- I want to observe myself in relationships, see how I treat others, see how I settle conflicts, and see if I am the one who creates the problems. I want to develop a plan of self-renewal and find the person in me who has always been there but got left behind and covered up by years and layers of what and who others thought I should be. I want to finally be my true self and bring that person into this real world where I have to take care of myself and others for whom I have great love: my family.

So, look inside, then outside. What model are we projecting to our children, to our neighbors, to our workplace, to our family? Each and every family must remain strong and connected with other families. This connection is what builds healthy communities and countries; you can see how vital it is to start with the self. Love, of course, is at the root of successful families, but so many people define love in so many ways, and not all of them are not good. It takes more than love. It takes the stuff of the healthy individual, awareness, self-development, attitude, looking in the mirror, and cleaning the "closet." It takes a single person to show interest; care for others; cooperate instead of creating conflict; and have a genuine desire for a connection with family members. We can bring all of this into the New Year with a spirit and commitment that will remain throughout the year and throughout the rest of our lives.

Individual parents are the leaders. YOU are the foundation. YOU make the difference. YOU make the family work. Make it work even better this year in love, in courage, in strength, in knowledge, and in genuine care. And, **don't lose heart!**

Check the mirror each day.

Who do you see?

Anybody you like?

FEBRUARY

Connections of the Heart

Feel-good moments. You know what those are? I'm sure you've had them. Everyone does at some time or another. You have them when you see certain movies that touch you, lift you up and give you hope. You have them when you read a moving poem that brings soft tears or memories of what has been or what could have been. You experience good feelings when you see a job well done, great effort, and accomplishments by underdogs, and when you witness people being kind and caring to each other.

I find it interesting and surprising that we all can recognize those feel-good moments when they happen, applaud them, and reward them, and yet, for some reason, we seem to have trouble creating them ourselves on a regular basis. We know what to do and we know how meaningful certain behaviors are to ourselves and to others, yet we can't seem to practice what we know in our hearts to be right! Why is that? This is that odd month when so many of us think about hearts. February is filled with images and goodies about being someone's Valentine. The best I can figure about what that means is that we offer and hope to get new or renewed friendship, love, and care from others in our lives. We want people to "like" us or "love" us more than they normally do and show it by giving us a sweet or clever card, some heart-shaped candy, dinner out (or in), or some suggestive or romantic article of clothing or trinket that will get a laugh or a giggle and then get tossed.

What we really want is simply to be thought of in a special way by other people. To be singled out for a moment as someone special is a powerful way of communicating that we think that person is worth the effort, time, and money. Maybe that is why valentines are so exciting for children and are meaningful for adults. Someone is thinking about us in a special way, even if it's only for one day.

I also think about how the word "heart" is used in other ways. You get "heartaches" when you miss someone. You get "heartbroken" as a result of someone's actions or tragic events. You might say your "heart hurts" for the plight of others. Some people behave in "heartless" ways at home and at work. Others give "heartfelt" thanks for compliments or recognition of deeds done well. "Heartbeats" can measure time, can determine health, and hearts can go "a mile a minute" when certain stimuli touch our lives. Some people actually "give their hearts" to others both figuratively as in romantic love and literally as in a heart transplant. Songs are filled with all types of references to hearts, from restless ones to evil ones, from soft ones to hard ones. Our language has come to make our most vital body organ mean so many different things. Some writers actually sign off their essay columns with a reference to losing or finding one's heart. I'm one of those. For more than fifteen years, I closed my parenting column each month with a hope for you: "Don't lose heart." When I first chose that phrase, I meant it to be a cheer for parents in their constant efforts to be the most effective parents they can be, the kind you want to be. The word "courage" comes from the Latin word "cor," which means "heart." So the root of courage is literally in the heart, and that's what I want it to mean for you. I want you to have and keep the solid courage that it takes on a daily basis to be an effective parent for the adults of tomorrow (your children). It takes desire, commitment, dedication, patience, understanding, and lots of courage to perform the duty of parent in the best possible way.

I have on countless occasions written and talked about how vital parenting efforts are to the future of children, community, and country. But after thinking about the other ways "heart" is used, I can add meanings in addition to "courage" for you to consider. Consider "speaking from your heart" when you are talking with your spouse or children (or anyone, for that matter). That means simply to speak the truth, to be honest, and to use care. People often say "I feel this deep within my heart." This has to have something to do with our true, real, and authentic feelings about a person or a situation, don't you think? When you are sometimes confronted with a major decision, you say or think "I'm going to do what my heart tells me to do." What do you think that means? It means you're going to do what feels "right." These three statements using heart can be felt and used in the pursuit of good relationships with your children. They are at the "heart" of the matter when it comes to building your home into a place where all members of the family want to be, where they feel safe, and where they feel welcomed, loved, cared for, and valued for being themselves.

This heart month is also a great opportunity to continue your never-ending search for knowledge. The focus in this special selection on heart stuff and how important emotional health is to the health of hearts applies of course to the health of your family. It is almost impossible to have healthy, loving, and caring families if there is someone in the family who is "heartsick" about his or her own sense of self or about his or her place in the home and in the world. Dr. William S. Pollack states in *Real Boys' Voices* (1998), "What teenagers need most to survive the tribulations of adolescence is knowing that they have meaningful connections, not only with their peers, but also with their parents and other family members." He goes on to say that "it is the family that can make all the difference in this society as to whether our youth grow into happy, well-adjusted adults or whether they become depressed, dysfunctional or even violent and hateful (mean-hearted) ... the tip of the iceberg, beneath which lurks all too much pain, heartache (there's that heart stuff again) and potential crime/violence ... pain that the emotional glue of family love can ameliorate or eradicate."

In the National Longitudinal Study of Adolescent Health (1994-1995), a survey of close to 100,000 adolescents in various stages, researchers found that what affected adolescent behaviors most was social context, most often in the family. Other factors affecting behaviors were whether the parents were present during key times of the day and whether the parents had high or low expectations of the child's academic performance. But these factors were not as significant as the "connection factor." This connection involves "closeness to mother and/or father and a sense of caring coming from them as well as feeling loved and wanted by family members" (joined at the heart).

It is reassuring that a loving and caring home can make connections not only for a lifetime, but also can instill compassion, empathy, and emotional involvement in millions of people, adults and children alike. Take the tragedy of Hurricane Katrina, for example, and the concern and care for the affected region that continues to be remarkable. I am encouraged that maybe there is hope for our world and that there will be connections of the heart throughout our planet in the years to come.

I once conducted an all-day workshop called "Connections of The Heart." The workshop was about how being connected in that place from which you symbolically create love and care, the heart, bonds us together like nothing else, whether in the home or in the workplace or across the world. When those connections happen in good ways, homes become places of warmth, growth, open discussion, responsive understanding, thoughtful and mindful boundaries, and a better environment for all members of family to explore themselves on the way to an identity for which they feel comfortable and thankful.

Wouldn't it be nice if we could be connected at the heart every day instead of just one day in February? Wouldn't it be fine if we let our hearts mix with our minds in more thoughtful ways? Most of the time, most people know what to do and what not to do when it comes to choosing a behavior. So, if we "let our heart speak" and let it speak thoughtfully and carefully, we most often would make decisions that don't hurt, don't cause pain, don't deform, and don't disconnect the folks in our lives who are "the heart of our heart." We would indeed experience more "feel-good" times in our lives. Ask your children and your sweetheart to be your Valentine. Tell them what it means to you to connect your heart to theirs; when your hearts are connected, the world is a much better place, because it then will be Valentine's Day all year long with an everyday presence of love. Have a sweet day all this month and beyond.

And, don't lose heart!

MARCH
Spring Cleaning!

It's spring already! The year is flying by and I sincerely hope it is a good one for you.

There's a story I would like to share with you that I tell in many of the workshops I facilitate in my community. I was helping with a youth conference at Coastal Carolina University a few years back, and I had the responsibility of preparing the refreshments for the break. As I was trying to open a large bag of potato chips, I noticed a 9 year-old boy looking at me; he seemed quite puzzled. As I continued to try to tear the plastic bag with my teeth, a technique I had used all of my considerable life despite the fact that it usually resulted in a mess of spilled chips and a bag with a rip so untidy it looked as if I had blasted it with dynamite, he could no longer hold his tongue. "Mr. Rogers," he said, "why are you opening that bag with your teeth?" "Well, that's the way to do it. It's fast and that way we can get to eat them sooner," I smiled at him with my wise and clever answer. "Besides, that's the way I always open chip bags." "But," the boy said carefully, "there's a lot better way to do it." Taken aback, I responded with "Oh, yeah? Well, show me then." And he did. He grabbed the bag on opposite sides and simply but deftly pulled with a jerk, and the top popped open quite easily and cleanly, leaving no mess and a nice-looking bag, as well. I was impressed and somewhat shocked. I swallowed my pride and told him so as I thanked him for showing me a new way to do something that I had been doing so wrong for so long.

Another young person told me one day that if I double-knotted my sneaker strings, they would stay tied longer than the half-hour that seemed to be the length of time I could count on before stopping what I was doing to tie up again. Learning that has added hours to my life that have been put to a lot better use.

Have you ever been in a restaurant and tried to get mustard or ketchup out of one of those squeeze bottles? You wait long, unpleasant minutes squeezing out bubbly air with attention-getting sounds before the real stuff finally begins to ooze. If you were to take the time to turn the bottle upside-down for a few seconds first, then you could get on with the eating much sooner. And speaking of restaurants, think about the last time you were in the restroom and after washing your hands you spent some frustrating minutes trying to get the paper towel out of the dispenser. You, like others before you, evidenced by the shredded pieces of towel scattered all over the floor, become frustrated when there is no tab or edge of the towel to grab on to and pull. There is just plain seamless paper there which you have to pinch and pull and tear to get out. Do you know why? Whoever put the paper in put it in upside-down. The paper stack and the dispenser are made to have a pull edge showing. Paper napkins in a dispenser can frustrate us too, for the same reason. The worker responsible for putting the paper in correctly either was not trained to know better; was not interested in doing a good job; or was in too much of a hurry to make sure it was done right.

The point of these scenarios is that there are right ways to do things and better ways to do things. If we stop and take stock of what's going on, what seems to be the trouble, and what we might do differently, that could make things better, things might get better. Someone once said that the definition of insanity is when a person continues to do the same thing over and over and still expects better results.

As spring bursts out, and some spring cleaning may be in order, I offer you a challenge. I would like for you to start off the new season by taking some time for yourself. Give yourself permission to stop the hectic world around you for a few hours and go for a walk or a ride out in the warming spring air, but don't listen to the television or radio. Just be with yourself and reflect. Think about who and what kind of person you are. Ask yourself if you are finished yet. Are you done, or are you still a work in progress, still cooking, still growing and learning every day, sorting out what's really important to you and deciding how you can make that your priority in life? Think about what you are happy with and what you are unhappy with and then take the first step toward making change.

The first step is becoming aware of and admitting to yourself that you, your life, your family, and your surroundings are just not what you had hoped for (if that is the conclusion you reach after your time of self-reflection.) **You might find that there are too many disappointments, too much pain, too much arguing, and too much conflict. You might realize that you had hoped for more love, fun, kindness, laughs, and harmony in your life and that some good stuff is missing.**

Do this "me test" first by yourself. Ask others in your family to do the same thing, especially the other parenting partner(s). You can ask your children to do it, too. Any child older than six ought to be able to give it a try and report back to the family. You and your partner start first. Be honest and open with each other, which is possible if there is a bond of love, trust, and respect. If those bonds aren't there, ask for work to be done on both sides to put them there. The two parents work on what they perceive is not right with the family. And there will be some things; even families in pretty good shape can find room for improvement when the future of children is at stake. Then get to work on making it better.

What does your family stand for? If you don't know, ask. What does your family want? Ask. What is missing? Ask. Ask a lot of tough questions about the state of your family. What condition is it in? Talk about what mood exists in the home and what attitudes exist and where those feelings originate. Look at schedules. Are family members overwhelmed by everything that is going on? Set a limit on things that take family members away from each other. Spend more unhurried time together. Children especially need unstructured time, so build in time for relaxation and free time. It's spring – get outside and enjoy the weather together!

When you think about your home life, what comes to mind? Love, warmth, laughter, cooperation, and moments of togetherness that you will cherish forever? Or are there mostly angry times, conflict, and manipulation? Are all of the family members working together so everybody is respected and considered part of the team? Or is the daily agenda one that pits "them" against "us," parents against children and vice versa? Are you allies or enemies? If there are more negatives than positives in your family life, then you and your family members should consider change. The future of your family and its members depends on making things work better. The longer you wait, the more difficult change becomes. I know there are many barriers, but barriers can be overcome. I've seen families that made it through some troubled times with desire, commitment, and hard work; their lives seem now to be miracles.

Changes can be made. It's almost never too late to turn over a new leaf. Children are resilient and naturally respond to love and nurturing. Parents can change, too, since the children will seldom find ways of dealing with life that are acceptable without the love and proper guidance of the caregivers. Think of it as if your family is shaking off the doldrums of winter and blooming into a beautiful, loving, and caring unit.

Remember the stories from the beginning of this essay? There are right ways to do things and wrong ways to do things. If you're not sure of the right way to make positive changes within your family, don't be afraid to find some help. There are many ways caring, understanding, knowledgeable and committed people can increase their effectiveness and improve their lives and the lives in their care. There are books, counselors, and educators, to mention a few, as well as all of the resources counselors and educators can provide. My *ABC's of Parenting* (at the end of the book) is an example and a resource for you. There are plenty of other resources, but efforts have to be made in order for those resources to work. Brains, souls, and hearts have to be put to good use. While you're doing the cleaning...

Don't lose heart!

APRIL
Times to Forget BUT Remember

So much has been said in the aftermaths of school tragedies, like the horrific shootings at Columbine High in Colorado that happened in April 1999. The talk has continued with other tragedies in Virginia, Oklahoma, and most recently Arizona, Colorado, again, and Wisconsin. There are many other school "incidents" that occur every day in schools and towns that don't get national and international attention, incidents that disrupt towns and communities and change lives forever. In fact, the topic of youth violence is one of the most serious concerns in the world today. As a Parenting and Family Life Educator, I feel a responsibility to the community and to parents to make a few comments founded in research, education, and experience with a wide cross-section of families. Just what has caused youth violence and what can we do about it?

It's clear that no single factor is the cause for the violence in our society. Certainly, no single gun law, or juvenile justice bill, or new security plan in schools with metal detectors, or the display of any religious signage, is the answer. But if I were pressed to give just one reason for the violence in our society, it would be, in a word, "adults." The adults have caused pretty much all of the questionable pieces. Adults are usually the culprits and the youths are the victims. In our society, what children witness all around them is adults modeling a variety of ways of existing in the world.

In sports, athletes are taking drugs, cheating, fighting, and complaining. "Pro" wrestling fosters physical and verbal conflict, even if it's just for entertainment purposes. More recently, something called Ultimate Fighting has taken the country by storm. Grown men fight with almost bare fists and almost no holds barred in cages until one beats the other into submission. It's ugly and scary. Most children under 8 years old find it difficult to separate reality from fantasy. They watch adults who are totally immersed in a battle between two or more adults while an audience screams and yells for blood. In hockey, fighting is an expected part of the game. Missing teeth is an honor.

Arcades are filled with electronic games that depict people and non-people killing, shooting, beating, and tearing each other apart. Adults create and make those games available. Popular games of team competition that involve shooting and killing each other for fun are available, not only as video games, but in real life through the use of paintball guns. Laser battles and green laser "guns" are now creating havoc all over the roads and skies. Movies are certainly on the list of factors provided by adults, and not just the R rated ones. Underage children do get in to see these movies, no matter what the management says or what the rules are. They are often taken to such movies by their own parents. Even movies that are rated PG or G, so-called contemporary comedies, have inappropriate content for young children. In the Colorado late night premier showing of the 2012 installment of Batman, "The Dark Knight Rises", pregnant women and families with small children, even infants, were in attendance to be exposed to the incredible sights and sounds of violence. Not to mention the unmentionable...the real gunfire and killing of twelve people and the wounding of many more. What about the abundance of G-rated animation films? They are filled with violence, beatings, mis-behavings, and ugly scary things that go bump in the night. Family fun.

Older teens are having babies and disposing of them in a variety of ways, and extended families encourage this behavior by taking care of the children themselves, taking away or decreasing the biological mother's responsibility. There seem to be no repercussions or consequences for the teens' actions. Adults are killing their children daily through abuse, neglect, and cold-blooded murder, and adults are beating and killing each other for a variety of irrational reasons.

TV, not just the prime time shows, is loaded with negative ways of living life. Take a look at cartoons, teen shows, talk shows, music shows, court shows, soap operas, and the ever increasing "reality" shows. They are filled with mean-spirited people who act out in angry, devious, and evil ways. They teach revenge, rebellion, hatefulness, and terrible ways to solve problems. Legal people and school administrators and countless other authority figures respond with sarcasm. These experiences create fears and cynicism, and disillusionment for young people about the world in which they are expected to live.

Magazines offer teen fashions and images that can create eating disorders and depression in young people. Why do such things get published? Because we buy them.

Media, as in news shows and newspapers, are spending time and space reporting tragic crimes and seemingly insurmountable problems from down the street to the other side of the world. We cannot even venture a guess on how much fear and hopelessness this implants in our children and adults. What impact does this have on the choices children make? Preachers from the pulpits talk about forgiveness and understanding, then ignore or belittle some children they encounter, or they preach tolerance and inclusion but don't live it. Religious leaders are actually being sentenced to jail for crimes against their own people, even children, and others are making claims that make them appear foolish and silly.

Adults brag about getting away with unpaid taxes, or being undercharged by a store and not pointing it out, or putting people down with hate language that would make the devil blush. There are people who model that the way to solve problems is to duke it out or sling more mud. There are adults who are negative about school and teachers, or who talk about how important school is yet never find the time to be involved in their child's education process or any activities at the school. There are those who bad-mouth work, supervisors, and people who are different, and there are those who are just bad examples of getting along with all decent and lawful people.

There are government officials who lie, who philander, who act in most immature ways as they conduct the business of a country or community and who show and receive little respect. Politicians talk a lot about the plight of the poor and what a valuable resource our children are, but there are still areas of our country that are deplorably impoverished and our children are still looked upon as just problems that need to be summarily handled, controlled.

Some businesses tend to squash working folks by keeping wages low, working people unreasonably long hours, and offering no medical help or any other benefits. These are circumstances that can lead to despair and criminal behavior.

There are parents who say don't smoke, don't drink, don't lie, cheat, or steal, and yet by their own actions, live a lie. There are parents who break promises; show disrespect for each other, for their parents, relatives, and neighbors; and who seldom, if ever, involve themselves and the family in any kind of community activity to help others.

Children don't decide what clothes to wear. Adults do, by giving in to their pressures. Children don't decide what movies to see. Adults do, by letting them go. Children don't decide what TV to watch. Adults do, by letting the TV be the baby-sitter. There are TV sets in children's bedrooms, and parents can't find the off switch.

Parents of course have to give freedoms to build independence, but with freedoms come responsibilities. Adults aren't involved enough with the lives of their children in positive ways. We react a lot when we have to, but we don't respond. We have **Response-Disability**, but what we have to have is **Response-*Ability***.

All of this, as you know, is about role modeling. We do whatever we want to do, what gives us pleasure, what feeds our self-centeredness, or what makes money. Children simply copy us until they are adults themselves. Then children copy them. It's a cycle.

Remember this? **Home is where the *start* is.** Many of these ills could have initially been addressed in the home by the parents or the caregivers. When each adult commits to live a better, more informed, and caring life, and pass these values along to young people, then problems of violence in this country will begin to decrease. When we bring back a sense of individual responsibility to family and community, creating opportunity for everybody, we will be able to start reducing the violence and crime that we fear will destroy us. Legislation will not change morals. Posting the Ten Commandments on a wall will not likely change students' lives. However, *living* the Ten Commandments or any other rules of decent behavior just might cause some positive change. In order for children to want to live by any excellent guideline, they have to see that their leaders hold the guideline in high regard.

A past president had hopes for "a kinder, gentler nation." That's the only way we will ever turn the tide: one person at a time, from the inside out. Children need us to lead the way. That's why we must hang in there and **Don't lose heart!**

MAY

May Is For Mothers! They Deserve More!

The most important people in all of humanity just have to be mothers. Practically speaking, of course, none of us would be here without them, and sometimes we forget that. I can think of no other group of people who deserve to have a day of celebration more than mothers. In fact, the day should be declared an international holiday! We would close down businesses (even the retail stores and especially the golf courses), take the day off from routines, turn off all the television sets and computers, and after some quiet moments of silent, calm gratitude, joyfully dance in the streets and have parades in honor of mothers.

While not meaning to belittle anyone else, I think those kinds of events and accolades for moms are far more important than doing them for our past presidents. Maybe we should combine Mother's Day and Thanksgiving Day and call it Giving Thanks for Good Ole Mom Day! I think mothers would like that. There would be a required gift for all families to give mom on her day – a box of "thank-yous" and a day out of the kitchen. Workplaces would even give working moms the day off!

But, alas, moms are taken for granted by too much of society and even by their own families. A calendar day of recognition is, of course, quite nice. The card, chocolate, and flower companies love it. Husbands and children actually take the time to go to a store and pick out something special for mom. It may be the only time in the year they do that, so that alone makes it special. **But wouldn't it be nice if we all thought more about mother and all that she does, all that she is, and all that she means to us at least a hundred days of the year instead of just one?**

Of course, as a parenting educator and children's advocate, I'm talking about a certain kind of mother. I've known all kinds of mothers in my many years on earth and in my various businesses in many towns. There are many "good" mothers and there are many "not so good" mothers. It's hard to imagine that there could be "bad" mothers, isn't it? For example, in my previous career as a commercial director/producer, I encountered hundreds of so called "stage mothers" who wanted to make their children (infants even) into stars, whether the children were interested or not. Those mothers were determined to reach that goal at almost any price. They were pretty obnoxious and pretty sad. Many times, crying, kicking, screaming toddlers were pushed before the video camera while the mothers roughly coaxed an unheard line-reading of the script, I firmly but kindly excused the mother from the room, determined if the child really wanted to be there, and if not, thanked them, hugged them, and sent them on their way back to play. The mothers would almost always be upset with the child for "blowing the audition." In most cases, the child should not have been there in the first place. I also knew many mothers who were in "show business" and were so consumed by their own ambitions that the immediate and future needs of their little ones were often ignored, neglected, or rationalized into delay.

In my present work I have gotten to know a much larger variety of mothers. Some are "great" and some are "terrible," but most are on the scales somewhere in between. Mothering might be the most difficult job any human being ever has. The care, welfare, and development of another human being is an awesome responsibility. The prospect of the job alone is enough to scare the daylights out of some women (and most men!). I think when women and men get married and start thinking about having children, that they *should* be scared. Even though having children can be the most joyful of all experiences, future parents have to know that along with that joy can come much frustration, confusion, anger, depression, iso- and deso-lation, sleep deprivation, terminal fatigue, and on some days, the "I can't go on another day" syndrome. The existence of these and other temporary challenges should not keep couples from having children, of course, but the awareness of the necessity of knowing what to expect, what you're doing, and what will be required is vital.

I know mothers who do not want their children for a variety of reasons. They conceived during a "fling"; or while mom was altered, either from alcohol, drugs, or escapism; or from a desperate desire to be held, loved, and cared for, which many men feign to get what they want. The child may not be wanted for other more personal and deeper reasons. Some mothers-to-be say they do not want their children, but when they have the newborn miracle in their arms, they change their minds and hearts. Others who are still children themselves, and still others, older, but who are immature, irresponsible, self-centered, void of the understanding of the importance of being a parent to a human being, still consciously and deliberately don't want their children and proceed to act that way at the extreme expense of the children and often society at large.

Most other moms want and love their children and want to be good mothers, and then there are too many who love but don't have a clue about what to do with it. So while they are learning how to be with their children by trial and error, a lot of damage can happen for the child, for the mom, and for the relationship. That's where education comes in, and that's when moms become the fully realized persons they always wanted to be. "Good" moms take their roles seriously, realize their importance in the life of another, want to be the best that they can be and work hard to become so, all the time realizing that they are not perfect. Being human, moms will make mistakes, but they will learn from them because of their high level of "response-ability." Good moms will know that they should take care of themselves, and they will know how to do it. They know that there will always be good days and bad days, but with effort, hope, help, faith, and love, the good days will outweigh the bad.

Mothers are a combination of: egg provider; careful carrier; strong and courageous deliverer; natural nurturer; doctor and nurse; decorator; outfit procurer; materials provider; food source; warmth source; welcoming source; security source; trust builder; brain function jump-starter; needs meeter; provider of love, care, and guidance; teacher; disciplinarian; psychologist; sociologist; logistician; sleep walker; tenacious task completer; day preparer; and more, and all of those responsibilities are just for one child. When there is more than one child, add to that list: referee; wise negotiator; efficiency expert; juggler; miracle worker; Job's patience; understanding; empathetic listener; and on and on. Then, what about all those other jobs, like a career; a wife; a daughter; a friend; a community member; a church member; a choir member; a committee chair; a driver; a coach; a class mom; a chef; a waitress; a laundry mistress; an ironer; a check-book balancer; a hurt feelings fixer-upper (for husband); and a boo-boo kisser for the kids. And she often does these duties when she herself is sick and tired. Literally.

Women who are mothers with all these jobs or any combination thereof are indeed the "sheroes" of our times. I have great admiration and respect for all you moms who are out there every minute of every day and night giving your dead-level best to make it all work for yourself

and all those loved ones around you. Frankly, I don't know how you do it as well as you do. Please give yourself a long, large hug and pat on the back. I hope you will get appreciation from lots of others, but if you don't, give it to yourself. I applaud your efforts and accomplishments loudly. And, I have an humble ode to you.

M   *is for the extra MILES you go to.*

O   *is for the OTHERS who know you care.*

T   *is for the TIME you freely give them.*

H   *is for your HEALTH which you must show.*

E   *is for the EARS with which you listen.*

R   *is for your RESPONSE-ABILITeeeeee...*

S   *is for the STYLE you use to raise us....*

Put them all together, it spells MOTHERS – the wonderful people who nurture the world. Have a great, special day!

Don't hold my singing against me!

And, don't lose heart!

JUNE

Fathers Are Parents, Too!

It's June! Now, time to celebrate fathers!

Yes, those guys. Those guys who just don't get enough praise and credit for the good work they are doing these days being true partners, or soloists, in parenting and helping to raise children to be successful. Fathers are getting better and better at being the champions of their children, which means they are standing up for, looking out for, advocating for, doing the best they can for, and helping to create the good life for their children.

Finally, men are claiming bragging rights about being good dads! It's something about which they are beginning to feel good and proud. Time was when men wanted to feel good about themselves it was because of what they achieved as far as business or career success, how much money they had, and how many toys they accumulated. Those were ways of how men measure themselves as men. And many still do. They never got too much recognition from others and society for being a good father! It's a good thing times are a- changing!

Change does not come easy. Even good changes are often hard to handle, difficult to accept, and frustrating in the re-programming of the self and others. So many years have passed with so much history presenting fathers and mothers in their roles in ways that were rigidly defined and protected by society. Whenever we thought of parenting, we most often thought of it as the mother's job. Whenever we thought of breadwinner or head of household, we most often thought of fathers. Generally speaking, the mother has always been the nurturer and the father has been the bill-payer and disciplinarian. The mothers were always seen as the "senior partner" of the parenting team.

All too often, "parent involvement" really meant "mother involvement."

When my children were growing up, I was what is called today an uninvolved father. I was part of a generation that thought the man's job was to sire the children, bring home the bacon, house, feed, and clothe the family, do the disciplining and punishment, and that was about it. Sure, I played with my young children from time to time, and as they grew older I tried to make it to as many of their school activities as possible, but I would say as I look back on it that I was not a very active participant in the raising of my children. I worked hard, traveled a lot, did all of the exterior home chores, repairs and improvements that were not beyond my abilities, but ask me to change a diaper, put my paper down, or turn off the TV, and I'd balk with a clever quip like, "daddy's too tired" or to their saintly mother, "can't you do that?" My wife was a registered nurse but chose to be a stay-at-home mom and she had three children in diapers for about two years. She was a true homemaker, keeping house, preparing meals, and even ironing shirts! To this day, I don't know how she did it, but she did, and she did it well. When I think about those times today, I get sick to my stomach. I'm actually embarrassed about the kind of father and husband I was.

Well, look at what has happened in the last few years! Those defined "father" roles have been turned upside-down by forces of needs and a variety of other real and unreal reasons and I am here to applaud you guys and encourage others to do the same. Fathers are finding out that when they are better fathers, they have better marriages or relationships. When their values shift from emphasis on the materialistic to the interpersonal, they care more about people and less about the tangible or material measure of success. They feel freer, they become more sensitive to the feelings of others as well as their own; they will be able to teach good values to their children because they will be demonstrating them by their own behavior. **Fathers are discovering that paternal praise, support, and encouragement are associated with better behavior and achievement in school, while father absence often increases vulnerability and aggressiveness in children, particularly boys.** And, when I say "absence," I'm not talking about just not being in their lives physically. I call it "absent in place": being there but not being there for them emotionally, psychologically, and spiritually. This type of emotional and supportive absence can lead to a child's distress, causing problems academically, in social interactions, and in healthy self-development. Rejection can affect the child's sense of self-worth, and there is a definite connection between father absence and crime, violence, drug abuse, and teen suicide. Many times, too, the father forces himself to become involved with the children, but in ways that are more damaging than they are helpful. The "fix everything" father, the "read my lips" father, the "why should I listen to you" father, the "you'll do it because I say so" father is not going to be effective in raising his children to adulthood, and today's fathers are finding that out and embracing that truth.

The fact is that many fathers have changed in really good ways. Awareness of the importance of being involved with the children and the whole family on a daily basis is increasing. Many fathers want to be better, want to know their children on a deeper level, want to create a more important and lasting relationship, and want the enrichment that such a relationship gives to both the children and the father. And the mother.

Fathers today are reflecting on their childhood and how their fathers were involved or not in their lives. Today's fathers feel that they can make change without dishonoring their own fathers, or blaming them for any lack they may have had. They look at what was, learn from it, and hopefully improve their lives by re-parenting and self-help programs to make their roles of father better, which therefore improves the lives of their children.

Ask any man who is truly connected and engaged with the lives of his children, and he will tell you that there is nothing that quite compares to the feelings that fire his commitment to being the very best dad he can be. Dads are not here to just stereotypically sit around and watch TV, or play golf, or go fishing, and bring home bacon. They are meant to be a mutual partner in the vital role of parenting in addition to being a team player in all the many other ways a successful and healthy family operates.

Parenting is not just for mothers. Know that as we celebrate Father's Day this month, while children desperately need their mothers, they also no less desperately need their fathers. Many fathers have never been fully present in their children's lives. They say they don't know how. If you say that, then it's up to you to find out how. It's your job. Thank goodness more men are doing it. Keep up the good work!

Not too long ago, I had the occasion to meet a couple who had 4 year-old twins. During our get-acquainted conversation, the father asked me what I did for a living. When I told him that I was a parenting educator, he looked rather puzzled and asked what that meant. I told him that I tried to help parents with raising their children. "Oh," he said, "then go talk to my wife. She needs all the help she can get."

I hope you don't mind my sharing some personal stories. It's about the only way I can honestly and candidly speak to the fathers out there. As a father of three and a grandfather of four, I have to tell you men that if you are not involved with the raising of your children, you will regret it. Parenting is not just for mothers. Further, parenting daughters is not just for mothers, either. The extent and quality of father-involvement with the daughters' lives does much to determine what kind of woman she becomes – just as with their sons. They learn from their fathers how girls and women should be treated, that they are just as "good" as boys, and that they, too, can have full opportunity to be themselves in life and pursue whatever goals they may desire.

There are, of course, many fathers today who are very active parents and who have been since they coached the mother and held her hand tightly when she delivered their child to the world. Many change diapers, take their turns with night feedings, fix boo-boos, and do car pooling, while also helping wash dishes, clean house, do laundry, and a multitude of other teamwork duties that today's working parents agree upon. Parenting indeed is a team sport (although it certainly can be done and done well by only one parent), and the team has to pull and push together to better assure the relationship remains strong and healthy, the home operates as smoothly as possible, and the children reach their full potential. Although some men will fight it with their very lives, as if it were some sort of holy entitlement, it is time for men to give up that old-fashioned role of the macho loner who doesn't do "woman's work," which they have mistakenly come to believe includes taking care of the children. A father has to be as involved with the children of today as much as the mother. Of course, there are certain areas or topics where one parent might be more qualified than the other, but they have to do the parenting together, presenting a united and loving front, modeling their relationship and the treatment of each other and others as a goal for their children. This is also extremely important and more difficult, but necessary, when the children are being raised in separate homes.

I truly believe that deep in the hearts of most men there is a desire to be as involved as the mom with the raising of children. But they have to deal with the expectations of society. Despite the biased attitudes, fathers do have the potential to be as involved and nurturing as mothers. Their styles may be somewhat different, but the father's special participation contributes to the well-rounded development of their sons and daughters.

Just before I started putting this section on fathers into the collection, I was catching up on my back reading of the New York Times Sunday features and it seems that we are now uncovering even more evidence of the importance of the male in the lives of children. There is dramatically increased interest in and study of epigenetics! Look into it. You'll see that who the father is physically, nutritionally, socially, healthily, and many other ways can make definite differences in the children's lives.

A loving father does more than foster positive masculinity in his son. A father's care, attention, and encouragement are vital to his son's intellectual development. Studies of especially bright school-age boys have found that the underachievers tend to be those who had poor relationships with their fathers. Many of these men worked long hours and were rarely available to their sons. When they were home, they dominated and controlled their sons by means of excessive discipline and physical abuse. This kind of behavior can destroy a son's love and respect for his father and, in effect, take away a boy's desire to make his father proud of him. Involved fathers are especially likely to have sons who are strong in problem-solving abilities and have high grade-point averages. The quality of the father's behavior, particularly his loving acceptance of his son, appears to be the important ingredient. When a father spends time with his son, he serves as a model and he shows his son by his behavior how to "be" in the world.

The best way for a father to foster competence in his daughter is to give her positive feelings about her being female, appreciating both her social and intellectual endeavors. Encourage her so-called feminine traits, her expressiveness, warmth, and sensitivity, but also encourage her assertiveness, independence, and achievements. A father's close involvement with his daughter is especially important because it is he, not her mother, who has the greatest influence on her ability to relate to men. A father gives a daughter a chance to compare her femininity with his masculinity and to have her femininity rewarded by a man who is special in her life. A girl who is constantly frustrated in her interactions with her father may develop a negative attitude toward men. The quality of the father-daughter relationship is crucial if a woman is to be successful in both her relationships with men and her creative and professional life. Most successful, achieving women had fathers who were personally secure, vital, and achievement oriented. They treated their daughters with respect and valued who they inherently were and who they would develop into whether or not they were a fit for the expected societal role.

So, fathers, know that your job is crucial. You are important in the parenting process in many, many ways. Turn off the television, put down the paper, and pick up your child. Thirty years from now, you won't be regretting that you missed the most wonderful part of your life. And, **don't lose heart!**

A father is neither an anchor to hold us back, nor a sail to take us there, but a guiding light whose love shows us the way.
– *George Webster Douglas*

JULY

Summertime and Freedoms

Summer is now in full bloom, and I hope you are enjoying yourself. Packed in the summer months is July Fourth, when we celebrate our freedom as a nation. I wish you safety and happiness as you find your way to give thanks and honor our independence. Most people, whether they were born here or have been re-born here, realize that this is a great country, even with all its troubles and challenges. The freedoms this nation enjoys have been fought and died for by many generations in many ways. Among those freedoms is the right to choose. Choice is always there. Follow the rules, don't follow the rules, or try to change them. You can choose to behave or misbehave. You can choose to stay put, go forward, or fall back. You choose the direction of your life. You choose the values you will live by. You choose how to treat your fellow human beings. You choose the work you hope to do and you can choose to quit (or to keep trying). You have the choice to belong to a religious group; to speak your truths in public; to live in community or in isolation; to help out or sit on the sidelines. You can choose to marry (and choices are getting more diverse) or stay single. You choose when to try and have (or not to have) children. You choose your parenting style. You choose how you are going to raise your children and how to make sure your family has healthy environments, and you choose to try and learn more or you choose not to.

> *"Coming together is a beginning, keeping together is progress, working together is success."*
> – Henry Ford

Just as you have the freedom of choice, so do your children as they become aware of the world around them and what it has to offer them. As a parent, it is up to you to help your child learn how to use this freedom of choice by setting rules and expectations based on the parenting style you have chosen.

Take caution when doing so, however, because there may be such a thing as too much freedom when it comes to your children. One thing that often happens in the summertime is parents get relaxed and let the children have a full life of freedom with no guidelines for anything and minimal expectations. Or some parents may go the other way and over-schedule the children in an effort to take care of them and keep them occupied. The children then end up not having enough "self" time to think, to play, to just do nothing, and find creative ways (other than e-devices, computers. and television) to enjoy being in the world. It's not easy to reach that fine balance and maintain it but it's so important to make good efforts. I hope you continue to have rules, routines, and structure, and that you continue to stress learning, reading, and being dependable and responsible. I'm talking about family function and I want to share with you some wonderful information I have accumulated over the years, some of it from the Clemson University Extension Service in South Carolina, regarding resilient family life. One of the important ways we can create and maintain healthy families is to decrease conflicts and problems. One way to do that effectively is to prevent problems before they start.

Poor family management skills lie at the heart of the breakdown in the family and in child/parent relationships. These breakdowns in the family system can lead to problems and disconnections within the family and within the community, such as chronic despair and stress; child abuse and neglect; drug abuse;

juvenile delinquency; teenage pregnancy; mental illness; school failure; crime and violence; and teen suicide.

Poor family management skills translate into:

- the inability to recognize and cope with a child's development stages
- potential for abuse and neglect
- poor communication among family members
- children and adults unable to recognize their full potential
- lack of respect for each other
- lack of interest in the child's education
- inability to effectively solve problems
- lack of knowledge
- lost hope and motivation

Regardless of how one defines family, the family is the basic institution through which children learn who they are, how to behave, where they fit in society, and what kinds of futures they are likely to experience. Within the basic family unit, many family management skills are necessary to ensure that each member of the family successfully completes the transition into the next stage of life. Five qualities that characterize a strong family are:

- spending substantial amounts of "good" time together
- insisting on respectful and continuous communication among all members
- showing appreciation and affection for each other
- dealing with crises positively and effectively
- maintaining a strong commitment to family life

Family management skills are necessary for maintaining a happy and successful self, marriage, and home for raising children and for interacting with one's extended family, including the community at large. These skills include such things as:

- effective communication
- promotion of self-esteem and respect for self and others
- emphasis on education
- effective problem solving
- building a foundation of principles and values
- personal involvement of both parents or extended caretakers
- modeling healthful behaviors
- providing a safe environment
- an understanding of the different developmental stages of life

The developing of a healthy self, caretaking team, and home, (three of the four keys to effective parenting), lead toward the desire for and commitment to gaining more knowledge (the fourth key) about the most important job an adult will ever have – parent. The degree of health to which a parent grows will determine if that parent will have a high level of response-ability instead of remaining in conflict and confusion with a high level of response-disability. The more competent a parent becomes in responding to the inevitable growth behaviors of adults and children, the more their lives will come together in good and healthy ways. The most important of all the criteria for being an effective parent is indeed the condition of one's self.

Don't lose heart!

AUGUST

School Is a Family Affair

By now, most schools are gearing up to welcome back their students, all of whom come from some form of family. There are thousands of scenarios being played out daily as children leave for school in the morning and return home with homework, school stories, and school influences.

There are those families whose members live and work and play in harmony most of the time. (Nobody experiences harmony all of the time). Many of these families value all aspects of education and the pursuit of knowledge. The parents or caregivers in these families have great concern that their children get the best education possible and they do what they know is best to help the children throughout the educational process. They model the value of learning by reading for themselves and having family conversations in which many topics of daily life are discussed. The parents supply a good home library of dictionaries, encyclopedias, magazines, newspapers, and informational, educational, and fun books to read.

These families go out to places together, to a museum, an art exhibit, or a music show. They take walks together, have picnics, take trips, and genuinely have a good time being with each other. They do watch television, but they watch it selectively, knowing in advance what they are going to watch; they often watch programs together, discussing what they see and using the time for interaction as well as entertainment or education. These families don't have TV sets in their children's rooms; the main set is in an area where many can watch together. These families with children under two years of age don't allow the little ones much TV at all. (These last two suggestions come from the American Academy of Pediatrics, and I couldn't agree with them more).

The parents in these families let their children know in no uncertain terms just how they feel about education. They make it clear that getting a good education and doing their very best in school is a clear-cut expectation, and that nothing happens in the home after school until the school work and study is done (there could be a cookie break in there somewhere.) The parents and children have together decided (depending on the child's age) when they are going to do their school work, where they're going to do it, and how the parents are going to be involved. The parents are also involved in the schools themselves, know the teachers and administrators, volunteer to be there as often as possible, and help the children carry out the prescribed lessons at home.

Sounds like a fairy tale, doesn't it? There are many families whose homes work this way, or almost this way. Many families do parts of the scenario and other families incorporate other parts of it. Because of a variety of reasons, family priority lists do vary, but I want to tell you that education and working with the educational process with your child needs to be somewhere close to the top of your priority list. More than thirty years of research has shown that when parents or caretakers are effectively involved with their children's education, the children do better academically, socially, and behaviorally and are more cooperative and agreeable at home. Check out the national Parent-Teacher Association website, as well as your local organization's information.

Unfortunately, there are families at the other end of the scenario spectrum who are living in disharmony. The parents are so pre-occupied with themselves and their own problems and/or achievements, that working with the children in a focused, dedicated time period on learning happens seldom, if ever. The family members feel disconnected and go their separate ways and seem to have nothing in common. The parents lead through dictatorship and expect more from the children than the children are emotionally ready to handle. This alienates the children who don't get enough rest, comfort, nutrition, or love, and those children go to school already hurt and already behind. There are even families who don't have books around and whose lives are spent eating, sleeping, watching TV, running here and there, fussing, yelling, and screaming at each other, and generally disagreeing about any and everything, often at how the school is not teaching their children very well.

Both family examples I offer are a little extreme, even for me. Most families are somewhere in the middle. Most families want to do their best for the children, it's just that they don't have time or they don't know how. Both reasons are valid, but both can be overcome with desire, knowledge, and effort. As the schools and families interact on behalf of the students this year, it is my hope that everybody involved will approach the interaction with attitudes of cooperation, respect, collaboration, involvement (both ways), kindness, and partnership. Such combined attitudes will lead to more effective communication, more learning, and safer, more productive environments. With a hand from the Practical Parent Education programs developed in Texas and the Family Information Network and Children's Hospitals & Clinics of Minnesota for Family Information Services (1999), I'd like to offer parents, caretakers, and schools some thoughts for action to ponder.

Getting off to a good start at the beginning of the school year can give children a boost and the motivation to do their best during the school year. However, even with "experience," each new school year is an adjustment for all family members. Changes may include:

- bedtimes
- friendships
- activity levels
- expectations (academic, social, athletic)
- activities (TV, homework, school meetings and functions)
- diet (hurried breakfasts and school lunches)

Many children will attend school for the first time, and the whole experience is new. For other children, there may be new interests, new doubts, changing family dynamics, and new developmental needs since the previous school year. Changes at school include new classrooms, teachers, and subjects. All of these and more mean that the child must re-design at least a few aspects of his or her life. This is easier for some children than others. A child may adjust well one year and may struggle the next with noticeable changes in attitude, mood, and socialization skills. Patience, understanding, and encouragement are called for as each school year begins. Given this, most children adjust in a few weeks or a month.

Here are a dozen practical ways parents can help make the transition easier for themselves and their child:

- **Encourage the love of learning**. Tell your child about teachers who inspired you and the interesting things you did in school. Don't support negative stereotypes about school and teachers.
- **Treat school as a normal part of your family's activities**. Answer questions and discuss issues, but keep school preparation in

perspective. Don't force enthusiasm or unwanted conversation.
- **Visit the school and bus stops with your child**. Walk to the school or drive the bus route to familiarize your child with pertinent landmarks. Play or have a picnic on the school playground. Visit the child's classroom and meet school staff members. Coordinate visits with the schools.
- **Adjust bedtime schedules**. Bedtimes have often been less consistent in the summer months. Experienced parents use different approaches to make the adjustment. One approach is to gradually move bedtimes back for two or three weeks before school starts. Another method is to wake the child earlier in the morning for three to four days until the child automatically goes to sleep earlier.
- **Provide your child with an alarm clock (or let the child pick it out) and instructions on how to use it**. Have the child set it each night after choosing clothing for the next day.
- **Shop for school supplies together**. Make a list before you go to avoid conflict during the outing. Allow your child to make as many choices as possible. Use the excursion as an opportunity to discuss academic goals and organizational needs. For children in kindergarten through second grade, anticipation and fun should be the focus.
- **Hold a family meeting** to discuss the schedule, expectations, and new rules that will go into effect during the school year. Talk about bedtimes, morning rituals, bus rules, homework times, play and television limits,

and school lunches. Also, discuss clothing, supplies, and plans for involvement in school activities and fun events. Along with expectations has to come the discussion of appropriate consequences for missing the marks and unacceptable behaviors.
- **Establish routines** for bed and wake-up times, getting dressed, after-school activities, meals, and homework. Children thrive with routine if it leaves room for personal creativity and is not too rigid.
- Help your child **identify potential "helpers" at school** – people to talk to if your child is scared, upset, or ill.
- **Try to get involved in your child's school**. Studies show that kids are more motivated to learn when they see their parents involved at school.
- **Plan to be easily available to your child**, especially the first few weeks of school. Keep the early weeks as free from outside activities as possible, and pamper your child a little with favorite foods or extra reading time with a parent.
- **Enjoy** this very special process as a family, because education is best when the entire family is involved. Everybody wins! And...

Don't lose heart!

SEPTEMBER

A Little More Schooling Never Hurts

The start of a new school year comes with mixed emotions for everybody in the family. It can be a time of stress and strain on the family system and emotions can run high and wild. Mistakes in relationships between parents and children can be made, mistakes that might last forever or mistakes that can be turned around into lessons and growth. The best preparation for keeping these "back to school" stresses from damaging a family is for the family to be healthy and solid to begin with. That's what every offering in this book is about: how to build strong families and minimize damage.

Here are some thoughts on effective parent involvement/engagement in the education of children. Effective involvement in their lives of children pays off for all concerned, and one of the areas that impacts a family most is **school and the educational process.** For more than thirty years, research has shown that the quality of home is one of the most powerful factors in determining student success. Parents working with their children at home, modeling interest in learning, and embracing new knowledge establish expectations and build the foundation of belief that education is a key to a better life.

Home is where the *start* is. If your child goes to school each day tired and confused about disharmony in the home place, the child does not enter the classroom prepared to learn. A tired, discouraged, de-valued child will mire deep in low self-worth and become a "problem child" because she/he is having trouble making it. Even the best teachers can only do so much; it is up to the parent to prepare that child for the teacher. The teacher doesn't have the time to teach *and* parent, although, thank goodness, many of them somehow do both and literally save lives that would otherwise be lost.

Studies show that when parents are involved with the education of their children, the children will often enjoy the learning process and school life in general much more. Involvement/engagement improves the skills and attitudes of the child, and therefore the child's grades and achievements. It helps develop more confidence and self-esteem, which all lead to a better future in the adult world. Parents should see themselves as part of the team, along with the teachers, that is working for the benefit of the child. A parent may have had an unhappy experience in his/her school days. That's unfortunate, but caring and aware parents will either put those experiences aside or learn to deal with them; the problems they experienced shouldn't interfere with the educational process of their own children.

Parents should try to create a home atmosphere where the child feels loved, cared for, and where his/her interests are of concern for the whole family. Forced learning is fleeting; a love of learning will lead to a lifetime of growth. Parents need to get to know the teachers, the subjects being taught, and important and applicable school policies regarding discipline, expectations, and any codes of conduct by which the school operates. Parents need to be involved in the school activities and should participate with the child whenever possible, which shows the child that the parent values education and expects the child to do the same. Parents also need to help the child make the most of study time. Parents are a child's first teacher and can be the most important one. Remember: Children imitate parents. Two powerful gifts that parents can offer their children are a positive attitude toward education and involvement in the learning process, both in the home and in the school.

Schools are among the most vital institutions in communities. Whether communities will be strong or weak depends a great deal on the condition of the schools. Teachers for the most part are hardworking, dedicated professionals who are concerned about quality education of children. If all children are educated well, communities will not only survive, but will thrive. Parents and all members of the community need to support the schools and the efforts of the teachers and administration by letting them know that they and their important roles are valued. Parents should thank teachers as often as they can and be available to provide help whenever it is needed, whether inside the classroom, on field trips, or raising money for the school. Everybody wins when everybody works together. Parental attitude about the value of learning is of prime importance. Children need to know that their parents are big believers in education, and one good way to do that is to always be interested in what's going on at the children's home away from home. But tread carefully: An over-zealous parent can be unintentionally too demanding on a teacher's time, and too many questions of and pressures on the child can be intrusive and evoke a possible response of "whose school is this, anyway?" from the child. Awareness and sensitivity on the parents' part, and, of course the age of the child, are the keys to keeping the balance.

In addition to the teachers, parents should get to know the principals, counselors, and other staff members at their child's school. Attend open houses and other school activities, like sports events, concerts, plays, and other happenings that involve students. Even if your children are not actively participating, you are showing your support for the school and the students, creating a "this-is-our-school-and-we're-proud-of-it" spirit.

Teachers will schedule regular conferences as they are able, but you are encouraged to schedule a parent/teacher conference for yourself, one that's convenient for you both. This should be done as soon as possible after the school opening has settled down. It's an especially good practice if there are things about your child's life that you would like your teacher to know, like any particular stresses, unusual situations, or unique conditions. It would also be a good time for compliments and teacher encouragement. Like all of us, teachers need to know they matter. Be prepared for such meetings with specific questions and concerns and keep the time to a minimum. Let your child know that you're going to meet with the teacher because you're interested in building a good relationship and ask the child if he/she has questions for the teacher, too. The better the teachers know you and your child, the more they can be help, but remember, don't wear out your welcome. Attend as many PTO or PTA meetings as you can, and be an active member and volunteer in the organization's plans and activities. The meetings are a good time to exercise your voice in what's taking place at school.

Of course, the first thing to do after establishing a team-connection with the teachers and/or principal is to talk with them about what they need or what you can do. There are all kinds of possibilities. Some schools have organized volunteer programs. Find out about them and how you might be able to fit in. Maybe you could help out with some activity or project. Most teachers welcome parent visits to the classroom. Perhaps teachers need help with phone calls, setting up conferences, or the coordination of some logistics. Newsletters are popular and require some expertise and creativity. This might be a fun project while executing the important task of building a relationship. Being a tutor one-on-one, especially in reading, is a wonderful way to get involved, and it's a great area for grandparents, too. Many retirees are making themselves available, and intergenerational lessons are added benefits. With the diverse cultures we have in today's schools, opportunities abound for sharing rituals, foods, clothing, and fun activities. It could be exciting and educational. Teachers and staff need parents to do what they can to promote learning at home. Here are some ideas.

EFFECTIVE HOME ENVIRONMENT FOR SUCCESSFUL CHILDREN

WORK HABITS OF CHILDREN AND PARENTS
Children from homes with routines, structure, clear and simple expectations and shared responsibilities do better in school.

ACADEMIC GUIDANCE AND SUPPORT
Children need someone at home who will offer them encouragement in their schoolwork, be responsive to their needs and frustrations, understand their strengths and limitations, and be aware of what they are studying and how they are doing.

STIMULATION TO EXPLORE AND DISCUSS IDEAS AND EVENTS
Children need someone who provides them opportunities to know about events in the world through print materials at home, trips to libraries, discussions about current events, managed screen time, and participation in family hobbies and activities.

LANGUAGE DEVELOPMENT AT HOME
Children need opportunities to see and hear adults use good oral and written language in the home, to hear and see role models of effective relationship building, problem solving, and team work.

ACADEMIC ASPIRATIONS AND EXPECTATIONS
A child needs an adult at home who will set high but realistic standards for the child's school efforts and encourage the child to aspire to the highest levels of education.

LOVABLE, VALUED, AND ABLE
Children need adults who truly love them, think they are special and unique, and who help them know that they are capable of achievement and success.

Good study habits are vital to your child's successful education and for establishing the foundations for lifelong learning. To develop those habits, the child needs first and foremost to feel good and rested. Make sure proper health care is maintained, including nutritional meals, appropriate exercise, and plenty of sleep. Set a regular bedtime for your child and stick to it. Being in good physical condition will enhance other needed skills, like listening carefully to instructions, interpreting them accurately, taking good notes, managing time properly, and reading effectively.

Make the home a **learning center**. You and your child set up a study place at a desk or a table that has good lighting and provide supplies, including reference books, a variety of reading material, books, magazines, and newspapers. (Ask teachers for suggestions if you need ideas of what materials to provide.) Make sure the study area is free from distractions, like television, radio, video games, and toys. However, we certainly know now that some learners, young and old, learn pretty well with music or "sound" somewhere around. Depends on the person. With your child, set a specific time each day for study and let him know that studying is a top priority: "Nothing else happens until the school work is done!" Of course, there will be times when flexibility is necessary. When the study schedule is interrupted, then reschedule with the child for the missed time. Make it always a trade off, never a loss of study time and getting work done. Permit the child to be involved in helping to make decisions about the time, place, and materials. When they have a "say" in the rules, they are more cooperative.

Homework is given to help the child. Don't do it for her. Answer questions, consult, support, and encourage resourcefulness, but try not to give specific answers. Ask questions that will provoke thinking and problem-solving instead of just finding the answers for the next test or quiz. Learning is not memorizing something just to forget it after getting the grade. Review, critique, and make sure a task is completed, but be careful not to concentrate on weaknesses; rather, highlight the strengths.

If your child is a procrastinator, or has trouble staying focused, set a **time limit for completing a task**. A very young child needs a break about every ten to fifteen minutes. An older elementary child can often work up to thirty minutes before taking a break. Establish a reinforcement system and choose a reinforcement that has meaning for the child, such as watching TV or a movie, going out to play, or some other privilege. It's vital to set the rules, stick to them, and have specific consequences for compliance and for non-compliance. **Monitor and limit** the amount of screen time your child enjoys, and try to talk with them as often as possible about the shows, texts, and Internet offerings they do watch. Even better, watch some programming together and discuss it with them without becoming a "kill-joy." Make the discussions part of the fun. If you can't, or if it turns into some more "parent preaching," forget it. You'll do more harm than good.

Expect your child to complete all assignments on time and to be in school every day. Make your expectations clear. Show a **genuine interest** in any and all work the child has to do for school. Ask about projects and events and what's going on at school in general. Have conversations about the school and learning as often as you can without prying, spying, or forcing when the child is not ready. Be able to truly listen when your child wants to talk. They will feel valued and encouraged.

Put **encouragement** at the top of your list and something you always do. Praise and compliment your child's efforts at tasks and assignments. Avoid phrases like "well, you're just not very good at math" or "you know, it runs in the family." Encourage your children to read, read, and read. Read with them or to them daily if you can. Reading and the love of it is not only vital to school success but to life success. It's the root of life's literacy abilities. Encourage your children to write, either in diaries, journals, notes to family, or letters to friends and grandparents. Try it yourself. Every now and then, write a note to your children and let them know how much you love them and how proud you are to be their parent. You can even try it with your spouse.

Encourage your children to be independent. Help them learn how to budget their time and make decisions. Encourage interest in hobbies and activities. Encourage a zest and love of life. Show them how. Ask for their opinions and their help. You honor them and respect them when you do.

Set realistic goals together and plan them. Remember that your child is not grown yet. Don't expect too much too soon, or too little. Don't concentrate on the weaknesses and shortcomings. Concentrate on positive skills and behaviors. We have to learn to learn. Encourage your child to try and do the best he can. Don't bail her out of tough spots that she could handle with a little more effort or patience.

Always be a **positive influence**. Talk about school and teachers and the importance and difficulty of their jobs. Be a role model with healthy habits that can be shared, like exercising or cooking meals. Find the positives in school assignments and don't make them look like "just more stuff to do."

Express your love freely without qualification and avoid comparing your child to others, especially other siblings. Spend time with your child by giving him your undivided attention and talk *with* them, not *at* them. Listen carefully to what he has to say.

Instill a love of learning, but don't expect perfection. Mistakes are part of the learning process. The establishment of enjoyment for learning will last a lifetime. Keep grades in their place. They don't mean everything. Effort and improvement are important. Applied stress and pressure to achieve can be discouraging. A boundary between encouragement and pressure for perfection has to be drawn.

Learning is a positive venture, and each child is able and capable of achieving his or her full potential. It is in a very large way up to parents to help children reach that goal. Every child has positives, and it is up to the parent to constantly build on those positives. Too often, children only hear from adults when they have done something wrong or they are not living up to expectations, which may not be entirely the truth of the matter. Think about how you are responding, and why. Be mindful. Be careful. Be firm, but fair and kind. Remember when you were where they are. And,

Don't lose heart!

OCTOBER

There Is Violence in Society

A few years ago, I received a statement and a set of questions asking for my responses from a local newspaper journalist on the topic of violence in society. After careful reflection as to whether or not I should comment, I decided to share some of my thoughts since I felt, and still feel, that the topic is of great interest to parents and families. As I was in the process of rereading and editing this entry, two other horrific acts of senseless violence have just taken place; the July 2012 tragedy in Aurora, Colorado, and another, seemingly of religious nature, in Wisconsin. Lone young men, one excessively armed in a warrior uniform, [and the other in aggressive tattooed markings,] attacked the audience attending a midnight premier showing of "The Dark Knight Rises" and the second man-a gathering of attendees at a Sikh Temple; the latest sadness of mass violence referenced in my earlier essay for April. So this piece on violence is even more timely as the acts appear to be increasing rather than decreasing. I've duplicated a version of the question-and-answer session for you in this special section on violence in society as October's offering because of the prevalence of commercial and mischievous violence that tends to occur around Halloween time.

Question: Parents are barraged with news of school shootings, Internet predators, children snatched from their beds while they sleep, politicians, respected church and sports people preying on young people, etc. With all of that, we, the public, are asking these questions: Are parents raising their children differently today than the way they were parented because of increased violence against children, or are today's parents just more aware of the violence because of more thorough media coverage?

Answer: Most parents are definitely raising their children differently today, but not because of the violence, since we have always had isolated occurrences of violence. It's the other way around: The epidemic of violence is being caused by the way we parent and raise our children and the weakness of homes and families. We are now a larger population; there is more of everything, including unhealthy people, identified mental illness, reactions to being a member of the "have-nots" or disenfranchised population, and the seemingly uncaring power wielding of those in the "haves" population (a gap that seems to be getting wider and wider), and all of these incidents can be reported almost instantaneously to the entire world, especially the "newsworthy" ones.

We are such a reactionary society that even after a violent episode hits our neighborhoods, it doesn't take a long time for a return to normalcy and becoming close to complacent again. We hurry to "fix" the symptoms of deeper problems, ignoring the root causes.

The media definitely needs to be more responsible and accountable, both entertainment and news media sectors. There are so many media outlets today that are all competing for audiences to increase their profits and staying power. Not only do they simply report a news event, but they also banter it all day and night long, making it much more important than it truly needs to be, and some media actually create news from the news. Look at what the media has done to two young women not long ago who battled internal demons of some kind that created for them sad and confused lives, and the media uses them to sell themselves, calling it news.

Those were specific woman at that time, and by now there could have been many more individuals who have been "used" by the media. I also believe that media exposure can and has created violent events by unhealthy persons wanting the notoriety the coverage provides. Media fuels terrorism. Many perpetrators live and die for the publicity they get. Media also fuels social violence, from the images of "professional" wrestling to "in your face" athletics, juvenile sports, players, coaches and fans, to Spike TV fist fighting and macho stereotypes. Is it any wonder that our children and our adults accept and practice violent behavior as "the way it is?"

We have changed the way we parent for lots of reasons. Mostly it's due to corporate control and money/survival driven lives. We live in a 365/24/7 world. It is always open for business and we all find ourselves running to just keep up. Parents spend less time in the home, less time with children, less time developing vital relationships with their spouses and sons and daughters and community, less time for self-reflection, and less time for personal growth and learning. Family members all drag themselves home at the end of the day, and it's sometimes all they can do to be civil to each other. Their duties are endless, and the times for just being together in good and healthy ways have greatly diminished. Too much parenting today is done on the run, hurling snatches of guidance and direction at their confused and needy offspring with few interactions, and even those are often not well thought out. Parents too often "react" to their children's needs, with what I call "response-disability," rather than being effectively responsive to their needs, which is "response-ability." We are often too harsh, insensitive, too rigid, inconsistent, impatient, and not willing to stop, listen, and attempt to understand and guide. We don't even try to develop true relationships with each other; we just order, dictate, command, criticize, complain, and talk – all the traits that undermine the purpose of effective parenting, which is to prepare a child for adulthood. How do we think we get to be adults? We adults teach our children how and who to be. Who do you want your children to be? What kind of lives do you want for them? We are creating childhood memories for adults now. What kind of memories do you want them to have?

Question: Has this increased awareness bred paranoid parents at risk for creating a generation of paranoid youngsters? Or are parents justified in their vigilance?

Answer: Paranoia is running wild...television, motion pictures, cell phones, and Internet media help create it and fuel it. Electronic media is always there and available and attacks most of our senses: sight, sound, and emotions. It can dramatically tap into our imaginations and fears in an instant, and the image can remain, maybe forever. The print media is also guilty, but we can put it down, read it in small doses, or not read it at all; there is very little visual and no auditory impact, the emotion has to be created by the reader. You don't find many teenagers sneaking around to buy a newspaper. Mass media gives us something new to fear and worry about almost daily, even hourly. If we allow ourselves to be a "regular" habitual user, there is no way that we cannot feel anxious, stressed, frustrated, worried, depressed, and fearful when we try to close our eyes at night. It is all too much, too constant, and too negative. We are not only raising a new generation of paranoid children, but anxious, hopeless, aimless, and depressed ones, as well. We cannot possibly be our most effective selves if we are always looking over our shoulders or feeling like the sky is going to fall any minute. And if we aren't our most effective selves, then we are not giving our best as a parent, a spouse, a child, a worker, a citizen.

Question: We have parents equipping their young children with cell phones as a way to have immediate communication. Is this a good parenting tactic or are parents using today's electronics to babysit their kids and avoid having to spend time with them?

Answer: Just like television, computers, video games, air rifles, sling shots, and other potentially harmful popular commodities, the cell phone is not bad in and of itself, but rather it can have good and bad consequences; it all depends on how it is used. Too much of anything is too much. Proper, informed, purposeful uses are all good. Cell phones are incredible tools for good, but they can be misused and can be tools for illegal, inconsiderate, and obnoxious behaviors. When so called social media can be used as a learning, gathering place for children to exchange ideas and opinions, it's good. Used as a controlling, bullying, gossiping, and spying tool, or as Betty White called it "an awful waste of time," it can cause major problems. Many parents use many commodities, schedules, lack of time, and other distractions to avoid spending time with their children. Too many parents would rather be some place else. Being with our children in positive, helpful ways can be time-consuming, hard, frustrating, and boring. So can going to the dentist, but they are both necessary parts of our healthful lives. Nothing can replace the genuine "unhurried" time that we give our children. Nothing.

Question: How should parents handle the bad news of the world (school shootings, Internet predators) when discussing this with their children? What's your advice for how to have that discussion?

Answer: We cannot raise our children in a vacuum. We cannot pretend that bad things don't exist. If we don't inform them, someone else will. Of course, they will be informed by others as well as parents anyway, but parents have to manage the information and relate it to how that family believes, what it values and how it feels about any given subject in the neighborhood and world. Parents have to design, manage, modify, and execute rules, as well as behavior expectations, discipline, structure, routines, and how their family adapts to and lives in and with the world. There are many positive examples of living in this wonderful world, and they need to be pointed out and emphasized. Help children understand that life is not what they see on television or in the movies. Help them sort out the difference between reality and make believe, if we can do that ourselves! Depending on the age of the children, be open and honest with them. Tell them what you think they need to know based on their age and maturity level. Answer their questions, but don't elaborate unnecessarily. Talk about certain events minimally. Try not to make it fill the day or all of your time. Try to maintain normal schedules and routines. Above all, maintain your own cool and maturity about the events. Don't go around all day hand-wringing and bemoaning the state of the world. Check your judgments, your reactions, your criticisms, and your conclusions. Remember that you are role modeling and teaching your children how to handle emotions, how to think, how to consider, how to wonder, and how to grow in self-assurance and confidence. The more strength and courage you show, the better the children will grow into those healthy places, and then they will be able to handle the inevitable events that will greet and bash them in their present and future everyday living of life. And most of all...

Don't lose heart!

NOVEMBER

The Blessings of the Early Years

Happy Thanksgiving! This is one of my favorite times of the year because it's all about family members getting together and giving thanks for the blessings in their lives. If I could have one wish, it would be that all families could come together in love and harmony to count their blessings. Realistically, all families will not be able to do that. Many feel they have no blessings to count, with nothing for which to be thankful. Our country is filled with such families; there is a lot of sadness and suffering. Of course, there is a lot of happiness, too. I hope those of you who are more blessed will not lose sight of those who do not feel blessed and will always seek to find a better balance in giving of yourselves, your time, talents, energy, and money to lessen the gap between those who have plenty and those who have little. I believe most citizens in this country actually do a lot of good work for those who might be considered less fortunate, less able, less motivated, and less served. But not enough is being done. So when you are being thankful for all you have, vow to put aside some time to volunteer and offer an organization some material resources or some extra dollars to help another family help itself toward love and harmony.

Almost every day, I work with parents who are near "the end of their rope" trying to raise their children. I empathize with them totally. Raising children well can be the most difficult job a person has. In some of the workshops I facilitate, I talk about the four key elements of effective parenting. I'm going touch on them briefly here to make a point about why some families have a lot to be thankful for and others don't.

In order for families to even have a chance at harmony and happiness those in charge have to be in charge. I'm not talking about being controllers or wardens or drill sergeants. I'm talking about being good managers of a home, of a schedule, of your life, and of others' lives. The first key there is **the self**. The individual who decides to bring children into this world needs to be a fairly healthy person physically, emotionally, and mentally, a person who is able to realize the importance of the choice to become a parent. Then the **couple (or caregivers)** and their connection needs to be healthy, as well. A parenting style should be discussed and all people engaged in the care of the child should be reading from the same page while supporting and enriching each other. Some parents I work with aren't in the same library, let alone on the same page! Healthy parents and caregivers will most likely then create a healthy **home**, which is a warm and nurturing place with minimum friction, conflict, and combat; where relationships are cooperative, loving, and respectful rather than adversarial, discouraging, and mean-spirited.

The final key to the most successful parenting is **knowledge**. If parents and their homes are healthy, then most likely they will want to gather knowledge about how best to perform their roles as parents. Which brings us to this point: Home is where the *start* is. If you do not have the knowledge and health to create environments that allow and encourage your children to grow and find their way to their full potentials, then you are not building the strong foundation of life your children need. This failure can lead to future dysfunction and cause unhappy family situations where there are indeed few, if any, blessings to count. (Read more about the Keys in Group 3.)

I was motivated to write about this subject because of some new research on the importance of the early years of life. The science of early childhood development calls on parents, teachers, family educators, and the nation to thoroughly re-examine policies that affect children and bolster its investment in their well-being. Children undergo tremendous intellectual, emotional, and physical development from birth to age 5. Providing safe, loving, and enriching environments for children at this age is crucial to development. The first weeks and months of life are crucial in setting the stage for what happens in later life. It is shocking to me that our nation, state and local governments, and too many parents, teachers, and schools are not taking advantage of nearly fifty years of research on early childhood development to help raise and educate young children. Whenever people talk about their children, much of the focus is on their academic advancement. But research shows that children's social and emotional development is just as important – maybe even more so. If a child has a solid foundation of self-worth, his ability to become educated increases proportionately. Scientific study shows that even very young children are capable of experiencing deep anguish and grief in response to trauma, loss, and personal rejection.

- Early experiences affect the development of the brain and lay the foundation for intelligence, emotional health, and moral development. Those are the basics that help lead us toward fuller, healthier lives and relationships that build the healthy families that are the core of society.

- Healthy early development depends on nurturing and dependable caregivers (parents) who are able to focus on the role and gather the knowledge the role requires.

- How young children feel is as important as how they think, particularly with regard to school readiness. In most situations in which a student is having trouble at school, there is nothing biologically wrong with the child; there are no apparent learning problems. Most of the difficulty comes from behavioral problems based on emotional instability which in more cases than not is born in the environment (the home) and in the fragile and negative relationships modeled in the home. Effective interventions are necessary to keep those children from falling in the gaps and getting on a path that leads to a future full of unknown problems.

- Although society is changing, the needs of young children are not being met in the process. Too many parents and caregivers are too self-centered, too immersed in work and schedules and to-do lists, and too distracted by anything away from the number one priority: parenting the children.

Unfortunately, many early childhood education and child-care programs have failed to apply such findings to everyday dealings with children and the severe shortage of professionals with training in children's mental-health issues makes the situation even worse.

I'd like to offer a suggestion for you this Thanksgiving. I'd like for you to make a thank you list. Too often people spend much of their time complaining about... whatever. Here's a typical complaint list: "I have to get up too early, it' still dark outside"; "The cereal is not crispy and the milk is sour"; "The car is too old"; "The children are too slow getting ready in the morning"; "The work at my job is too hard, boring, and doesn't pay me what I'm worth"; "The days are just too short to get everything all done"; "Nobody helps around here and I have to do everything." And on and on and on it goes. We all tend to fill our lives with negatives and when we fill our lives with negatives, we are not very happy people and the others in our lives are not very happy, either.

So, instead, let's make that "thank you list." Get a group together and assign each person to go through the day and make a special list of all the positive things about his life; a list that will help him focus on the pieces of life he has for which he is grateful. Groups get together all the time to do a variety of things: Why not get together to grow thank yous?

Here's a start: I am thankful that I have a bed to sleep in. I am thankful that I didn't have to go to bed hungry or wait too long for breakfast. I'm awake again and alive again, able to start my day with a clean slate and forget about mistakes and try to do better. I am thankful that the sun is up, that I am not freezing and that I have clothes to wear. I am thankful for the basics of life that keep me going from day to day. I am thankful for the people in my life who love me, who care for me, and who take care of me. I have people to love, too. It gives my life meaning to have others to think about and talk with and listen to and learn from.

Spend a day before Thanksgiving compiling the lists, maybe a week before. Take a note pad and a pencil and actually write things down, your thoughts, your feelings, your pleasures, your successes, your smiles. If you can go along with the idea of making a thank you list, go a step further and make one specifically for your family, too. When you're sitting at the Thanksgiving dinner table or whenever you all get together, make serious and sincere efforts to thank each other. Thank mother for the million things she does, thank father for his million, too, and thank your brother and sister and your teachers and your grandparents and aunts and uncles. Give thanks to all of your family for being family and for being yours. You may not like everybody and certainly not everything that everybody does, but you can still be nice and find something to say "thank you" for. If everybody can't be in the same place, write a note, or get a card and send your thanks via mail or on the Internet if you have to.

And, to you parents, I want to give you a special thank you list. Examine yourself and your parenting styles, looking closely at how you are with each other and with your children, and give thanks-a-plenty if you have these characteristics on your list. If you don't, you can work toward putting them on your list.

Be thankful if you have knowledge, skills, and personal qualities essential for practicing effective parenting. Some of them are:

- patience
- human relations skills
- understanding
- confidence
- self-health
- genuineness
- concern
- openness
- honesty
- objectivity
- friendly firmness
- a sense of humor
- an understanding of child and adult development

- the factors that affect your personal development throughout your life
- respectful and effective communication, which includes listening
- an understanding of the goals of effective discipline and how it differs from punishment
- an understanding of the meaning of behavior and how parents need to always use response-ability and not response-disability when guiding and teaching children about how to be in the world successfully.

The most important item on your self-thank thank you list just might be this statement for you to commit to memory and practice daily:

> **"Parents hold their children's hands for just a little while, but they hold their hearts forever."**
>
> *– Anonymous*

I hope you will try the thank you list suggestion in a group, at work and at home, and I wish for you and your families a month-long, a year-long, a life-long time of Thanksgiving. Remember to put your family at the top of your list and keep it there. Be sure to also remember those who have less to be thankful for and reach out if you can. And, whatever you do,

Don't lose heart!

DECEMBER

Home for the Holidays

You know the words of the song: "Oh, there's no place like home for the holidays?" It's one of the many holiday songs we'll be hearing this month. The sociologists, family researchers, and parenting experts have all come to the "duh" conclusion that what matters most in order to create those great memories is the condition of the home. So, that's what parents and grandparents are doing now – creating memories for their children. As I was thinking about the topic this month, I wanted to see what most people think "home" means. Of course, the Internet is full of definitions; I'll stick mostly with the ones about family.

HOME:

1. A place where one lives; a residence.
2. The physical structure within which one lives.
3. A dwelling place together with the family or social unit that occupies it; a household
4. An environment offering security and happiness.
5. A valued place regarded as a refuge or place of origin.
6. Family: a social unit living together.
7. The place, such as a country or town, where one was born or has lived for a long period.

I particularly like numbers 4, 5, and 6 because they all indicate a safe haven for family happiness and renewal. I also like these two for their unique application:

- an environment offering affection and security; "home is where the heart is"; "he grew up in a good home"; "there's no place like home"

I use a modified version of "home is where the heart is" frequently: "home is where the *start* is" with thanks to the N.C. State Extension Service and poet T.S. Eliot. I believe that the home you come from is critical to who you become as an adult. I think this definition applied to basketball could fit many of our lives perfectly, since that's where we began and hopefully have flourished;

- Home: A place where something began and flourished; "the United States is the home of basketball"; the place where something is discovered, founded, developed, or promoted; a source.

So, what's my point? Home **is** where the *start* is, and the home environment, the traditions, and the family relations in the home are the foundations of great memories that you want your children to have when they are parents themselves. What kind of home will you be having for the holidays? What kind of home will your family be living in, visiting, being re-nurtured, remembering the good times and what life is all about.

I would like to share some thoughts with you. Isn't it an odd thing that these are the places and times when most family conflicts happen. Homes and holidays. Feelings get hurt; we don't get or give enough positive attention; we feel left out or leave someone else out; we get jealous and disappointed; we open old wounds; we put people and practices down; we judge, blame, complain, disrespect, lie, and are inconsiderate, self-centered, and selfish; we fail to remember the good times; we concentrate on mistakes, instead of positives. These toxic situations have to be avoided at all costs especially during the holidays. In these complex modern times, home takes on new and different meanings with multiple marriages and divorces; increased levels of family relations (half, step, adopted, foster); and all kinds of combinations of people being together through blood line, marriage, and friendship. With new combinations come new ways of trying to make the connections work. It takes considerable maturity to not only participate but to do so willingly and warmly as the struggle to find good ways of giving to each other begins to grow. Don't forget that whatever you do, you are creating memories of home. Again I ask, what kind of memories do you want them to be?

I hope you will think about the fact that every day we are helping to create memories for our self and our family members. When our children are adults, they will look back on their early years and they will have memories. You have yours from your childhood. Are they good ones? Are they not so good? Do you wish they had been different? Are we living our lives in ways that will better guarantee our children some memories they will cherish?

Take a look at how you are contributing to your children's future memories with you and in their home. A good way to build memories is to create traditions or family rituals. These traditional ways of doing things a certain way or behaving in certain ways can be the glue that holds a family together. Bonds can be made between family members that will last a lifetime and bring deep meaning to relationships between parents and children, between fathers and mothers, between brothers and sisters. These rituals are activities or practices that have meaning and significance.

To quote Dr. William Doherty from Minnesota, "in a world in which we are often isolated, family rituals give us connections to one another, a sense of identity, and a sense of values." Having certain things we all do together in expectation of pleasure, fun, purpose – whether those actions are symbolic or real – on a regular basis provides reassurance, regularity, and order, as well as a sense of feeling comfortable and safe in an environment with people we can trust.

As we grow into adulthood, many of our traditions in the core family are left behind and no longer practiced for a variety of reasons, but the memories of the experiences will always be with us. The memory of family meals together could be a treasure; taking turns reading stories; or the annual trip to the grandparents' home. Even revisiting the family photo album for the umpteenth time can be something we can count on and enjoy over and over.

Here's just one example I want to share from my personal memory. My sister-in-law took her daughter, her mother, and her granddaughter on a summertime tour of interesting places in North and South Carolina. The grand-daughter Eva, a first-grader, enjoyed one particular area the most, a museum in Winston Salem. She wrote an essay in school and drew pictures and talked about it all the time. Her grandmother wrote to the museum to tell them the story, and here is an excerpt from the reply of their executive director:

> *"Current research among museum visitors indicates that early childhood museum experiences that are reinforced with subsequent visits, conversations, and memories have a profound and positive impact on the way in which adults grow up to participate in the arts. You are playing an important role in Eva's life experience. Keep the memories alive for Eva; there's no telling what her future in arts and museums will be! Your story and Eva's is so wonderful, I'd like permission to share it with others."*

We can never know how the experiences we offer our children can impact and influence their future lives in positive or negative ways.

What I'd like to offer you for Christmas is a reminder to examine your parenting style, and look and think about what you are doing in those few precious moments of time you spend with your children.   Think about the fact that your children are children for a very short period of time. Think about the fact that they will be adults for much longer than they are children. What kind of adults do you want them to be? What kind of a relationship do you want to have with them? What you as a parent and caregiver are doing now with your children is impacting their lives in many ways. Who your children will become as they grow is determined by many factors, but one of the most important ones is you – who you are, how you behave, how you live your life, how you spend your time, and how you continue to add knowledge about your role as parent. When you are with them, do you consider it a privilege or a burden? When you are with them, do you hurry through that time on your way to something else? Do you put them off to get to something higher on your priority list? When was the last time you reviewed your priority list?

We are raising, training, developing, and growing the next generations. Our children will someday be in charge and I believe we want to make sure that we give them the absolute best foundation that we can. How they get to that place is in no small part due to parents and the storehouse of knowledge that parents have and how they continue to learn and grow and add to that storehouse. Now is the time to give them the greatest gift we could ever give them-our educated selves! If we give ourselves and our knowledge in the best possible ways, what they will feel from us is that they are lovable, capable and able; confident that they can be successful in their world because they have self-worth and realize that they are indeed valuable.

I hope you have a wonderful holiday season. I offer you these words and ideas to keep in your heart and mind as you interact with your loved ones, especially your children. Give them the gifts of good memories. Have patience. Slow down. Reduce your "to do" list. Focus on what's important. Don't go overboard on material remembrances. Don't over-promise. Don't over-expect. Don't wear your feelings on your sleeve. Don't bring up past experiences that will create hurt and allow negative and painful emotions to emerge. Stay away from the subjects that will fire up conflict. Spend a lot of "unhurried time" with your children. Show them how to enjoy a joyous season, how to build and maintain friendships, how to love, and to care for themselves and others. Teach them how to bring purpose and meaning into families spending time together and creating memories that will last forever. Those memories build the foundation for solid lives as solid adults and positive contributors to the world.

Don't forget (and how many times have you heard this from me?) that whatever you do, you are creating memories, both for yourself and for your children. Here's that question again, what kind of memories do you want them to be? How much of your own knowledge about life and living will you share with them and in doing so, teach them how to be successful and find their own joy? It's not an easy task...so

Don't lose heart!

"Here is Edward Bear coming downstairs now, bump, bump, bump ... on the back of his head behind Christopher Robin.
It is as far as he knows the only way of coming downstairs. But, sometimes he feels that there really is another way, if only he could stop bumping for a moment and think of it."

"Winnie the Pooh"

The ABC's of Parenting

*A is for **accepting** yourself and your children as **able**.*
*B is for **behaving** so your children feel they **belong**.*
*C is for the **courage** you have to make **choices**, to be **consistent**, to **cooperate** and to truly **care**.*
*D is for the **dignity** you give with **discipline**.*
*E is for the **effort** and **energy** to **encourage**.*
*F is for **family**, **flexibility**, **forgiveness** and allowing **feelings**.*
*G is for the **goodness** you show with **guidelines** and **goals**.*
*H is for the **honesty** and **honoring** you teach as you do, and **hugs** go a long way, too.*
*I is for the **interest** you show and the **intentions** you have to **influence**.*
*J is for the **joy** when **justice** is found **jointly** without **judging**.*
*K is for **kindness** in all that you do.*
*L is for **love**, the greatest of all, and two ways to give it are to **listen** and to **limit**.*
*M is for **modeling** the **messages** you send.*
*N is for **nurturing**, a **need** we all have.*
*O is for the **obligation** to our **opportunity**, with **optimism**.*
*P is for the **patience** we need to be **positive professionals** as we **praise** and **protect** and **prepare**.*
*Q is for **questioning** our **quick** reactions.*
*R is for **responding** with **respect** to the **rights** and **responsibilities** with **reasonable rules**.*
*S is for **sharing** our ways of **solving** and **surviving** that create for all a healthy **sense** of **self**.*
*T is for the **time** it takes to **teach**, to **trust** and to show how to **thrive**.*
*U is for **understanding**. To give it is to get it.*
*V is for the constant **vigil** it takes to **validate** the **value** of your children and yourself.*
*W is for the **wisdom** you need to keep the **wonder** of parenting **warm**, **whole** and always **worthwhile**.*
*X is for **xenogenis**, the production of an individual who is completely different from either of the parents. Your child is not a **xerox** of you. She/he is unique in all the world. Be **eXcited**!*
*Y is for **you**, the most important person to **your young**.*
*Z is for your **zeal**, the eager endeavor of devotion to your purpose, to keep you from the **zig-zag** sharp turns away from your critical course.*

© 1995 Jim R. Rogers, **ParentsCare**
still learning, inc.

EPILOGUE ❦ ❦ ❦ ❦ ❦ ❦

The Greatest Gift for Your Children: You!

As I begin to slowly and with futile foot-dragging move into my elder years, I often reflect on my life; the successes that have brought me great happiness and of course the mistakes and poor judgment calls I made that produced too much sadness for myself and for others. All in all, though, I would say that I am one of the fortunate because on my balance sheet, the positives far outweigh the negatives. I only hope those who have been connected to my life will say the same. And I hope you can say the same about your own life and those others who are in it with you.

In case you haven't guessed, I'm talking mostly about my children. As I sat down to write more entries for this collection my computer screen-saver presented me with a picture of my daughter when she was just two years old. What a precious child she was! What a precious adult she is today, and I have mixed emotions about all those years in between. She is a few days away from being 50! And she's my youngest child! Those years went by like a Japanese commuter train. That speed at which we live our lives too often leads us to what I call "parenting-on-the-run." May I offer you an "anytime" gift, a truth or two of mine which just might touch a part in you as parents that will ask you to examine your parenting style and look and think about what you are doing in those few moments of time you spend with your child.

Think about the fact that your children are children for a very short period of time. Think about the fact that they will be adults for much longer. What kind of adults do you want them to be? What kind of a relationship do you want to have with them? What we as parents and caregivers are doing now with our children is impacting their lives in many ways, some obvious and some not so clear. Who our children will become as they grow is determined by many factors, but one of the most important ones is you-who you are, how you behave, how you live your life and how you spend your time. When you are with them, do you consider it a privilege or a burden? When you are with them, do you hurry through that time on your way to something else? Do you put them off to get to something higher on your priority list? When was the last time you reviewed your priority list?

One of my goals in the past twenty years, since I have been in the parenting education world, is to shed light on the vital role that parents have in society. We are raising, training, developing, growing, whatever you would like to call it, our next generations. Our children will someday be in charge and I believe we want to make sure that we give them the absolute best foundation that we can for being great human beings. They will be our doctors, lawyers, politicians, firemen, scientists, and teachers, hard-working citizens, and I don't know about you, but I want the persons who will be taking care of me and leading our communities to be really smart and really caring. How they get to that place is in no small part due to us.

I don't think most of us spend enough good, what I call "unhurried," time with our children. I don't think we respect them enough, or listen to them with interest and care. I don't think we respond to their feelings and needs in the best possible ways. I think we don't think they have enough sense or courage to solve their own problems, and we too often indulge their whims and wishes. I think we think that our role is one of dictator, controller, expediter, scheduler, fixer, when what might be better is to think of ourselves as guides, nurturers, disciplinarians, caregivers, managers, providers of truth, sensitivity, care, and of course, love.

A selection from Dr. Jane Healy's Failure to Connect posted on May 9th, 2001 in *American Society, Education, Kids, Psychology /Psychiatry* (jmhneuro@drjanehealey.vpweb.com) offers a word of advice for teachers and families with children in school or about to be in or out of school. On the surface the book seems to be about technology in schools and in education and in the homes (computers in particular), but it's about more than that. She reaches deep for words worth wondering about and words that support what I'm talking about here. She says; ["We seem to care more about how fast our children can learn than how deeply they can feel. Instead of offering children our own thoughtful companionship, we saturate them with the noisy and temporarily self-gratifying objects of an electronic world, hooking them on artificial stimulation and self-gratification. As we thus drown out their inner voices and their inner selves, should we be surprised if they lack a stable core? Parents and teachers today must prepare children for an unfamiliar journey to technological frontiers, far from traditional choices and boundaries. How should we equip our children for this journey? In the long run, the best preparation may be simply to help them become as human as possible."]

I don't want to alarm you and ask you to second guess every little move you make, then feel guilty when you think you've goofed, but, I am suggesting that you slow down, think about what is most important, how you are spending your time with your children, how you are directing them to spend time with you, what words you choose to use with them. What tone of voice will they hear? What attitude toward them will they feel? I hope you will be aware that you are creating memories for your children, now; memories of childhood. And I sing my old familiar tune, what kinds of memories do you want them to have?

Now is the time to give them the greatest gift you could ever give them...yourself! If you give yourself in the best possible ways, what they will feel from you is that they are lovable, capable, and able, confident that they can be successful in their world because they have a sense of self-worth and realize that they are indeed valuable.

I loved my children when they were young. I thought I did. But I was taught the way to show it was to work hard, make the money for a home and clothes and good meals, and the rest would take care of itself. I was so wrong. Looking back, what my children wanted most and what I gave too little of was me...my time, my presence, 100 percent with them, believing in them and who they could be. I wish I could go back and correct the mistake of absence with my children. I think I could have been present more often and in good ways, and truly LISTENED to them, if I had only known how important it was. I think I would be better for it today. Maybe they would be happier, too. I wish I had hugged them more. I hope they will forgive me some day. I hope your children will never even have to think about it.

And oh yes...

Don't lose heart!

BIOGRAPHY PLUS

MORE FROM THE AUTHOR

My first career, which I held for almost forty years, was as a commercial video/film producer then a director/writer. I am a retired member of the Director's Guild of America and won two Clios for best commercial in certain categories. It was a dream career and I actually worked in what I studied in college at the University of North Carolina at Chapel Hill and earned a bachelors degree in mass communications. I was in television, advertising and production for almost forty years in Charlotte, Atlanta, New York, and Los Angeles. Then one chilly, rainy, L.A. morning, I decided that maybe there just might be something better to do with the rest of my life and with the energies and cares that had begun to fuel me. My three children were grown and on their own pursuing their lives. My second marriage was over and I was free to make major decisions about what to do with the rest of my productive years. My concerns for the future of our country and my interest in humans as a pretty neat species were growing more intense day by day.

In my considerable lifetime, I had seen and continue to see many changes; while some are indeed good ones, I was and still am very concerned about changes in our lives that are not too healthy. You know what I'm talking about. We hear about it every day: discourse about family values; violence in the schools, on the street, on TV, and in our music; youth's disrespect of adults; adults' disrespect for youth; disregard for others' rights; teenage pregnancy; bullying and school dropouts; mean-spiritedness; the absence of random acts of kindness. And our leaders leading in directions that amaze and confuse us all. Divisiveness reigns big time with our country and her people are split pretty much down the middle. The list is long, scary, and disturbing.

A national parenting movement has been going on effectively since the early 1990s, with more interest and commitment to the importance of the profession of parenting and family life educator being created every day. I am proud to be a part of that movement. NPEN, the National Parenting Education Network, and many state network tie-ins are operating with the mission of advancing the field of parenting education. Each and every member of the volunteer organization works diligently offering the best research, knowledge, commitment, and practical applications so that all "parents/families will have the information, resources and support needed to provide a nurturing relationship and an optimal environment that will encourage their children's healthy growth and development."

What astonishes me most as I continue to pursue growth and knowledge is that there are so few parents who are actually interested in the study of parenting. Since you have read these words of mine (or are planning to!) you are not one of them, so I hope you will join me in passing the word along to other parents that there is no stigma in wanting to learn how to be a more effective parent. Why wouldn't we want to be? I will continue working toward helping to make "Parenting and Family Life" a required course in high schools and colleges. All of us who believe in the importance of effective parenting and responsive homes can work together to form a strong front to encourage our communities, our schools, and our legislators to develop and fund resources available for our learning about how to help our children reach their full potential.

With this book, I want to challenge citizens of this country to start today to begin to rearrange their priorities. I challenge parents to be better at practicing the art of effective parenting. Opportunities for education are plenty. You just need to want to be better. I challenge educators to work with the whole child as you educate him or her, and that means taking the child's family and circumstances into consideration for meaningful partnership. I challenge all businesses to consider their employees more as family members, respect them, and help them in ways that you can to better balance their work and family lives by acknowledging that they have personal lives. If you can help them be happier in those roles, they will be happier in the workplace. I challenge each faith organization to reach out to a broader community, embracing them with love and encouragement. There is plenty of missionary work right here at home, right down the street.

Thank you for reading this book, or for planning to. I am hoping that you will tell others about it and remind them that **home is where the start is**, and how important it is to be developing memories now for our children's adult years and…all together now…

WHAT KIND OF MEMORIES DO YOU WANT THEM TO HAVE??

BOOKS, ARTICLES, STUDIES, REPORTS, INTERNET SITES, CONFERENCES

REFERENCES

RESOURCES FROM WHICH THIS WORK WAS BORROWED, INFORMED, INSPIRED, MOTIVATED, INFLUENCED, AND AFFIRMED

As this manuscript was on its way to the publisher, I found another article that I had been waiting to read, and my enthusiastic recommendation to you has to be noted here or this book offering would not be complete, and I didn't know that two hours ago. Please find and read the incredible article "What Ails Us" in the August 2012 issue 440 of *The Sun*, a most important magazine from our good neighbors in Chapel Hill, N.C. It's an interview with Dr. Gabor Mate by Tracy Frich. Dr. Mate practiced in Vancouver for 27 years and his discoveries and views offer overwhelming support to the basic premise of this book in that our lives in the early years have enormous bearing on who we are as adults. I encourage you to read this article at http://www.thesunmagazine.org/issues/440/what_ails_us.

Albert, Linda (1992). *Coping With Kids*. NY: Ballentine Books.

Alden, Ada (2004). *Parenting on Purpose: Red, Yellow, Green*. MN: Crane.

Allen, Eileen K. & Marotz, Lynn (1994). *Developmental Profiles: Pre-birth Through Eight*. Albany, NY: Delmar.

Alvy, Kirby T. (1995). *Parent Training Today.* Universal City, CA. CICC.

Alvy, Kirby T. (2008). *The Positive Parent.* NY Teachers College Press, CA: CICC.

American Academy of Pediatrics, Shelov, Stephen P.; Hannemann Robert E. (1994). *Caring for Your Baby and Young Child.* NY: Bantam.

American Academy of Pediatrics, Schor, Edward L. (1996). *Caring For Your School-Age Child.* NY: Bantam.

American Academy of Pediatrics, Greydanus, Donald E. (1991). *Caring For Your Adolescent.* NY: Bantam.

Beatty, Barbara; Cahan, Emily D.; Grant, Julia, editors (2006). *When Science Encounters The Child.* NY: Teachers College Press.

Blaney, Sue (2008). Practical Tips for Parents of Young Teens. MA: ChangeWorks.

Bowlby, John (1988). A Secure Base. NY: Basic Books, Inc.

Boylan, Kristi Meisenbach (2003). Born to be Wild. , NY:The Berkley Publishing

Branden, Nathaniel (1994). *The Six Pillars of Self-Esteem.* NY: Bantam.

Branden, Nathaniel (1998). *Self Esteem Every Day.* NY: Touchstone/Fireside

Brazelton, T. Berry (1992). *Touchpoints, The Essential Reference.* Reading, MA: Addison-Wesley.

Brazelton, T. Berry; Greenspan, Stanley (2000). *The Irreducible Needs of Children.* MA:DeCapo Press.

Brazelton, T. Berry; Sparrow, Joshua D. (2003). *Discipline The Brazelton Way*. MA:Perseus.

Breckenridge, Marian E. & Vincent, E. Lee. (1950). *Child Development: Physical and Psychological Growth Through The School Years*. PA: Sanders.

Breen, Michael J. & Fiedler, Craig R. (1996). *Behavioral Approach To Assessment Of Youth With Emotional/Behavioral Disorders*. Austin, TX: Pro-Ed, Inc.

Briggs, Dorothy Corkille (1970). *Your Child's Self-Esteem*. NY: Doubleday.

Brooks, Jane B. (1996). *The Process Of Parenting*. Mountain View, CA: Mayfield.

Brown, Jesse; Adams, Arlene ed.; Rogers, Jim R., et al (2001). *Constructivist Teaching Strategies,* IL: Charles Thomas.

Brunk, Jason W. (1975). *Child and Adolescent Development*. Wiley and Sons.

Budd, Linda S. (2003). *Living with the Active Alert Child (3rd Edition)*. WA: Parenting Press.

Buscaglia, Leo (1982). *Living, Loving & Learning*. NY: Ballantine.

Butler, Annie L. et al (1975). *Early Childhood Programs*. Columbus, OH: Merrill.

Canfield, Ken (1996). *The Heart of A Father*. Chicago, Ill. Northfield Publishing.

Carlson, Richard; Barley, Joseph (1997). *Slowing Down to the Speed of Life*. CA: Harper.

Carr, Tom (1996). *A Parent's Blueprint*. NC: Professional Press

Carr, Tom (1992). *Keeping Love Alive in the Family*. NC: Professional Press.

Carr, Tom (2008). *Got Grit?* SC. Youthlight.

Child and Adolescent Behavior Letter, The Brown University. (1997-current). Multiple articles providing the link between behavioral research and clinical work.

> Begley, S. "Child Growth and Development, Annual Edition." (1998-99). *Newsweek*.
>
> Brown, Larry J. & Pollitt, E. "How To Build A Baby's Brain." *Scientific*.
>
> Kilpatrick, W. Malnutrition, "Poverty and Intellectual Development." *American*.
>
> Collins, J.; The Moral Power of Good Stories *American Educator*.
>
> Crockenberg, S. "The Day Care Dilemma: Zero To Three." *Time*.
>
> Gallo, N. "How Children Learn To Resolve Conflicts In Families." *Child*.
>
> McCormick, M. and John. "Why Spanking Takes The Spunk Out Of Kids." *Ingrassia*.
>
> Werne, E. "Why Leave Children With Bad Parents." *Newsweek*.
>
> Werner, E. (June 1995*)*. Resilience in Development. *Current Directions in Psychological Science*.

Clarke, Jean Illsley (1978). *Self-Esteem: A Family Affair*. San Francisco, CA: Harper.

Clarke, Jean Illsley (1986). *HELP! For Parents Of School-Age Children and Teenagers*. San Francisco, CA: Harper.

Clarke, Jean Illsley (1986). *HELP! For Parents of Children From Birth To Five*. San Francisco, CA: Harper.

Clemens, Sydney Gurewitz (1983). *The Sun's Not Broken, A Cloud's Just In The Way*. MD: Gryphon.

Cline, Foster W. & Fay, Jim (1994). *Grandparenting With Love & Logic*. Golden, CO: The Love & Logic Press.

Cloud, Henry & Townsend, John (1998). *Boundaries With Kids*. Grand Rapids, MI: Zondervan.

Coles, Robert (1997). *The Youngest Parents*. NY: Norton and Co.

Coles, Robert (2003). *Children of Crisis*. NY: Little Brown and Co.

Coles, Robert (1990). *Spiritual Life of Children*. Boston: Houghton Mifflin Company.

Collections. (1991). *Parents Are Teachers, Too!* Atlanta, GA.: Southern Bell.

Comer, James P. And Poussaint, Alvin F. (1992). *Raising Black Children*. NY: Plume.

Coopersmith, S. (1967). *The Antecedents of Self Esteem*. CA: Freeman.

Crary, Elizabeth. (1994). *Love & Limits*. Seattle, WA: Parenting Press.

Crary, Elizabeth (1993). *Without Spanking or Spoiling.* WA: Parenting Press.

Daniels, Harvey (1996). Building Parent Partnerships In Chicago. Alexandria, VA: *Educational Leadership, Vol. 53. No.7.*

Dimensions of Early Childhood (1994).

> Stamp, L. & Groves, M. M. Strengthening the Ethic of Care, Planning and Supporting Family Involvement.
>
> Swick, Kevin J. Family Involvement: An Empowerment Perspective.
>
> Sexton, D. Aldridge, J. Snyder, P. Family-Driven Early Intervention.
>
> Lindle, J. C. Kentucky's Reform Opens Doors To Early Intervention.
>
> Wilson, S. & Wilson, J. Kentucky Parents Respond To Primary Education Reform.
>
> Latimer, D. Involving Grandparents and Other Older Adults in the Pre-school Classroom.
>
> Dodd, E. & Brock, D. Building Partnerships with Families Through Home-Learning Activities.

Dinkmeyer, Don Sr. & McKay, Gary D. *STEP: Systematic Training, for Effective Parenting.* Circle Pines, MI: AGS.

Dreikurs, Rudolf. (1987). *Children: The Challenge.* NY: Dutton.

Early Childhood Education, 88/89.

> Honig, A. S. Emerging Issues in Early Childhood Education.

Schweinhart, L. Child-Initiated Activity: How Important Is It In Early Childhood Education?

McCoy, E. Childhood Through The Ages. Where Have All The Children Gone?

Frost, J. Children In A Changing Society: Frontiers of Challenge.

National Association for the Education of Young Children: Position Statement on Developmentally Appropriate Practice in Early Childhood Programs Serving Children From Birth Through Age 8.

Eimers, Robert, and Aitchison, Robert (1978). *Effective Parents, Responsible Children, A Guide To Confident Parenting.* NY: McGraw-Hill.

Elium, Jeanne and Elium, Don (1994). *Raising A Daughter.* Berkley, CA: Celestial Arts.

Elium, Don and Elium Jeanne (1992) *Raising A Son.* OR Beyond Words Publishing.

Elkind, David (1993). *Parenting Your Teenager In The 90's.* Rosemont NJ: Modern Learning.

Elkind, David (1984). *All Grown Up and No Place To Go.* MA: Addison Wesley.

Erikson, Erik H. (1963). *Childhood and Society.* N Y: Norton.

Evans, Robert. (2004), *Family Matters: How Schools Can Cope with the Crisis in Childrearing.* CA: Josey-Bass.

Faber, Adele and Mazlish, Elaine (1987). *How To Talk So Kids Will Listen...And Listen So Kids Will Talk.* IL: Nightingale-Conant Audio.

Faber, Adele and Mazlish, Elaine (1998). *Siblings Without Rivalry,* NY: Avon.

Forehand, Rex & Long, Nicholas (2002). *Parenting The Strong-Willed Child.* McGraw-Hill.

Fromm, Erich (1956). *The Art Of Loving.* NY: Harper & Row.

Garbarino, James; Bedard, Claire (2001). *Parents Under Siege.* NY:Touchstone.

Gardner, Howard (1991). *The Unschooled Mind.* NY: Harper Collins.

Gardner, Howard (1990). *To Open Minds.* NY: Basic Books/Harper Collins

Gay, L.R. (1992). *Educational Research.* NY: MacMillian.

Gershoff, Elizabeth T. (2008). *Report on Physical Punishment in the United States: What Research Tells Us About Its Effects on Children.* Phoenix Children's Hospital. Phoenix, AZ. Center for Effective Discipline, Columbus, OH.

Ginott, Alice; Goddard, Wallace, Ginott, Haim (1965, l995, 2003). *Between Parent and Child.* NY: Macmillan., NY: Three Rivers Press.

Goleman, Daniel (1995), *Emotional Intelligence.* NY: Bantam Books.

Gonzalez-Mena, Janet (2002) *The Child in the Family and the Community.* NJ Merrill-Prentice Hall.

Gordon, Thomas (1975). *P.E.T. Parent Effectiveness Training.* New York, NY: New American Library.

Gordon, Thomas (1976). *P.E.T. Parent Effectiveness Training in Action.* NY: Putnam.

Gottman, John and DeClaire, Joan (1998). *The Heart of Parenting: Raising an Emotionally Intelligent Child.* NY: Simon & Schuster

Green, Ross W. (2001). *The Explosive Child.* NY: Harper Collings/Quill.

Grevan, Philip (1992). *Spare The Child.* NY: Vintage Books.

Greydanus, Donald E. (1991). *Caring For Your Adolescent: The American Academy Of Pediatrics.* NY: Bantam.

Hagstrom, David (2004). *From Outrageous To Inspired.* The Josey-Bass Education Series. CA: Josey-Bass Wiley Imprint.

Harris, Judith Rich (1998). *The Nurture Assumption.* NY: The Free Press.

Hart, Louise (1987). *The Winning Family.* NY: Dodd, Mead.

Hass, Aaron. (1994). *The Gift of Fatherhood.* NY: A Fireside Book

Hershman, Dyan, McDonald, Emma (2000.) *The ABC's of Effective Parent Communication.* TX: Microsoft 2000.

Hewlett, Sylvia Ann & West, Cornel (1998). *The War Against Parents.* MA: Houghton Mifflin Company.

Holden, George, W. (2010). *Parenting A Dynamic Perspective.* CA: Sage.

Hulbert, Ann (2003). *Raising America*. NY: Alfred A. Knopf.

Hyman, Irwin A. (1997). *A Case Against Spanking*. CA: Jossey Bass.

Hymes, James L. Jr. (1952). *Understanding Your Child*. NJ: Prentice-Hall.

Keim, Robert E., Jacobson, Arminta L. (2011). *Wisdom for Parents: Key Ideas From Parent Educators*. Canada: De Sitter Publications.

Kelly, Joe (2002). *Dads & Daughters*. NY: Broadway Books.

Keogh, Barbara, with foreword by Stella Chess and Alexander Thomas (2003). *Temperament in the Classroom*. MD: Paul H. Brooks.

Kohn, Alfie (1996). *Beyond Discipline*. VA: ASCD.

Leman, Kevin (1993). *Bringing Up Kids Without Tearing Them Down*. NY: Delacorte.

Levine, James, A. & Pittinsky, Todd L. (1997). *Working Fathers*. MA: Addison-Wesley.

Linderman, Mike, with Gary Brozek (2007). *The Teen Whisperer*. NY: Harper Collins.

Louv, Richard (1993). *Father Love*. NY: Pocket Books.

McDermott, Dana; Heath, Harriet; Palm, Glen (2006) Parenting Education and Support: Advances in Theories, Research and Practice. *Journal of Policy, Practice, and Program. Child Welfare League of America, Vol. LXXXV, Vol.#5, September/October*.

McDermott, Dana (2008). *Developing Caring Relationships Among Parents, Children,Schools, and Comunities.* CA: Sage.

McNair, Charles (1993). *Midstream: Navigating The Middle Years With Your Child.* Atlanta, GA: Southern Bell.

Margolin, Edythe (1982). *Teaching Young Children at School and Home.* NY: MacMillian.

Marston, Stephanie (1992). *The Magic of Encouragement: Nurturing Your Child's Self-Esteem.* NY: Pocket Books.

Maslow, Abraham (1962). *Toward A Psychology of Being.* NY: D. Van Nostrand.

Monte, Christopher F. (1991). *Beneath The Mask.* IL: Holt, Rinehart, Winston.

Montessori, Maria (1970). *The Child in The Family.* NY: Avon.

Nelsen, Jane & Glenn, Stephen H. (1992). *Time Out: Abuses and Effective Uses.* CA: Sunrise.

Nelsen, Jane (1999). *Positive Time Out,* CA: Prima Publishing.

Nelsen, Jane; Lott, Lynn; Glenn, Stephen H. (2000), *Positive Discipline in the Classroom.* NY: Random House,

New Carolina: South Carolina's Council on Competitiveness, *Increasing Parent Involvement in Education: A Resource Guide for South Carolina Communities. (2006)*

Nicholson, Barbara and Parker, Lysa (2009). *Attached At The Heart.* NY: iUniverse.

Olweus, Dan (2004). *Bullying at School*. Blackwell.

Paley, Vivian Gussin (1986). *Mollie Is Three: Growing Up In School*. IL: University Press.

Palmer, Parker J. (1993). *To Know As We Are Known*. CA: Harper.

Patrikakou, Evanthia N., Weissberg, Roger P, Redding, Sam, Walberg, Herbert J. (2005), *School-Family Partnerships for Children's Success*. NY Teachers College Press.

Pawel, Jody Johnson (2000). *The Parent's Toolshop*. OH: Ambris Publishing.

Payne, Ruby K. (2001). *A Framework for Understanding Poverty*. TX: aha! Process.

Pierangelo, Roger & Jacoby, Robert (1996). *Parents' Complete Special Education Guide*. West Nyack, NY: The Center for Applied Research In Education.

Popkin, Michael H. (1983, 1994). *Active Parenting & Active Parenting Today*. Atlanta, GA: Active Parenting.

Popkin, Michael H. (2007). *Taming the Spirited Child*. NY: Simon and Schuster.

Powell, Lane; Cassidy, Dawn (1992), *Family Life Education*. MN: Mayfield.

Purkey, William W. And Novak, John M. (1984). *Inviting School Success*. CA: Wadsworth.

Rapp, Doris (1996). *Is This Your Child's World?* NY: Bantam.

Rich, Dorothy (1988). *MegaSkills*. MA: Houghton Mifflin.

Rief, Sandra F. (1993). *How To Reach and Teach ADD/ADHD Children*. West Nyack, NY: Center for Applied Research In Education.

Riera, Micahel (2003). *Staying Connected to Your Teenager*. MA: Life Long.

Rogers, Carl R. (1951). *On Becoming a Person*. Boston, MA: Houghton Mifflin.

Ross, Peter (1999). *New Approaches to Problem Beahvior*. RI: Manisses Com Grp.

Sasse, Connie R. (1997). *Families Today*. NY: Glencoe, McGraw-Hill.

Schickedanz, Judith A.; Hansen, Karen; Forsyth, Peggy D. (2000) (1997) *Understanding Children (And Adolescents)*, Allyn & Bacon.

Schor, Edward L. (1996). *Caring For Your School-Age Child: The American Academy of Pediatrics*. NY: Bantam.

Shelov, Steven P. & Hanneman, Robert E. (1994). *Caring For Your Baby And Young Child: The American Academy of Pediatrics*. NY: Bantam.

Simpson, Rae A. (2001). *Raising Teens: A Synthesis of Research and a Foundation for Action*. Boston: Center for Health Communication, Harvard School of Public Health.

Smith, Roger Allen, et al (1978). *The Puzzle Of Parenting*. Columbia, SC.: S.C. Dept. of Education.

Stone, Joseph L. and Church, Joseph (1957*). Childhood and Adolescence*. NY: Random House.

Swick, Kevin J. (1994). *Parent Education & Family Literacy Programs in Early Childhood*. Columbia, SC: SICA

Swick, Kevin J. (1993). *Strengthening Parents and Families During the Early Childhood Years*. Champaign, IL.: Stipes.

Tannen, Deborah (2001). *i only say this because i love you*. NY: Random House.

Taylor, Joyce (2004). *Intervention With Infants and Toddlers*. IL: Charles C. Thomas

Thomas, A. and Chess, Stella (1963). *Behavioral Individuality in Early Childhood*. NY: University Press.

Turecki, Stanley and Wernick, Sarah (1994). *Normal Children Have Problems, Too*. NY: Bantam Books.

Turnbull, Ann P. & Turnbull, III H. Rutherford. (1997). *Families, Professionals and Exceptionality,* Upper Saddle River, NJ: Prentice-Hall

United States Department of Education (1994). *Strong Families, Strong Schools: Building Community Partnerships for Learning*.

Waldburger, Jennifer, Spivack, Jill (2007). *The Sleepeasy Solution*. FL: Health Communications.

White, Burton L. (1986). *The First Three Years Of Life*. NY: Prentice Hall.

Wright, Kay and Stegelin, Dolores A. (2003). *Building School and Community Partnerships Through Parent Involvement*. NJ: Merrill Prentice Hall.

Zigler, Zig (1985). *Raising Positive Kids In A Negative World*. Carrollton, TX: Zigler Audio.

RESOURCES AND LINKS FOR PARENTS, TEACHERS, CAREGIVERS AND PROFESSIONALS

Active Parenting Publishers

www.activeparenting.com Michael Popkin founded Active Parenting Publishers in 1983. Soon after, he introduced the first video-based parenting education program, *Active Parenting*. Recently revised, *Active Parenting Now* has helped millions of parents develop cooperation, responsibility and courage in their children.

University of Arkansas-Center for Effective Parenting

www.parenting-ed.org/parent-handouts.asp

www.parenting-ed.org/parent-links.asp

www.parenting-ed.org/conference.asp

www.arfamilies.org/family_life.htm

www.arfamilies.org/family_life/parenting/default.htm

Bellevue College

www.bellevuecollege.edu/health/staff.asp

Be There

www.bethere.org - Be There is a national movement that inspires parents to become more involved in their children's education.

Birth To Three

www.birthto3.org Birth to Three is highly respected early childhood parenting education with this specific program

Bonnie Harris

www.bonnieharris.com - dedicated to guiding parents in the discovery of why both they and their children behave and respond the way they do

Born Learning United Way parenting program

www.bornlearning.org

The Bowdoin Method of Parenting

Boys Town

www.parenting.org a service of Boys Town. Parenting Help - Free Tips, Advice, Resources & Guidance. Residence programs

California Evidence Based Clearing House

www.cebc4cw.org/search/by-topic-area Website from CA with deep research and resources on many topics.

Children's Services of Wisconsin on Prevent Child Abuse America...long list of resources.

www.preventchildabusewi.org/showlinks.jsp?sectionid=2&id=241

Center for Parenting in Tennessee part of the university system, lots of resources in variety of areas. Positive Parenting

www.center4parenting.org/Positive_Parenting.cfm

Center for Parent Education and Family Support, unt.edu, Center for parenting education (ROPER), cpe.unt.edu

Center for Effective Parenting,

www.parenting-ed.org

Cornell University extension programs, Parenting skills, teens as parents of toddlers and babies www.cce.cornell.edu (cooperative extension)

Commonwealth Parenting Center

www.commonwealthparentingcenter.org/services

Child Welfare League of America.

Excellent programs for community and parenting.

www.cwla.org/programs/trieschman/pride.htm

Children's Defense Fund of America

www.childrensdefensefund.org

The Challenge of Difficult children, www.elainegibson.net

Child Development Institute International network for children and families redirecting children's behaviors-coaching,

www.incaf.com

The Children's Trust Fund of America. Many states enjoy benefits of this org

CICC. Center for the Improvement of Child Caring Los Angeles. Confident Parenting, Effective Black Parenting and Effective Hispanic

Parenting. Certifications in parenting education. One of the parenting education pioneers

www.ciccparenting.org

Connect For Kids

www.connectforkids.org/index.htm Connect for Kids is a virtual encyclopedia of information for adults who want to make their communities better places for kids. The award-winning Web site, e-mail newsletters, radio, print and TV ads help people become more active citizens — from volunteering to voting.

Cooperative State Research, Education, and Extension Service (CSREES)

CYFERNET

www.cyfernet. National collaboration of extension services offering great general resources and info. Children, Youth and Families Education and Research Network, research based information from the nation's leading universities

Dads At A Distance

www.daads.com

Dads And Daughters

www.dadsanddaughters.org Dads and Daughters is the national nonprofit organization for fathers and daughters. DADs provides tools to strengthen father-daughter relationships and to transform the pervasive messages that value girls more for how they look than who they are.

DePaul University School of New Learning

www. snl.depaul.edu

The Early Childhood and Parenting Collaborative at the **University of Illinois Urbana- Campaign** is the home of more than a dozen research projects focused on early childhood education, child care and parenting.

www.ecap.crc.uiuc.edu/about.html

Edutopia- George Lucas foundation

www.edutopia.org

All Family Resources (Navato CA) All Family Resources

www.familymanagement.com

Family Resource.com Variety of resources

www.familyresource.com

Family Support Network

www.parentssupportnetwork.com

Family Development Resources, Utah

www.nurturingparenting.com

Fatherhood - The National Fatherhood Initiative encourages and supports family and father-friendly policies, develops national public education campaigns to highlight the importance of fathers in the lives of their children.

www.fatherhood.org

Gottman Institute

www.gottman.com/parenting Dr. John Gottman. At the Gottman Institute parenting is one of the most important, intense challenges adults with children have.

In the preface to Dr. Gottman's book on parenting, *Raising an Emotionally Intelligent Child*, he explains, "Before I became a father, I had spent nearly twenty years working in the field of developmental psychology, studying the emotional lives of children. But it was not until our child arrived in 1990 that I began to truly understand the realities of the parent-child relationship. Intense love. Frustration. Joy. Disappointment. Vulnerability."

The Go-To Mom

www.thegotomom.com
Kimberley Blaine's parenting shows were one of the first grass-roots parenting series launched in 2006 – The "how to" short-format segments (syndicated to an audience of more than 2 million) are for families with young children birth to seven.

GrandsPlace

www.grandsplace.org Grandsplace is for grandparents, aunts, uncles, step-parents and foster parents who are raising children they did not give birth to; they are raising children for one reason or another. Being a parent the second time around is not an easy task and this wonderful site discusses the many issues involved with being a "grandparent." They provide GrandPlace Resources, Legal Resources, GrandPlace Connections and Everyday Living. They also have a site "just for kids": Grandsplace Kids.

Grass Roots. Resources to help charities succeed

www.parentsupport.net (grassroots.org)

Greater Baltimore medical center programs for families

www.gbmc.org

Grow Parenting, cultivating healthy families

www.growparenting.com

Growing Healthy Kids is a comprehensive guide that shows what families, schools, communities, workplaces and governments can do to promote healthy child development.

Hand in Hand, nurturing the parent-child connection

www.handinhandparenting.org

Head Start early childhood programs

www.acf.hhs.gov/index.html

Hippy USA   A Love of Learning Begins at Home. Home Instruction for Parents of Preschool Youngsters (HIPPY) is an evidenced-based parent involvement, school readiness program that helps parents prepare their three, four, and five year old children for success in school and beyond.

www.hippyusa.org

The Incredible Years

www.theincredibleyears.com National resource site.

Jean Illsley Clark

www.overindulgence.info When it comes to the subject of overindulgence, Jean Illsley Clarke, Connie Dawson, and David J. Bredehoft are recognized experts. In both keynotes and workshops (individually and collectively), they offer creative and convincing examples on how overindulgence affects the lives of children and what to do instead. She is one of the pioneers of parenting education.

Kansas State University

www.k-state.edu/wwparent/programs/index.htm

Kansas State University great resource for a variety of programs.

Life Skills 4 Kids

www.LifeSkills4Kids.com This website and its newsletters provide first-rate resources for educators and parents teaching life skills to children in grades K-6.

LEARN : Literacy, education and resource network

www.learnwebsite.com

Love and Logic parenting programs

Microsoft resource library

www.msnfamily.com

Minnesota Parents Know is a resource filled with convenient and trusted child development, health and parenting information.

Minnesota University Extension

www.parenting.umn.edu The University of Minnesota Extension develops programs that foster the effective parenting of children and youth, with an emphasis on positive parenting for children birth to young adulthood, divorce issues, violence prevention, and other information to help understand the complex social issues facing families today. They offer: *We Agree: Creating a Parenting Plan A workshop for parents who care for their children in separate homes* When families change – through separation, divorce, re-marriage or a paternity action, a whole new set of challenges arises for parents and their children.

MIT-Rae Simpson

www.hrweb.**mit**.edu/worklife/**raising-teens** Dr. Rae Simpson. Raising Teens : A Synthesis of Research and a Foundation for Action is the culmination of a groundbreaking initiative to pull together current research on the parenting of adolescents and to distill from it key messages for the media, policy makers, practitioners, and parents. In creating Raising Teens, particular emphasis was placed on identifying those conclusions about the parenting of adolescents about which there is widespread agreement among researchers and practitioners.

MPC, Minnesota Parent Center, Parent advocacy coalition for educational rights,

www.pacer.org

NEPEM and NEPEF

National Extension Parent Education Model (NEPEM) set forth six categories of priority parenting practices to be learned by parents and taught by parenting educators (Smith, Cudaback, Goddard, and Myers-Walls, 1994).

www.k-state.edu/wwparent/nepem

National Extension Parenting Education Framework (DeBord Bower, Goddard, Kirby, Kobbe, Myers-Walls, Mulroy, Ozretich, 2002). This framework builds upon the National Extension Parenting Education Model (NEPEM).

http://www1.cyfernet.org/ncsu_fcs/NEPEF/NEPEF.pdf

National Alliance of Mental Illness, NAMI

http://www.nami.org

National Association for the Education of Young Children

www.naeyc.org

NPEN The National Parenting Education Network. Great site for educators

www.npen.org

NCFR National Council on Family Relations CFLE, Certified Family Life Educator source. Research and policy along with practitioners

www.ncfr.org

This New York University Child Study Center offers scientifically-based child mental health and parenting information.

North Carolina Parenting Education Network

www.ncpen.org/index.shtml North Carolina Parenting Education Network. Credentialing programs for parenting educators.

North Caroline State University Extension

www.CES.NCSU.edu/depts/fcs NCSU Extension Service - Family and Consumer Sciences views the family, in all its diverse forms, as the cornerstone of a healthy society. Faculty members within Family and Consumer Sciences hold appointments with the NC Cooperative Extension Service and work across the spectrum of family needs.

North Texas State University

www.coe.unt.edu/cpe University of North Texas State. Educational program and educator training. Tied into ROPER, parenting education network

NPR Parenting. Parenting and Parenting and Families

www.npr.org

Nurturing Parenting, Nurturing Programs out of NC. One of the most highly respected programs.

www.nurturingparenting.com/calendar/facilitator_calendar.php

One Tough Job parenting program

www.onetoughjob.com

ParentsCare, Putting Parents and Children First Through Family Enrichment Programs

www.stilllearning.org

Prepare Tomorrow's Parents.org, promoting and facilitating parenting education for children and teens

www.parentingproject.org

The Parents Journal, with Bobbi Conner

www.theparentingjournal.com

Parents Support Network

www.parentssupportnetwork.com

Parent News, an opportunity for parent information

www.parent.net_parentnews.com

parentingcenter.com, state by state resources for parents

Parents as Teachers Parents as Teachers helps organizations and professionals work with parents during the critical early years of their children's lives, from conception to kindergarten

www.parentsasteachers.org

Minnesota Early Learning and Development,

MELD, meld.org

Parent Training and workshops, Washington State University

www.parenting.wsu.edu

Parenting Adolescents Wisely, PAW University of Ohio

www.strengtheningfamilies.org

Parenting Now! in Oregon

www.birthto3.org

Parentingtoolbox educate, inspire and inform

www.parentingtoolbox.com

PRC Parents Resource Center

www.learnwhatsup.com/prc

Partnering with Parents, Iowa State University Extension

www.iastate.edu/pwp

Parenting101- multiple sites

Parenting Wisely

www.parentingwisely.com

Parent Wise-Collection of Google Help sites

www.parentwise.com

Parenting Now! Early Childhood parenting education program. Home visiting

www.parentingnow.net

Parents Forum Parents Forum is a non-profit, community-based organization that provides workshops focusing on emotional awareness. Parents Forum was founded on the principles that raising children connects all families, regardless of background or social status, and that all families can be strengthened by improving communication and increasing emotional awareness

www.parentsforum.org

Parents As Teachers

www.parentsasteachers.org   One of the top programs in the country for facilitating parents of young preschool children

Parents Tool Shop The goal/philosophy of Parents Toolshop programs is to empower parents to think for themselves by teaching them a unique, reliable problem-solving method that helps them find individualized solutions to their parenting challenges. Jody Pawel.

www.parentstoolshop.com

PBS Parenting

www.pbs.org

PTA

www.pta.org National Parent Teacher Association. PTA Mission is to be a powerful voice for all children, relevant resource for families and communities, and strong advocate for the education and well-being of every child

Parenting Teens Info-Sue Blaney

www.pleasestoptherollercoaster.com – www.parentingteensinfo.com Sue Blaney empowers, educates and connects parents of teenagers. She is the author of Please Stop the Rollercoaster! How Parents of Teenagers Can Smooth Out the Ride, a guide for parents and a parent discussion group program

The Parenting Doctor

www.theparentingdoctor.com

Parenting Possibilities-Coaching through your intermittent parenting and family difficulties with Dr. Karen DeBord

www.possibilityparenting.com

Parenting Teens Online

www.parentingteensonline.com

Positive Discipline-Jane Nelsen program for certification for parenting education. One of the most effective certification programs available.

wwwempoweringpeople.com

www.positivediscipline.com

Practical Parenting Excellent program in Plano Texas

www.practicalparent.org/professional_trainings.htm

Practical Parenting Partnerships Practical Parent Partnerships. Excellent resource for material and training in education and community building

www.pppctr.org

Prepare Tomorrow's Parents formerly *The Parenting Project,* is a non-profit 501(c)(3) organization dedicated to addressing our nation's crises of child abuse, neglect & abandonment, teen pregnancy & overall violence by working to bring parenting, empathy & nurturing skills education to all school age children & teens

www.preparetomorrowsparents.org

Prevent Child Abuse America

www.preventchildabusewi.org/showlinks.jsp?sectionid=2&id=241

Promoting Good Health for Latinos

www.esaludtoday.com

Putting Family First Putting Family First - works to raise awareness about the crucial connections between parents and children, and helps families find balance in their lives. For resources on positive youth development and the 40 Developmental Assets from Search Institute. http://www.search-institute.org

www.puttingfamilyfirst.org/index.php

Resources for Teaching Relationship Skills to Teens

www.dibbleinstitute.org/our-programs

SafeKids USA

www.safekids.org

Strengthening families, SEP, University of Utah,

www.utahmarriage.org

Strengthening Multi-Ethnic Families and Communities: A Prevention Parent Training Program, Dr. Marilyn Steel,

www.strengtheningfamilies.org

Stop Hitting-Center for Effective Discipline

www.stophitting.com/index.php?page=answers-main

Shoulder To Shoulder: raising teens together - is dedicated to helping to make our job easier by connecting fellow parents and caregivers, and sharing the insight of those who have been there before.

www.shouldertoshoulderminnesota.org

STEP Publishers STEP. Systematic Training for Effective Parenting pioneer parenting facilitator training.

www.steppublishers.com

Talaris Research Institute on parenting/families

www.talaris.org

Teams for Early Childhood Solutions, TECS,

www.uscm.med.sc.edu/tecs/index.htm

The Thinking Child

www.thinkingchild.com

Triple P Positive Parenting Program. Triple P is a system of easy to implement, proven parenting solutions that helps solve current parenting problems and prevents future problems before they arise.

www.triplep.net

Teaching Tolerance A project of the Southern Poverty Law Center is a principal online destination for people interested in dismantling bigotry and creating, in hate's stead, communities that value diversity. If you want to know how to transform yourself, your home, your school, your workplace or your community, Tolerance.org is a place to start — and continue — the journey. Through its online well of resources and ideas, its expanding collection of print materials, its burgeoning outreach efforts, and its downloadable public service announcements, Tolerance.org promotes and supports anti-bias activism in every venue of life.

www.tolerance.org

Tufts University Child & Family WebGuide – Tufts University: A directory of Web sites that contain credible research based information about child development. The sites, which are useful for parents, professionals, and students, have been evaluated by experts from Tufts University. Topics include family/parenting, health/mental health, education/learning, typical development, childcare/daycare, and activities by region.

www.cfw.tufts.edu

U.S. Alliance to End the Hitting of Children

www.endhittingusa.org

US Government Prevention Programs

www.childwelfare.gov/preventing/promoting/parent_ed_resources.cfm

Whitehousedrugpolicy.org will give hundreds of evidenced based prevention programs.

Wisconsin center for educational research, wcer.wisc.edu, FAST, Families and schools together Wisconsin Dept of Ed, Families Learning together Family living programs,

www.uwex.edu/ces

Yale University Parenting Center

www.childconductclinic.yale.edu

Zero to Three Early Childhood parenting education training www.zerotothree.org

DON'T LOSE HEART!

PROSE PRESS

The origin of the word prose is Latin, *prosa oratio,* meaning straightforward discourse.

Prose Press is looking for stories with strong plots. We offer an affordable, quality publishing option with guaranteed worldwide distribution.

Queries: E-mail only.

proseNcons@live.com

www.ingramcontent.com/pod-product-compliance
Lightning Source LLC
Chambersburg PA
CBHW022036290426
44109CB00014B/871